DRAMATHERAPY
Theory and Practice for Teachers and Clinicians

Dramatherapy

Theory and Practice for Teachers and Clinicians

Edited by SUE JENNINGS

CROOM HELM
London & Sydney

BROOKLINE BOOKS
Cambridge, Massachusetts

© 1987 Sue Jennings
Croom Helm Ltd, Providence House, Burrell Row,
Beckenham, Kent BR3 1AT

Croom Helm Australia, 44–50 Waterloo Road,
North Ryde, 2113, New South Wales

British Library Cataloguing in Publication Data

Dramatherapy: theory and practice for
teachers and clinicians.
  1. Psychodrama
  I. Jennings, Sue
  616.89'1523   RC489.P7

  ISBN 0–7099–1454–7
      0–7099–1477–6 (Pbk)

Brookline Books, PO Box 1046, Cambridge, MA 02238.

Library of Congress Cataloging-in-Publication Data

Dramatherapy : theory and practice for teachers
  and clinicians.

  Includes bibliographies and index.
  1. Drama — Therapeutic use. I. Jennings, Sue.
[DNLM: 1. Psychodrama. WM430.5..P8 D7635]
RC489.P7D73 1987   616.89'165   87–13211
ISBN 0–914797–36–0
ISBN 0–914797–37–9 (soft)

Filmset by Mayhew Typesetting, Bristol, England
Printed and bound in Great Britain by Mackays of Chatham Ltd, Kent

Contents

THIS BOOK IS DEDICATED TO THE MEMORY
OF MY FATHER,
THE LATE DR CHARLES JENNINGS

Contributors

Pat Brudenell, RMN, RDTh, CertEd, is a psychiatric nurse who trained and now works as a dramatherapist. She has innovated dramatherapy methods, in particular with profoundly handicapped people. Her recent book is called *The Other Side of Profound Handicap*.

Richard Courtney is Professor in charge of postgraduate studies and research in Arts Education at the Ontario Institute for Studies in Education and is also cross-appointed to The Graduate Centre for the Study of Drama, University of Toronto. He is the author of numerous articles, research reports and books including the two volume work, *Drama in Therapy* (edited with Gertrud Schattner). His most recent books are *The Quest: Research & Inquiry in Arts Education* and the *Dictionary of Developmental Drama*.

Martin Davis, MA, MD, FRCPsych, is Consultant Psychiatrist to Central Birmingham Health Authority with a special interest in group and individual psychotherapy. He trained in psychodrama with Dean Elefthery and has written extensively on dramatherapy and psychodrama.

Alida Gersie, RDTh, ME, is a Dutch dramatherapist resident in the UK. She is Course Leader of the Post Graduate Dramatherapy Diploma at Hertfordshire College of Art and Design. She has innovated her own method of therapeutic story-making and is shortly publishing a book on myths and stories.

Rosemary Gordon is a Jungian analyst in private practice in London. She has written extensively on the relationship between art and therapy including 'The Creative Process' in *Creative Therapy* (ed Jennings)

Sue Jennings, FRAI, RDTh(UK), RDT(USA), HonDipDTh, has been a pioneer in dramatherapy for over twenty-five years. From a background in theatre and group psychotherapy, she has integrated an anthropological perspective into dramatherapy thinking and practice. Until recently, she was Senior Lecturer and Course Leader in Dramatherapy at Hertfordshire College of Art and Design.

Currently, she is conducting research in dramatherapy with child abuse and into problems of infertility. She has a private practice in St Albans and London. Her publications include *Remedial Drama, Creative Therapy* and *Creative Drama in Groupwork*.

Dorothy Langley, RDTh, is a dramatherapist and psychodramatist. She is tutor on the Dramatherapy course at South Devon Technical College and is former chairperson of the British Association for Dramatherapists. She has published *Dramatherapy in Psychiatry* (Croom Helm).

Ross Mitchell, FRCPsych, FRCPE, MA(Cantab), is Consultant Psychiatrist at Fulbourn and Addenbrookes Hospitals, Cambridge, and has been external examiner in Art Therapy and Dramatherapy at Hertfordshire College of Art and Design. He has had a book published on depression.

David Powley, BA, RDTh, is Head of Drama, Film and Television at the College of Ripon and York St John, and is Director of the Postgraduate Dramatherapy Diploma. He is an executive member of the British Association for Dramatherapists.

Roy Shuttleworth, BSc, DipEd, ABPs, until recently was Principal Family Therapist at the Family Institute, Cardiff. He now works as a family therapist at a private clinic in London. He has published his work extensively both on adolescence, 'Dramatherapy and Adolescents' (in *Creative Therapy*, ed Jennings), as well as Systemic Family Therapy including 'Wheels within Wheels: A System Approach to Maladjustment' in the Journal of Maladjustment and Therapeutic Education, vol. 1, no. 2, 1983.

John Whitelock, RDTh, was formerly a deputy headmaster before training as a dramatherapist. Having practiced in a psychiatric hospital and day centre, he is now manager of a psychiatric day centre in London.

Preface

The incubation of this book has taken several years. As with any attempt to lay foundations for new concepts, there is always the dilemma of 'the right moment'. My first book on the wider understanding of creative arts therapies was in retrospect, published before its time. It has been of far more interest in the past five years by comparison to the first five. This book is in no way a final statement on dramatherapy. Quite the reverse! It is a first account to present some coherence to what often appears a very diverse and complex subject.

Not only is dramatherapy developing in new and unexpected ways, but also the milieu within which it is practised is changing too. Beliefs, attitudes and practices in all spheres of medical, psychological and social fields are undergoing transformation. Forms of treatment, care and custody are being challenged and new ideas are being tested as we discover more and more about the intricate nature of human beings and their environment.

Sadly, many changes are accelerated because of primary economic considerations rather than the well-being of the people concerned. Staff and clients alike are subject to very rapid changes and re-orientations without sufficient consideration of the immediate impact or long-term effects. However, on the optimistic side, arts therapies are now coming more strongly than ever into their own realm of established practice with accredited training, supervised professional practice and evaluative research.

We need to be careful that dramatherapy does not fall into the trap of attempting to make itself 'scientific' in order to gain credibility in the medical model. It could lose some of its unique qualities that contribute to a holistic approach to bring about change through people's own creative possibilities. However, because traditional scientific models are not necessarily appropriate, it is nevertheless essential that we keep a rigour concerning standards of practice, training and professional supervision.

I hope that all those who read this book are not just concerned with how drama happens 'out there', but also begin to understand their own relationship with the drama process. Only then will it make sense as a process relevant to all spheres of society, including 'us *and* them'.

Sue Jennings

Acknowledgements

As always in the finished production of creative endeavour, the people that have helped are too numerous to mention. Where does one start — with the beginning of one's life with the many influences that have shaped one's growth?

Maybe I should be more concise and thank those people in my more recent past and crave the indulgence of those who have not been mentioned by name. Firstly I must thank all the contributors for their creativity and patience with the lengthy preparation of this book and for their trust of my editorial judgement.

Margaret Davies, as always, is a solid backbone of assistance and help and excellent typing. All the people with whom I have had dramatherapeutic encounters have contributed to my own evolution in this work including students, clients and colleagues and especially too my clients involved in my research. The Senoi Temiar with whom I did my anthropological research have inspired me in many ways that I am still discovering especially in being able to wait for illumination.

There are some very special friends who have sustained me in my creative journey who I must mention — Harry Andrews, Gordon Wiseman, Tony Solomonides, Jane Puddy, Jill Anderson, David Bryan, Hugh and Jean Dickenson, Ase Minde, Yiorgos Polos and Bob Kingsley.

My children, by flesh and marriage, Andy, Jaqui, Ros and Hal always help me to hang in there when the going gets tough. My supervisor, Dr Murray Cox, has taught me so much from his own understanding of chaos and has helped me inestimably to believe in my own.

Sue Jennings

Introduction

It would be unrealistic to attempt to present a step-by-step guide to the evolution of dramatherapy. The many influences that have contributed to the emergence in recent years of dramatherapy practice do not have a uniform line of inheritance. Although current dramatherapeutic practice as we now accept it began in the UK in the early sixties, there were nevertheless, in most societies, dramatic rituals that were, and still are, used to bring about healing of mind, body and spirit (Jennings 1985, 1987).

It was in the early sixties in Britain that a development in the remedial application of drama within the educational framework began to direct itself towards work in clinical areas. This was initiated by such groups as the Remedial Drama Group, which toured Germany, Belgium and Holland, and Sesame Kats which took participatory performances into hospitals and homes. The Remedial Drama Group eventually became the Remedial Drama Centre in Holloway Road, London, where for the first time a centre was specialising in both training and practice of drama with a variety of disabilities and disturbances with children and adults.

This later became the Dramatherapy Centre, the forerunner of the now British Association for Dramatherapists, which is the validating body for dramatherapy training, as well as publishing a journal and promoting conferences. By the early seventies, training was becoming more sophisticated. The Dramatherapy Centre under the auspices of the Central London Polytechnic together with Playspace, offered part-time, one and two year courses, as well as weekend and summer schools. Dramatherapy Consultants was formed to provide specialised courses for professionals in the caring professions as well as leading initiatives in research. Sesame started a full-time course 'Drama and Movement in Therapy' at Kingsway College London.

Hertfordshire College of Art and Design took its first intake of Dramatherapy students in 1977 (where they had already established art therapy training). The College of Ripon and York St. John appointed a research fellow in dramatherapy, and began a qualifying course the following year. In 1980 South Devon Technical College established its own course.

Dramatherapy initiatives began in the USA in the seventies and there are now two Masters courses (Universities of New York and

Antioch), and a National Dramatherapy Association. Holland has had a long-term interest in arts therapies and more recently, Greece has set up it own training programme at the Arts and Therapy Centre, Athens, in collaboration with Dramatherapy Consultants.

Currently there are two post-graduate training courses in dramatherapy in the UK (see training appendix) and a variety of advanced and specialised programmes. The Association now insists on supervision as a requirement for full membership, which places dramatherapy firmly amongst the psychotherapeutic practices. This is in no way to negate the value of both drama as recreation and as a meaningful activity, but it is also an increasingly important form of therapy in the clinical sense of the word, and can be legitimately considered as an alternative to other methods.

Increasingly I hope that hospitals and other centres will consider that there is a choice of different arts therapies (music, art, dance and drama) as well as individual and verbal therapy. It is apparent in this volume that varying professions can now perceive and support dramatherapy in its several forms.

Dramatherapy as an emergent field is endeavouring to find ways to define and re-define itself. This collection of chapters by leading practitioners in the field presents several contrasting theories and forms of practice in dramatherapy. The temptation is to try and find an all embracing definition of dramatherapy and a clear under-standing of what it is and also what it is not. Perhaps in other subjects this approach may be possible, however drama in itself, does not allow us to be so finite. Our understanding of drama, whether it is a part of theatre, whether theatre is therapeutic, whether role-play is also drama, are the sorts of questions that have beset historians, practitioners, drama teachers, social psychologists and many others particularly during the last three decades. However, since the nature and form of the drama is culturally and societally determined, any possible definition is only adequate at this moment.

There was a time when drama and theatre were split in relation to drama in education, when drama was seen as techniques rather than process, when performance was seen as unrelated to the reality of human living. Recently, there has been a total reassessment of these assumptions, but, I must emphasise the reassessment is still going on. Just as there has been in the past an attempt to polarise arts experience from the reality of people's lives, there is now a danger of a fusion that prevents us being clear about the many component parts of the drama and theatre medium.

This book is intended to present a variety of approaches, both in how we perceive drama and also its application in remedial and therapeutic fields. Not all writers agree with each other, and some writers emphasise some aspects of the process more than others. However all, in a sense are 'true' statements about drama and dramatherapy — unless one insists on absolute truth. Drama is not an absolute entity and as such defies an absolute definition.

The chapters are broadly divided into two sections. The first half emphasises theoretical models yet draws upon many practical examples to illustrate the work. The second half concerns specific application and settings where dramatherapy can be a part of therapeutic intervention, yet uses theoretical understanding to underpin the practice.

People with a variety of orientation and background have been deliberately chosen to give the necessary perspectives if we are to attempt to understand the very complex process of drama. This illustrates that, although there is a profession and a practice of dramatherapy, an understanding of drama reaches far beyond a single discipline. As is demonstrated, psychiatrists, psychoanalysts, anthropologists, teachers, psychologists, family therapists, nurses who have training and experience of drama, as well as dramatherapists, have a contribution to make in our unending quest for something so fundamental as the 'nature of drama'. Of course this does not exclude the others for whom this book is also written, such as social workers, occupational therapists, probation officers and all those engaged in remedial and therapeutic work with others in need.

The first two chapters, Dramatherapy and Groups, and Playing on Many Stages, illustrate both group and individual processes that are part of the drama experience. The first chapter puts dramatherapy in the context of developments both in group psychotherapy and in theatre, drawing on sources from ancient Greece, but especially innovations in the first half of this century. Ritual is discussed in relation to drama and theatre and especially the concept of 'liminality' as being parallel to the therapeutic experience. The struggle for reconciliation between light and dark, order and chaos, are seen as belonging to the core of therapy, which can be experienced as a microcosm of the existential struggles of the forces of good and evil expressed in the great myths. Chapter 2 takes a Jungian perspective in charting the process of several clients undergoing psychoanalysis. Rosemary Gordon discusses the 'internal drama' and the 'external drama' as affecting each other through continuous links. She says:

drama is in fact ubiquitous and universal, happening as it does in the world inside all persons, in the world where man relates to universals, to the cosmic, to the good and the bad . . .

Alida Gersie in Chapter 3 on play discusses playing in relation to both healthy and unhealthy psychological development. She suggests that

The exploration of alternatives which is inherent to play demands centred freedom. This is a freedom that comes from our belief that the world will continue to exist whilst we absent ourselves to embark upon a journey of inner and outer discovery.

She makes the play-experience available to dramatherapists an essential dimension to their work and describes the transformation of time and space, the quality of absorption and the need for access to an inner sanctum.

In Chapter 4, David Powley again uses Greek sources to explore and clarify what we mean by drama. Through a careful evolutionary process he describes how we can encounter our many selves, our many roles, through engagement in drama. It is crucial for those engaged in dramatherapy to have this kind of understanding of the depth and breadth of drama at both a personal as well as a cross-cultural level. Drawing almost entirely on drama sources, from Aristophanes to Peter Brook, he establishes the fundamental 'drama experience'.

The following two chapters place dramatherapy within complementary theoretical constructs. Martin Davies looks at the similarities between dramatherapy and psychodrama and the seeming polarity between the two. He discusses Moreno's far-reaching contribution to the entire group-work movement and concludes by describing the 'depth' experience that both psychodrama and dramatherapy can provide. Perhaps a future work should also consider how creative drama in itself can provide a profound experience as is considered by Powley in an earlier chapter. Creative drama is often left outside the consideration of the psychotherapist working at depth. Roy Shuttleworth takes the debate in another direction when, through case histories, he considers family therapy and dramatherapy. Shuttleworth maintains a particular 'right brain' stance when discussing effective therapy and challenges the belief that dependency through transference is at all helpful. He separates out the cognitive from the affective experience, suggesting that change will only occur through the latter. His case work is all based on systemic family therapy and the importance of non-interpretation and metaphor is emphasised throughout.

In Chapter 7, Richard Courtney takes us on a personalised journey of his own development from teacher to therapist through the medium of drama. His contribution needs to be put in context to the many educational drama initiatives that are increasingly taking into account personal and social development as part of the education programme.

Chapter 8 focuses on dramatherapy with adolescents. Both Alida Gersie and myself base this chapter on clinical work in adolescent units and Intermediate Treatment (IT) centres, working with the most difficult of clients. From this experience we have attempted to formulate a working methodology both for a diagnostic and a treatment programme to help the practitioner avoid some of the most common and often painful pitfalls.

Pat Brudenell in Chapter 9 brings alive her highly motivated practice with people who are mentally handicapped. Brudenell stresses the importance of practitioners knowing themselves — being able to recognise their own handicap and their own helplessness. She questions much of the labelling that happens to handicapped people and pushes the limits of drama possibilities with conviction.

Dramatherapy in a Psychiatric Day Centre by John Whitelock provides the reader with the dramatherapist in context — both in terms of role-models, and multi-professional team work, but also within a psychotherapeutic framework of reference. Whitelock also emphasises processes that can be activated by drama which we may not choose to call dramatherapy *per se*.

Dorothy Langley brings us to the final age stage in her chapter on working with elderly people. Like Brudenell, she suggests that the therapist must have an understanding of their own attitudes and feelings towards ageing in order to work effectively with elderly people. Langley uses examples from both reality orientation and reminiscence theatre as well as other dramatherapeutic methods to describe appropriate structures for this work.

Finally, Ross Mitchell looks at dramatherapy within the wider context of the psychiatric institution rather than limiting it to how the dramatherapist works with psychiatric patients. He describes the dramatherapist within the wider system and suggests they should be a resource for staff training and dynamics as well as direct client work.

These chapters have a common aim in wishing to make dramatherapy more accessible both in understanding and practice. Most writers call upon sources from poetry and theatre and literature to highlight their meaning, and enable the dramatic metaphor to expand rather than to reduce the drama to a collection of techniques. If it were the latter, indeed we would all be technicians.

However the struggle for most people is to have sufficient framing to make the drama manageable. This rather parallels our life experience when we need terms of reference, and a framework of a family or social setting in order to know who we are. Since it is apparent that drama is not only of life, both internal and external, it is also larger than life. Not in the sense when we use the term 'acting out' or 'going over the top'. Drama is larger than life in the existential sense that it helps us make sense of the human dilemma.

These chapters present a series of frames or perhaps stages is more appropriate, at the micro, macro and epic levels to facilitate greater understanding of ourselves and the world.

Sue Jennings

REFERENCES

Foucault, M. (1967) *Madness and Civilisation*. Tavistock, London
Jennings, S. (1985) 'Dramatherapy'. In Burr (ed.) *Therapy Through Movement*. Winslow Press, Bucks
Jennings, S. (1987) *Drama, Ritual and Healing*. Unpublished thesis

1

Dramatherapy and Groups

Sue Jennings

Can this cockpit hold
The vasty field of France? Or may we cram
Within this wooden O the very casques
That did afright the air at Agincourt?
Chorus *Henry V*

Dramatherapy is a group process which explores, at many levels of metaphor, dramatic engagement between members of a group.

Before exploring the nature of dramatherapy groups and the nature of other groups which may have dramatic elements or activities, I want to consider the relationship between dramatherapy groups and other groupwork models. This relationship has not always been an easy one. There has often been a simplistic division between 'sit down and be quiet, you're acting out' or 'don't just sit there *do* something!' Dramatherapy groups are often considered 'fringe' activities in a theatre of medicine and dramatherapists are given marginal status. It is first necessary to consider the emergence of both groupwork and dramatherapy during the middle period of this century. Perhaps it would be more accurate to say that I shall look at the influences in therapy that contributed to the groupwork movement as well as the influences in drama that contributed to dramatherapy.

As human beings we find ourselves in groups for a variety of reasons. We are all born into groups — the first-born has the sometimes unenviable task of turning a couple into a group. We come together throughout our lives in a variety of groups of varying sizes. As small children we often join a structured playgroup, and then have free play with the neighbours' children. Structured forms of group games and group activities of all sorts take place in schools, clubs and societies. However, it is only the more enlightened of teachers who will actually teach *through* the group: usually we teach *to* the group, or even *at* the group, rather than through it. Most self-directed learning experiments are usually with individuals rather

1

than groups. Group projects are a more recent innovation in the classroom. Very early in life we instil the individual concept — 'Are you *sure* its your own work?' Yet pupils themselves often struggle on their own initiatve with group learning and understanding. This can reach difficult dimensions in teenhood, when the pull of the peer group can be strong enough to set up an opposition between the known authority of the parents and the fusion with the group identity. Or it can be that the parent/child identity is fused and will not allow for separation into peer-group identity. Many parents themselves are very ambivalent about the amount of separation they want from their children, and vary in their attitudes between boys and girls. Children who choose to read in their rooms are often hassled into 'get out and enjoy yourself'.

It would seem that throughout life there is a struggle concerning the individual and the group — about being alone and being together. However a closer look at ancient philosophy would show that societies have always struggled with the 'individual and the group' at both personal levels as well as societal levels. Although the study of groups of people by sociologists, anthropologists and psychologists has increased as these disciplines have grown, the notion of the group as a form of systematic treatment and change did not occur until relatively recently. First there had to be a shift from the treatment of the soma to the treatment of the psyche.

The turn of this century certainly saw the emergence of major new thinking in terms of treating neurosis and later, psychosis. The old asylums usually locked people up and, when necessary, manacled them for restraint. People who felt 'unwell' were given support or medicines of various sorts. People were put into mental hospitals for all sorts of reasons (for example, women for illegitimacy). There was still much folk medicine, with rural midwives and exorcism from the clergy. Brown and Pedder (1979) give a brief description of the historic background of dynamic psychotherapy and Foucault (1973) illustrates the wider medical context of the time. Many writers and philosophers knew of unconscious feelings but it was Freud in 1894 who crystallised this thinking and wrote extensively on the nature of the unconscious. This later formed the basis of psychoanalysis. Now we refer to psychodynamic psychotherapy, whether for individuals or groups, in contrast to task-centred therapy.

With Freud, Jung and others, the practice of treating patients in a one-to-one setting developed extensively and there was a whole wave of energy in psychoanalytic practice, research and writing.

However, there was already to be a reaction not only against the one-to-one treatment, but also that it was static and verbal. Jacob Moreno, born in Vienna in 1892, became frustrated with this non-interactive model of therapy and began to develop his own ideas growing from his studies in sociometry — the study of the 'social atom' of which people are a part. He soon developed the theory and practice of psychodrama and later sociodrama. Moreno could be said to be the forerunner of modern group psychotherapy, although his ideas of using action in groups rather than only words took much longer to be accepted.

I do not want to elaborate here on psychodramatic theory, which is developed in more detail by Davies in Chapter 5, nor will I repeat information described by other writers in the context of different approaches to working with groups (e.g. Shuttleworth on Family Therapy in Chapter 6). However, just as all psychodynamic psychotherapy must acknowledge the major contribution of Freud, so most groupwork approaches acknowledge the innovatory influence of Moreno on their thinking and practice.

During recent years there has been a plethora of innovations in the development of different approaches to groupwork. For the moment I want to focus on the emergence of the small group (which later influenced the emergence of De Mare's large-group concept, see De Mare, 1975) as a focus for treatment and change.

What has since come to be known as the Northfield Experiments, which took place in the military hospital with Jones, Bion and others, not only had an impact on the eventual practice of the small group but also on other innovations. Two in particular need mention: social therapy (Clark, 1974) and the therapeutic communities (Jones, 1968). The development of therapy in small groups led to the establishment of some major centres for treatment and training, including the Tavistock Centre and later the Institute of Group Analysis. The impetus came from a small group of psychiatrists and psychoanalysts who included Bion, Foulkes, Anthony and Main.

Brown and Pedder (1979) have suggested that the work can be contrasted in three ways: analysis *in* the group; analysis *of* the group; and analysis *through* the group. Analysis in the group was mainly operational in the USA and was the analysis of individuals in a group setting. Analysis of the group stems from the work of Bion and Ezriel with a particular emphasis on group dynamics. The term 'group dynamics' was first coined by Kurt Lewin in his involvement in the T-Group movement. Bion and Ezriel based their work at the Tavistock Centre and they not only worked with therapeutic groups but also with other sorts of institutions (Bion, 1961, Brown and Pedder, 1979). Therapy through the group is associated with the work of Foulkes who founded the Institute of Group Analysis. In group-analytic psychotherapy the individual is being treated in the context of the group (Foulkes and Anthony, 1973). Brown and Pedder suggest that Foulkes in fact anticipated recent understanding in family processes and therapy when he 'came to see the individual as at a nodal point in a network of relationships and illness as a disturbance in the network that comes to light through the vulnerable individual'. Foulkes maintained that groups function, often simultaneously, at several different levels. According to De Mare and Kreeger (1974) the group analysis of Foulkes is the most influential in Britain today; certainly it has a major European and international following.

In addition to the three forms of group psychotherapy and psychodrama mentioned above, there are other group methods including gestalt, encounter, T-groups and transactional analysis.

Group methods are now being used extensively in both the community and institutional setting. Not all groups are psychodynamic; there are many groups concerned with behaviour modification as well as activity groups of all kinds. Task-centred life and social groups have increased, especially recently with the work of Ellis and Whittington (1981) and others. Art therapy, music therapy, dance therapy as well as dramatherapy are all increasingly used. They are based on several theoretical models of practice.

In terms of workers we now have group analysts, group therapists, and group workers and psychodramatists. A useful description of verbal groupwork and action methods by Shaffer and Galinsky (1974) also describes the training for several of the methods. Before we start to look at the relationship of dramatherapy to other groupwork, I want to look at the recent developments of drama itself.

Just as people have always participated in groups, they have likewise always been engaged in drama to a greater or lesser extent. As far back as we can go in recorded history — and even earlier to the cave paintings in France which depict masked dancers — we know that people participated in some kind of dramatic ritual. Dramatic ritual has always enabled people to celebrate, heal, worship, to influence events, and to mediate between gods and mortals. Ritual drama has, until comparatively recently, had a central place in the affairs of people, it was belief, healing and worship in an integrated form. Drama has a unifying quality whereby the norms and values of the society are expressed within a context of heightened awareness and sensory experience, Turner (1969). Contrasting forms of dramatic expression in theatre have a more recent past but still can trace a history of 25,000 years from the classical theatre of ancient Greece. Thus we can see that dramatic expression has always played some part in the way we interact in groups with tremendous variation between cultures and continents.

For the present purpose I want to consider the influences in drama and theatre during the same period of time as Freud and the early group psychotherapists.

Just as Freud revolutionised the notion of 'treatment', extending it from static bodies that had things done to them to the possibility that there might be a psychic causality for the symptoms, and Moreno had set 'movement' in motion in psychodrama — Constantin Stanislavski was more responsible than anyone else for freeing the stylised and postured theatre of the times. When Stanislavski took over the Moscow Arts Theatre he developed a new approach to the training of actors as well as to the style of theatre production. He was the first person to develop the 'as if' concept. With his actors he worked primarily on their emotional memory in order to bring authentic feelings to their parts. If an actor had difficulty with certain parts, then the 'as if' principle would enable them to get in touch with appropriate feelings. Stanislavski (1937) emphasised lengthy, intensive training for actors, the importance of the unconscious and the reality of the actors' own lives. The work of Artaud, too, though revolutionary in its own right nevertheless has roots in the work of Stanislavski, as have most theatre innovations of the past eighty years.

Grotowski in the 1970s became more and more concerned with the creativity of ordinary people his 'para-theatrical' work. His concern is to remove the separation between actors and audience, remove the box office and to find new ways of rediscovering an experience of drama and ritual. Grotowski (1968) terms it 'A Theatre of Sources — bringing us back to the sources of life, to direct primeval experience, to organic primary experience.'

Roose Evans (1984) commenting on this says that:

> an attempt to create a genuine encounter between individuals who meet at first as complete strangers and then, gradually, as they lose their fear and distrust of each other, move towards a more

fundamental encounter in which they themselves are the active and creative participants in their own drama of rituals and ceremonials.

With the influence of Stanislavski, there are numerous theatre directors who made an impact and developed new forms during this century; they are concerned in their research not with formulations but with a continuous journey. Sometimes this journey takes an actual form such as Peter Brook's journey to Africa to the Ik tribe and Grotowski's journey to the Far East. There is a kind of restlessness which needs to go on discovering and resists formulation and static theory. Peter Brook in his book *The Empty Space* (1972) talks about the need to revitalise the theatre, to make it *Immediate* (as contrasted with other forms — Dead Theatre, the Rough Theatre and Holy Theatre). He says that we should consider the French word for performance 'representation' in order to reconcile the contradiction of repetition necessary in rehearsal. It is an occasion when something is 're-presented' and therefore not an imitation of a description of a past event

> It abolishes that difference between yesterday and today. It takes yesterday's action and makes it live again in every one of its aspects — including its immediacy. In other words a representation is what it claims to be — a making present. We can see how this is the renewal of life that repetition denies and it applies as much in rehearsal as it does in performance.

Recent innovators in the theatre have struggled to rediscover the active interaction between actor and audience, the 'genuine encounter'. However this encounter is not necessarily a fusion of the psyche of performer and observer, it may be by alienation — by a distancing such as described by Brecht in his work in Germany and America. Brecht never wanted the audience to forget they were in the theatre, that they were seeing a performance of events by actors and he would use various unexpected devices to remind them, such as the actors coming out of role. He thought the audience would be prompted to think about what they had seen and learn from it — he was attempting to change the nature of society. As Roose Evans (1984) says, 'For Brecht the purpose of the theatre was to teach us how to survive.'

Simon Callow (1984) warns of what happens when drama and theatre become institutionalised and belong to a directocracy rather

6

than the actors: 'The waste of the actors' intelligence and passion (how can you be passionate about something in which you have no involvement? All that's left for you is to concentrate on *your role*; unhealthy and counterproductive . . .'

Despite the influences of major theatre practitioners of this century there is still the institutionalised, director-centred theatre, just as there are institutionalised, leader-focused forms of therapy. Theatre and therapy can be an assault on the passive participant.

To summarise, so far I have reviewed the major changes that Freud and others have made on the emergence of new forms of therapy with a move away from the emphasis on passive somatic forms of treatment of the acknowledgement of unconscious, intra-psychic processes, the later development of groups in the healing process and the inclusion of action method within some therapeutic situations. I have then looked at the same period of time in the theatre when there was a major influence against the stylisation of the traditional theatre by Stanislavski, which stimulated a wave of new approaches and experiments. As with therapy, these experiments were not always in agreement, they often opposed or complemented each other.

In both areas despite many attempts to hold on to hierarchy and power in treatment and therapy there have been strong moves to democratise the process — to move to an interactionist model between patient and therapist, between actor and audience. Cox (1978) says:

The therapist can never be a merely neutral, impassive, facilitator of cognitive-affective self awareness for his patient, because he also shares the predicament of humanness. Paradoxically it is because of the ontological insecurity in the therapist, that the patient dares to trust him enough to risk 'abandonment to therapeutic space'.

Grotowski (1968) says:

I am interested in the actor because he is a human being. This involves two principal points: firstly my meeting with another person, the contact, the mutual feeling of comprehension and the impression created by the fact that we try to open ourselves to another being, that we try to understand him; in short the surmounting of our solitude. Secondly, the attempt to understand oneself through the behaviour of another man, finding oneself in him.

Although there are attempts to create a relationship through therapy and theatre, between thought and feeling, between givers and receivers, I am suggesting that verbal group-therapy and dramatherapy mutually distance each other from an understanding of their very natures. Dramatherapy is often seen as undifferentiated, uncontrolled, a collective emotional experience, and verbal therapy is perceived as being intellectual, formal, rigid and individualistic.

I do not think this is a recent debate. Just as we have struggled since ancient times with the relationship between the individual and the group, we have also moved between the oppositions of thought and feeling. Lévi-Strauss, the structural anthropologist, suggests this opposition as a polarity between nature and culture, a binary opposition in human thought. However, before I explore this further I want to look briefly at the drama of the ancient Greeks.

Plato in his writings vilified the person and nature of the actor and said that the art of acting could be morally damaging. If a person can represent a bad character on stage then it follows he cannot be a good person. In *The Republic*, Plato maintains that tragedy will excite in the audience emotions that should be curbed:

> Then is it really right, to admire when we see him on the stage, a man we should ourselves be ashamed to resemble? Is it reasonable to feel enjoyment and admiration rather than disgust?

Aristotle in his writing directly challenges Plato's view, and says that emotional impact of drama on an audience is a positive one. It was of course from this point that Aristotle developed his theory of catharsis.

So what are the themes that thousands of years later people still find disquieting about the nature of drama? There seems to be fear of a loss of control, of darkness, of antisocial forces, of unconscious feelings coming into the open. The Dionysian view of the drama is taken to exemplify the 'primitive' forces of 'nature', the collective frenzy that is set free within such an orgiastic drama.

Pentheus

Shrieking as long as life was left in him, the women
Howling in triumph. One of them carried off an arm
Another a foot, the boot still laced on it. The ribs
were stripped, clawed clean; the women's hands, thick red
with blood, were tossing, catching, like a plaything
Pentheus' flesh.

The Bacchae of Euripides

8

The characters within the Bacchae set up the polarity between individual thought and collective emotion particularly in the character of the herdsman who comes to report what he has seen on the hill side, when with other herdsmen and shepherds he witnesses the women breastfeeding wild animals, and then the frenzied collective orgy of the women. I have suggested elsewhere (Jennings, 1985) that there is a polarity of thought between group analysis and dramatherapy and that dramatherapy is seen as primarily Dionysian:

A medium that was ecstatic and revelrous, that contained darkness, timelessness, global intuition, expressing itself through chorus of rhythmic sound and movement. A fused experience of the collective relying on intuition and spontaneity, and dominated by the destructiveness of women.

It is a fantasy based on a Bacchanalian perception of dramatic freedom which was cathartic and without boundaries. However, in this perception of drama it is Apollonean aspects that bring the complimentary qualities of light, individuation, clarity of thought, and reason that are ignored. These are qualities attributed to the verbal analysis of the group process. However, in the Greek theatre, certainly in the fifth century, there was a constant attempt to reach an equilibrium between Apollo and Dionysus. The message of the play, the Bacchae, is that there is ultimate destruction in either extreme, and that if we *ignore* the passions of the collective, we do so at our peril. The problem with a polarity of this kind is that it becomes mutually exclusive whereas these two positions need to be in a dialectical relationship with each other. (See also Pines (1986) for a suggestion that the Apollo/Dionysian opposition is a way of understanding Foulkes and Moreno.) It is the space between them that is the crucial one for therapeutic interchange.

Conscious and unconscious do not make a whole when one of them is suppressed and injured by the other. If they must contend let it at least be a fair fight with equal rights on both sides. Both are aspects of life. Consciousness should defend its reason and protect itself, and the chaotic life of the unconscious should be given the change of having its way too — as much of it as we can stand. This means open conflict and open collaboration at once.

C.G. Jung (1916)

However, let us also further look at the binary opposition of the

9

structuralist anthropologists. As is well documented, early anthropologists and psychoanalysts were fascinated by the study of ritual drama and myths. Some of the early work was an attempt to prove an evolutionary basis of human development from the 'primitive' to the 'civilised'. Other writing sought to equate the workings of the 'primitive' mind with the manifestations of disturbed people. Writings by Freud and Bettelheim, to name but two, have been challenged for their ethnocentricity and for their reliance on second- and third-hand information. Malinowski, the forerunner of the Functionalist school of anthropology, maintained the field-work basis for the data of research. He posited another view of the Freudian Oedipal theory which was rejected by psychoanalysts at the time. Coming in the wake of the Functionalist school, with its emphasis on symbolism and utility, Lévi-Strauss developed his writings on the theme of *how* the primitive mind thinks, rather than what it thought. In *The Savage Mind* and subsequent writing he builds his theory of culture as an expression of the underlying structure of the human mind. Therefore cultures may vary considerably although their human thought processes are the same. His polar opposites become such contrasting pairs as raw versus cooked and light versus dark, and of course self versus other, which together with individual versus group returns us to our existential dilemma.

As I stated earlier, however, Lévi-Strauss formed many of these oppositions around the main focus of nature and culture. Although most people would recognise Lévi-Strauss's important contribution to anthropological theory, there are nevertheless some identifiable problems. He suggests within the nature/culture pair that we can also consider female/male. It looks convenient until we examine it more closely. By identifying women with the 'nature' side, all that is not human, uncivilised, we are making the same mistake of placing the female into the category of the wild, the dangerous, the undifferentiated and the collective. I do not want to elaborate here on the various interpretations of the use of the word 'nature' (see Bloch and Bloch, 1980), but point out a link with our early statements on Dionysian drama. What must concern us here is the parallel position of women being conceptualised in anthropological structuralism as wild (and also wicked and witches) with the collective and destructive imagery of the Dionysian position.

Therefore I would suggest that anthropologists and psychoanalysts generally have been guilty of what I term 'the Dionysian error'. They perceive the emotional aspects of dramatic ritual and early theatre, the arousal of archetypal images and the stimulation of uncontrollable feelings through powerful representations associated with destructive femaleness. It then follows that such expression needs to be *interpreted and verbally controlled* by the power of reason and logic within the classical intellectual framework. However Turner (1969) has pointed out that the central concern of ritual symbolism is the multiple meaning of its expression, that it is to do with both thought and feeling, that it can, at one and the same time, represent the individual, the group, the society and the cosmos at both a sensory *and* intellectual level.

Turner describes two poles of meaning which he calls the 'ideological' and the 'sensory'. He suggests that the ideological pole represents the norms and values for the maintenance and continuation of political, social and domestic life, whereas the sensory arouses the emotions and collective representations of human feelings. By bringing them into contact with one another, one will reinforce the other. As Turner (1982) says in one of his later writings: 'We *can* learn from experience — from enactment and performance of the culturally transmitted experiences of others — peoples of the Heath as well as of the Book'.

The paradox of the separation of the Apollonean and Dionysian aspects of therapy is that the very projections with which Dionysian drama is labelled, are the same themes that psychotherapists wish to explore — the darker recesses of the mind, the unchartered areas of unconscious and pre-conscious experience. It is only in a bringing together of these seeming oppositions into complimentarity, that we shall be enabled to contemplate the therapeutic journey.

All groupwork contains certain dramatic elements. As a complement to the description of the dramatherapy groups, I want to consider the dramatic elements in psychotherapy groups. Firstly, I would like to suggest that the transference element in psychodynamic therapy can be described as an act of dramatic imagination. When clients transfer feelings of parental love to their therapist they are engaging in an 'as if' communication; consciously they *know* that their therapist is not their parent, but they behave as if he or she is. It is the engagement of this dramatic relationship in its many dimensions that forms the very essence of the therapeutic relationship. Furthermore, the formal psychotherapy group uses the most primitive theatre form, the circle. The circle is used in many rituals and in the goat dance, an early form of Greek theatre. A ritual time and place is set aside for therapeutic interaction and the emphasis is on metalanguage and subtext. There is an adjustment of roles within the group that re-defines itself in relation to the group. The

11

psychotherapy group spends much of its time improvising. Time is also spent considering dreams, which are another dramatic form, and which, like at the Oracle of Delphi (the home of Apollo and Dionysus) can be made to yield meaning. Thus one could suggest that psychotherapy groups are, in fact, a stylised form of dramatherapy group!

All dramatherapy groups are based on the assumption of the therapeutic nature of the dramatic act, that there is a dramatic engagement between clients and therapists. Furthermore, a whole range of dramatic media will be the means of exploration and learning in the dramatherapy group. There are obviously specific models for practice which I have described in an earlier paper as the 'Creative/Expressive', the 'Learning' and the 'Insight or Psychotherapeutic' models (Jennings, 1984). These are described by Davies in Chapter 5.

I do not want to make value judgements concerning different types of dramatherapeutic practice, whether a 'depth experience' has more status than a 'social experience'. We are engaging in the art and craft of dramatherapy in contrasting ways, and some practitioners will be other kinds of therapists and group workers as well as dramatherapists. I am concerned that we are clear why we are running a particular type of drama-based therapy group, and why we have chosen the drama rather than another process? We may be emphasising the skills through the drama, or encouraging the social effects that coming together to make drama provides for us. We may feel dramatherapy ameliorates the effects of institutionalisation, or we may decide to use drama to explore a specific theme such as gender and role. There is a wide range of possibilities in the application of dramatherapy including psychotherapy, behaviour modification, re-education, rehabilitation, re-creation. Let us make the decisions which define the nature of the dramatherapy group, its overt contract, its intended aims and its duration (see Jennings, 1986d), or we shall be guilty of making the Dionysian error ourselves, and running undifferentiated dramatherapy groups with the vague idea that it is somehow good for us, or with the messianic zeal that it holds the answers to all individual and social problems.

For the remainder of this chapter I want to explore that area of dramatherapy of which there is least documentation. Depth experiences of the unconscious in dramatherapy comes close to psychotherapy, but is nevertheless one which is equated with loss of control. To set these experiences in context I want first to talk about *rites de passage* — the form of life–transition ritual described by

Van Gennep (1960). *Rites de passage* accompany our journeys through life from the womb to the tomb, and mark important changes in status — christenings, initiation, marriage, funerary rites, to name but some.

These rites have three important stages described by Van Gennep, separation, transition and re-incorporation. The transition or liminal time, is in between when learning and change takes place. I have discussed in a previous paper (Jennings, 1983) that the therapy itself, of whatever sort, can be described as a *rite de passage*, (see also Helman, 1984). As therapists we can accompany our clients on a journey from unwell being to well being. We may decide, as in some of the dramatherapy groups described above, to structure quite specifically the means of travel on this journey, which luggage is to be carried or disposed of. We may prescribe the route before we leave and decide to travel by the shortest possible route.

However I want to explore with the unchartered route, where the map may only be an impression. There is a notion that things could be better and a range of unexplained and sometimes chaotic feelings. Often our clients express desolation and despair or a nothingness. We are considering a journey from disorder to order, from darkness to some illumination, where the outcome cannot be prescribed, but we may have some idea when we arrive. We are talking of a journey that concerns inner change both for the clients as well as the therapist. This comes about through *interchange* between ourselves and others, we learn more of ourselves because of our interaction with others. The dramas of other people's lives also belong to our lives and the drama of the group's life is also the drama of Life itself. Whatever the moment of intra-psychic and inter-psychic reality we may be involved in with our clients, it has an existential reality as well.

Wilshire (1982) points out that the theatre is about the 'world' as well as the world. He says of the people assembled to watch Oedipus Rex that they

> were enabled to see what they were too inured to see, or too afraid to see, or too ashamed to see otherwise. It compressed and summarised in the 'world' of the play the wider context of sense which is the world itself; it was the absent given presence, articulation and precision through theatrical proxy. The 'world' stood for the world.

13

How may we learn about the 'world' and the world, the life and the Life through the experience of dramatherapy? Let us return to the liminal stage in our *rites de passage*, the stage where values appear to be turned upside down and where there is ambiguity. Turner says in *The Ritual Process* (1969)

> The attributes of liminality or of liminal personae (threshold people) are necessarily ambiguous, since this condition and these people are necessarily ambiguous, since this condition and these people elude or slip through the network of classifications that normally locate places and position in cultural space. Liminal entities are neither here nor there; they are betwixt and between the positions assigned and arrayed by law, custom, convention and ceremonial. As such their ambiguous and indeterminate attributes are expressed by a rich variety of symbols in the many societies that ritualise social and cultural transitions. This liminality is likened frequently to — death, to being in the womb, to invisibility, to darkness, to bisexuality, to the wilderness and to an eclipse of the sun or the moon.

From this vivid description we can already recognise many of the metaphors that clients will use to describe their disequilibrium and troubled selves, often expressed through disorientation in time and space. The liminal stage of the experience can be desert, jungle, ocean and mountain.

The dramatherapy group is the empty stage which enables these images to be represented at different levels. It symbolises the scenario of Life itself as well as the lives of the individual group members, and also the life of the group. Within the context of the dramatherapy group through many forms of dramatic expression, lives are re-created and re-presented in symbolic form. It is the polysemic nature of dramatherapy which enables the group's liminality to be expressed through the multiple metaphors. Whether they are expressed non-verbally or verbally, through role or projection, through myth or ritual, through mask or mimesis, they are the key to our understanding. These metaphors are the dominant symbols with which we begin to comprehend the human condition both specifically and generally.

Nevertheless, just as Turner described above the undifferentiated chaotic experience of the liminal period, he also says (1967) 'Liminality may be partly described as a stage of reflection.' It is a time when there are moments of clarity and illumination, when there is the possibility of discovering what we did not know that we knew. Although it may feel dangerous at times when boundaries move and signposts no longer contain coherent messages, nevertheless there are also times of understanding, when the experience of creativity in a seeming disordered form, can take shape and substance.

Nathan Scott (1985) also talks of the liminal period when he says 'However it is not merely a negative state of privation . . . it can be and often is an enormously fruitful seedbed of spiritual creativity.'

Therefore we can begin to understand that rather than the drama being the chaos, *the drama is both the container of the chaos and the means of exploring it.* Accompanying our groups through such dangerous territory may seem too frightening for the dramatherapist to contemplate, let alone the client. What can reassure us on these journeys?

Firstly, we need to remind ourselves that the journey will be about change in us as well as change in our clients. There is no way we can be in a dramatic engagement with our clients and stay static ourselves. Drama itself is a living organic medium and we will grow within it. We also need to know that it is our own liminality, our own experience of the dark, the desert, the fear, the chaos and the wounding that will enable the client to make use of their own experience. When Halifax (1982) talks of the 'wounded healer', it is the experience of our own wounding that will enable us to engage with our clients in a healing process.

This availability of our own experience can only be possible through our own creativity and poetic imagination. Often we need to *stay with* the metaphoric expressions of our clients rather than imposing control by interpreting them. Our need to explain and interpret is usually more about our own feelings of anxiety than our client's. My advice to dramatherapy students has been — 'stay with the chaos and allow the meaning to emerge'.

I did not realise how this had become a life-line, until I saw it written on a collage at a farewell celebration of my own transition from institutional life. This had been the advice I gave myself during anthropological field work when in the Malaysian jungle. I was surrounded by a plethora of symbolic material to which I could not get access for months. It would have been too easy to impose my own ethnocentric assumption as to meaning and to provide an explanation of the phenomena I was witnessing.

By having our creative poetic imagination at the service of others we must not neglect our own nourishment. We need also to be regularly replenished through art and literature, through music and painting, through gardening and poetry, so that we do not get trapped ourselves in an arid desert.

Ancient wisdom is in no doubt of the importance of the poetic imagination despite the criticism of Socrates and Plato. When Aristophanes asks quite simply in *The Frogs*

What do you want a poet for?
To save the City of course.

Artaud (1958) suggests that we must make a distinction between an expression of the senses and one of discourse:

I say that there is a poetry of the senses as there is a poetry of language and that this concrete physical language is truly theatrical only to the degree that the thoughts it expresses are beyond the reach of the spoken language.

The struggle to free imaginative expression from the strait jacket of rationality is permeating all disciplines. Beattie (1977) when looking at the similarity between early forms of theatre and spirit possession cults in Africa says that one of the problems of studying ritual is that we try and look upon it as a type of erroneous science rather than allowing it to be a kind of applied poetry. Murray Cox is the first psychotherapist I know who has explored the idea of 'The Poetry of Therapy' (1986).

However, in our search for greater understanding of the complexities of our clients' communications, we must ourselves not fall into the Dionysian error of perceiving all as chaos and darkness. We must stay in touch with our Apollonean nature, which has order and light. Apollo was also the god of arts, medicine and prophecy as well as for the care of flocks and herds. Constantly we find ourselves needing to rationalise, to find tools for explaining, to make something pocket size that we can take out and examine.

Perhaps it is more helpful if we remember that the epic metaphors of Apollo and Dionysus within which there is both differentiated as well as undifferentiated experience, are in themselves broad tropes with which we try and grapple with the human condition. Thus we may understand a little more of the balance between light and dark, individual and group, mind and body and order and chaos. The mediation of the dramatherapeutic experience will assist us in this transformation.

What is the point of being artists
If we cannot save our own life?

Alice Walker (1985)

REFERENCES AND FURTHER READING

Artaud, A. (1958) *The Theatre and its Double*. Grove Press, New York
Beattie, J. (1977) *Spirit Mediumship as Theatre*. R.A.I. No. 20
Bion, W.R. (1961) *Experiences in Groups*. Tavistock, London
Bloch, M. & Bloch, J. (1980) 'Women and the Dialectics of Nature in 18th-Century Thought'. In C. MacCormack and M. Strathern (eds) *Nature, Culture and Gender*, Cambridge University Press, Cambridge
Brook, P. (1972) *The Empty Space*, Penguin, London
Brown, D. & Pedder, J. (1979) *Introduction to Psychotherapy*. Tavistock, London
Callow, S. (1984) *Being an Actor*. Penguin, London
Clark, D. (1974) *Social Therapy in Psychiatry*. Pelican, London
Cox, M. (1978) *Structuring the Therapeutic Process*. Pergamon, Oxford
——— (1986) 'The Poetry of Therapy'. Title of Third Annual Lecture to St Albans Psychotherapy Association
De Mare, P. (1975) 'The Large Group'. In L. Kreeger (ed) *The Large Group — Dynamics and Therapy*, Constable, London
——— & Kreeger, L. (1974) *Introduction to Group Treatments in Psychiatry*. Butterworth, London
Ellis, R. & Whittington, D. (1981) *A Guide to Social Skill Training*. Croom Helm, London
Euripides *see* Vellacott
Foucault, M. (1973) *The Birth of the Clinic*. Tavistock, London
Foulkes, S.H. & Anthony, E.J. (1973) *Group Psychotherapy: Psychoanalytical Approach*. Penguin, London
Freud, S. (1894) *The Neuro-Psychoses of Defence* (1). In Standard Edition of Complete Works, Vol 3. Hogarth Press and Institute of Psychoanalysis, London
Grotowski, J. (1968) *Towards a Poor Theatre*. Eyre Methuen, London
Halifax, J. (1982) *Shaman: The Wounded Healer*. Thames and Hudson, London
Helmann, c. (1984) *Culture, Health and Illness*. Wright-PSG, Bristol, London and Boston
Jennings, S. (1983) 'Creative Arts Therapies in Psychiatry'. Paper presented to the Royal College of Psychiatry and the College of Occupational Therapy
——— (1984) 'Models of Practice in Dramatherapy' in *Journal of Dramatherapy*, vol. 7
——— (1985) 'The Ritual and the Drama, with Reference to Group Analysis'. Paper presented to the Spring Scientific Meeting of the Institute of Group Analysis
——— (1986a) 'Temiar Dance and the Maintenance of Order'. In P. Spencer (ed.) *Society and the Dance*, Cambridge University Press,

Cambridge

—————— (1986b) 'The Loneliness of the Long Distance Therapist'. Paper presented at the Annual Summer Seminar, Cumberland Lodge

—————— (1986c) 'The Angry Women in the Family'. Paper presented to the Norwegian Summer Seminar in Art and Drama Therapy

—————— (1986d) *Creative Ideas in Groupwork*. Winslow Press, Bucks

Jones, M. (1968) *Social Psychiatry in Practice: The Idea of the Therapeutic Community*. Penguin, London

Jung, C. (1916) *Collected Works*. Routledge and Kegan Paul, London

Lee, D. (1955) Trans. *The Republic* by Plato. Penguin, London

Pines, M. (1986) 'Psychoanalysis, Psychodrama and Group Psychotherapy'. In *Group Analysis*, vol. 19, No. 2

Plato *see* Lee

Roose Evans, J. (1984) *Experimental Theatre from Stanislavski to Peter Brook*. Routledge and Kegan Paul, London

Scott, N. (1985) *The Poetics of Belief*. University of North Carolina Press, Durham, North Carolina

Shaffer, J.P.B. and Galinsky, M.D. (1974) *Models of Group Therapy and Sensitivity Training*. Prentice Hall, Englewood-Cliffs, New Jersey

Stanislavski, C. (1937) *An Actor Prepares*. Re-published 1980 Methuen, London

Turner, V. (1967) *Forest of Symbols*. Cornell University Press, Ithaca, New York

—————— (1969) *The Ritual Process*. Routledge and Kegan Paul, London

—————— (1982) *From Ritual to Theatre*. Performing Arts Journal Pub, New York

Van Gennep, A. (1960) *Rites de passage*. Routledge and Kegan Paul, London

Vellacott, P. (1972) Trans. *The Bacchae and Other Plays* by Euripides. Penguin, London

Walker, A. (1985) *Horses Made a Landscape Look More Beautiful*. The Women's Press, London

Wilshire, B. (1982) *Role Playing and Identity*. Indiana University Press, Bloomington, Indiana

2

Playing on Many Stages: Dramatherapy and the Individual

Rosemary Gordon

INTRODUCTION

I want to explore in this chapter the question of man and drama in terms of what I, as an analytical psychologist, can contribute to an elucidation of it by drawing on my clinical experience and on my store of those theories that have proved to be useful models. Such elucidation may help towards a better and firmer assessment of the healing potential of drama when it is enacted on the stage, in the therapist's consulting room or in real-life situations.

Departing from the more usual and traditional procedure, I shall begin this chapter with a description of my analytic work with a young man, Bob, who was 32 years old when he started analysis. It was not until quite late in my work with him that I began to realise that many of the features of his case are, in fact, features that also characterise drama.

A CASE DESCRIPTION

Bob had been in analysis for several years. He was a designer and desperately anxious to become a good and inventive one; he longed to find, to reach and then to have and use his own creative resources. Longing to achieve this goal had been one of his main reasons for coming into analysis.

He was the elder of two boys. His father, an engineer, a quiet and somewhat withdrawn man, had been away fighting in the Second World War when Bob was between eight and twelve years of age — the very years when he most needed the presence, encouragement and inspired companionship of a man. His mother had been a professional ballet dancer who, after the birth of her two children and then the absence of her husband, became a teacher of dance and drama at a grammar school. She was, it emerged from Bob's description of her, a lively person, somewhat self-centred, devoted to her work and profession, with easy access to her feelings and her creativity, but not really interested in, or talented for, making a home, enriching such a home or giving much time and attention to her children. She had a close woman friend with whom she collaborated in her professional work.

Bob was a tall, thin, quiet, shy, timid, diffident, insecure and passive person, who looked ten to fifteen years younger than he actually was. He had great difficulty in asserting himself, either in his work, in relation to colleagues and superiors, or in his personal relationships with friends, partners and acquaintances. He seemed very cut-off from his affects and impulses and his feelings in the transference were subdued. It was only when he could tell me about some new failure or loss of prestige, achievement, argument or friendship that a note of triumph, of masochistic triumph, enlivened his verbal and facial expression. The analysis jogged along quietly. He had many interesting dreams; some were filled with quite strong emotions. There were several about giving birth, involving either himself or some domestic animal; but even this potentially optimistic and forward-looking theme tended to be vitiated in some way or other. Either there was not enough food for the new baby; or instead of milk the baby was offered faeces; or he, the mother, the birth-giver, was rejected and socially excluded and shunned; or else the baby was damaged or disposed of as rubbish. There was so much hurt and pain in the content of most of his dreams, but he would tell them in his quiet, gentle and bland manner as if they had actually been dreamed by someone else.

Strangely enough, my own feelings for him in my counter-transference remained consistently caring, affectionate and matern-ally protective. Why, I often wondered, did I not, at least sometimes, react with impatience, anger and irritation, as indeed his father had done when he returned from his war service and did not, as Bob remembered, seem to be particularly pleased with the way his eldest son had developed? Perhaps he experienced his son as a part of his own shadow, as a caricature of himself, representing his own lack of a positive masculinity.

I had come to suspect that there may be no lively and potentially creative centre to be found in Bob. When both of us came close to a loss of hope about it all, we decided that he should try his hand at some art therapy. The results were truly surprising. Bob brought his paintings to his analytic sessions. They were a revelation; for these paintings were quite remarkably lively, colourful and full of imaginative forms of persons and creatures and objects, expressing much joy and fun as well as fear and anger and violence. They showed a capacity to be playful — in Winnicott's (1971) sense of 'play' — that he had, until now, been unable to draw on and use and enjoy.

At first, as with his dreams, Bob displayed and discussed them without much affect, enthusiasm or even involvement. But now my own reactions to him became more fierce and challenging. I felt anger, as if on behalf of his pictures, at what seemed to me to be his dismissal of them and his churlish and almost sadistic refusal to acknowledge as his own the paintings before us. And, as I began to express some of these reactions, a father — a more potentially enabling father than he had experienced in his own personal history — seemed to become activated inside each one of us and between us. Bob reacted first by sullen, sulky and hurt withdrawal into more silence; but then, slowly, he rose to my challenge; he became more overtly resentful, a bit abusive and finally honestly hostile and aggressive. This then seemed to enable him to protect and defend what he had made and created, and also that part of himself from where his pictures had drawn their existence and aliveness. Thus did he extricate himself from the envy and the sense of total and hopeless impotence in relation to his lively, artistic mother, and from the delusion that all creativity is feminine and belongs to the woman — the mother who castrates the males and leaves them with only one way of associating with the forces of creation, that of being her vassal, her slave, or at best her flirty and admiring eunuch.

However, before Bob had achieved this extrication, which was to initiate the search for his own creative centre and his own 'true self', and while he was in the midst of his battle in and through the transference with both the mother-analyst-me as well as with the father-analyst-me, he was involved in a car accident. It was not altogether his fault, but had he been more alert and attentive he could have avoided it, as he himself explained to me.

It took several months to discover and understand the many meanings of this accident and to work through, in the relative safety of the consulting room, the emotional upheaval and the catastrophic emotional experience of this accident. It emerged that the accident was indeed a murderous attack on the much admired and much envied mother; it was also a murderous attack on the father whom he thought of as either absent and unavailable, or, if present, as inadequate because he was unable to tame and contain the mother or guide his son into true and enjoyable manhood.

But, in as much as Bob, when he was in a somewhat less hopeless and depressed state, was identified with the enviable mother, or, when in a more depressed state with the inadequate and impotent father, the accident was also a killing, the destruction of him who had been swamped and taken over by one or both parents. This was then a suicide provoked by the despair of ever being able to shed the introjected and incorporated 'others' and overthrow their domination inside him; despair of ever being able to find and to become his own self.

But as we worked further through the emotional experience and the symbolic meaning of the accident, it took on the quality not only of murder and suicide, but also of birth, of parturition and of sacrifice, that essential and always present constituent of all 'rites of passage'. The accident and our work on its actual, its manifest and its unconscious and potential meaning did lead Bob to the source of his central, his creative self, which then enlivened his work, his relationships and his feelings about himself.

What are then the features thrown up in Bob's analysis that seem to me to be so particularly relevant to drama?

(1) There are the conflicts engendered by the presence of alien 'not-me' personages inside one. This provokes conflicts and makes for confusion about what is one's own and true self.
(2) The actions that are — or are not — thought and felt to be appropriate in terms of one's own conscious intentions and prevailing circumstances and conditions.
(3) At the very heart of drama and of Bob's personal story is the struggle between life and death, hope and disillusion and the search to discover one's own destiny.

THE SELF

In order to discuss the theme of 'internal personages' and the experience of being 'oneself' — true and real or false and alien — one must discuss in some detail how the term 'self' has been employed, to give some of its history, but above all to commit oneself to a clearly defined use of this term, even if this may in the long-run turn out to have been an *ad hoc* definition only, but valid for at least this particular chapter.

The concept of the 'self' has actually remained very contro-versial. In fact, instead of gaining in clarity, it has become progressively more complex. It has the initial handicap of being a term that is part of the everyday language of the ordinary person, the ordinary man/woman in the street. But over and above this is the fact that more and more professional people in the analytic world — starting however from different premises and having different goals — have come to appropriate the term and to define it in a way that suits their particular purpose and need.

Thus, psychoanalysts, who at first used this term very sparingly, now rely on it more and more because they have, so I suspect, become increasingly interested and concerned with whether and how an individual experiences time, space, boundaries, authenticity and a personal identity that remains relatively consistent and continuous across space, time and circumstances. Rycroft (1968) in his *A Critical Dictionary of Psychoanalysis* has given two definitions for 'self':

> When used by itself: the subject regarded as an agent, as being aware of his own identity and of his role as subject and agent . . .
> The self refers to the subject as he experiences himself while the ego refers to his personality as a structure about which impersonal generalisations can be made.

Some psychoanalysts, and in particular, Hartmann, Jacobson and Kohut, have tended to use the term 'self' for what I have elsewhere called 'the introspective part of the ego'; they think of it as composed of self-representations, and as having the function in the psyche to make and guard the distinction between 'myself' and 'not-me'.

I myself regard the concept of 'the self' as an abstraction, as a metapsychological construct; that is, as a model which, like a geographical map, refers to and represents a whole system composed of varied phenomena. Jung derived this concept from a variety of fields of study — from observation of patients, particularly psychotic patients, from ethnology, from the examin-ation of religions, dogmas and rites, and from descriptions of mystical experiences. He used it in order to denote the origin in the psyche of those images and affects which relate to, express and symbolise unity, totality and immortality. He also used it to denote those experiences, which Freud had named 'oceanic' and which

Jung thought of as the origin, the matrix, of the dynamic processes that serve the goal of synthesis, such as the search for fusion, union, communion and bliss.

Being a pioneer, his concept of the self has never ceased to evolve and to be subject to modifications. Yet Jung did hold on to his initial thesis that it is only in the second half of life that man gives first importance to the development of the self as against the ego.

However a significant new look at the self has been initiated by Michael Fordham (1956, 1957). He has postulated that the self has in fact a beginning in an original state of wholeness and of relative undifferentiation. This can be shown to exist and to predominate in the new-born infant. Fordham has named this the 'original or primal self', in order to contrast it to that later state of wholeness, striven after through techniques of self-realisation, to which Jung had directed so much attention. This extension of the concept of the self helps us then to recognise that development is not really a matter of movement from chaos to order, but rather from simple order to ever-increasing complex order.

Both the self and the 'original self' can be thought of as the storehouse of the archetypal images, themes, drives and personages. These, so Fordham has suggested, lie in readiness to be activated and to emerge through a process that he has called 'deintegration'. It is through the process of deintegration that the original self differentiates and gives birth to the archetypal forms which then make up the nuclei of consciousness. Deintegration is a lifelong process, and the various archetypal themes have each a 'critical time' when their emergence is right and appropriate in terms of the stage an individual has reached in his life-cycle. They then enable him to be in contact with his own needs — be they physical, emotional or spiritual — and to recognise the persons and objects that can best satisfy these needs.

With the development of the concept of the 'original self' the way has really been opened to the inclusion of the 'self' in a more developmental overview. This has led to a closing of the gap between the Freudian and the Jungian conception and definition of the self. And indeed, among Jungian analysts and theoreticians the meaning of the term 'the self' has now come to cover a wider range — from the experience of personal identity and self-representation to the all-embracing self that was the object of Jung's thinking and reflections.

In order to clarify the way in which I intend to use the term 'self' in this chapter, I shall use an adjective as a prefix and speak about the *original or primal self*, as this has been defined and used by Fordham, the *little self* when I refer to the experience of personal identity and the cluster of self-representations, and the *big self* when I refer to the all-embracing and almost cosmic sense of the self that Jung has postulated and studied.

Looking carefully and deeply at the experience of 'one's self' seems to lead on quite naturally to an awareness that we carry inside us a number of different selves or different 'sub-personalities' as Redfearn has described it in his recently published book (Redfearn, 1986). He describes there how this feeling of 'I'

> migrates hither and thither to various locations in the total personality, like the spotlight at a theatre picking out first one actor and then another . . . each of which may take the stage and relate to other units in sometimes familiar, sometimes novel dramas and stories . . . I call these various actors in ourselves 'sub-personalities'.

These internal sub-personalities seem to derive from at least three different sources:

(1) The image of one's own body and the many different sensations we receive from its various parts.
(2) The objects and persons we encounter and relate to though they be modified or even distorted by the particular psychological processes through which they have arrived in our inner world, processes such as idealisation, denigration, rationalisation projective identification, etc.
(3) The various archetypal images which represent the themes and goals of our basic drives.

You will have noticed that when I described Bob's mother or Bob's father I was careful to refer each time to what I had learned of them from Bob himself; because what matters is who, how, and what they are in Bob's inner world, for it is in this form that he relates to them and has to exist and live with them. What they were really like remains finally an academic question. Also our perception of ourselves, our self-feelings, are themselves shaped by the interactions and inter-relationships that the various internal objects and persons have developed in our inner world. And there is the further question whether and to what extent we have identified with one or several of them; or whether they are experienced as 'the other' inside us, which makes them, of course, more available for projection upon the persons and objects in the world around us. There can of course be shifts and changes in our relationships and in our identifications and de-identifications with the various personages in our inner world.

We saw some of this happening to Bob, particularly when after the car accident the spell that had held his inner world static, as if frozen, began to break and lose its power. This, then, at last brought movement and change to the scene and the personages inside him.

Watching the ebb and flow of these inner states and reflecting upon them it is natural, appropriate and very illuminating that Joe Redfearn should have used theatre and actors as his metaphor to describe the intra-psychic world which he recognises to be peopled by our many sub-personalities.

CREATIVITY

Before I can discuss creative therapy and in particular the special form of it, namely dramatherapy, I need to say a few words about the place that creativity and the quest for it occupies in the psyche of man.

The need to create was regarded by Jung as one of the five main instincts in the human species — the other four being hunger, sexuality, activity and reflection. It is closely related to the need for order, continuity and meaning on the one hand, and the need for excitement and for discovering and making something new on the other.

According to the *Oxford English Dictionary*, to create means to 'bring into being, to cause to exist, to form, to produce'. The process of creation seems to depend on the co-existence of contradictory but mutually reciprocal qualities such as activity–passivity, receptivity–productivity, consciousness and un- or pre-consciousness, masculinity–feminity etc. In other words, a person must be available to freely moving oscillations between control and surrender, between periods of conscious work and periods of passive acceptance, and between periods of wishing or even demanding to be alone and periods of wishing for contact and communication.

Creativeness in the arts depends on the collaboration of such psychological functions as:

1. Perception

This is not a passive–receptive process that acts like a camera, but is a very active process involving the whole person — his needs, wishes, feelings, memories, expectations, etc.

2. Image–imagery

This refers to the mental representation of a sensuous experience *in the absence* of an actual stimulus that could have caused it.

3. Imagination

There is obviously a direct etymological link between image and imagination. Imagination refers to a cluster of images which have been brought together and 'produced' in association with other mental processes, such as past experience, memories, thoughts, intentions, wishes, hopes and the various emotions. Images are the essential raw material for imagination, but they stand to imagination in the same relationship as does the individual photograph, the still picture, to the moving picture, the film.

4. Fantasy

The boundary between imagination and fantasy is not clearcut, and so deserves a longer discussion. Fantasies 'embody' instinctual and archetypal experiences; that is to say, impulses, fears, wishes and so on that are predominantly in our unconscious world. They are thus still uni-dimensional — like dreams they hold sway and reign as if they were the only, the singular reality. In contrast to fantasy, imagination involves and depends on the interaction of both conscious and unconscious processes, and so carries both emotional urgency as well as cognitive functioning. Thus when we 'imagine', we are potentially aware that we live in, are part of and are able to experience the co-existence of different realities. When we imagine we can, if necessary, ask such questions as: Is this possible? Is this real? Does this belong to outer reality or to inner reality? Is this history or fantasy?

It is true that imagination is also, like fantasy, powered primarily by our inner world; it embodies and expresses this inner world and

27

it functions essentially in terms of this inner world. But imagination places us firmly into both the inner and the outer world. It involves, on the one hand, the experience, apperception, contemplation and enjoyment of our inner, private 'film show' — I often find myself speaking of 'film' when I mean to say 'dream'. On the other it involves an attitude of critical assessment of the products of imagination in terms of fact, reality, truth, consistency and so on. In the absence of such critical assessment we are in the world of hallucinations, delusions or dreams. Thus, in order to imagine we must be able to combine such ego functions as work, perseverance and effort with the more libidinal experiences such as enthusiasm, excitement and pleasure. In other words, imagination depends on the capacity to bear conflict and the bafflement of paradox. But it also depends on the existence of a certain amount of trust, as defined by Plant (1966) — trust that there is an inner world which is neither empty nor sterile, trust that the source of creation will continue to flow, trust that the loving, constructive and synthesising forces inside one are strong enough to outbalance the hating and destructive ones, trust that the world and the people outside one are relatively benevolent and sufficiently free from excessive envy so that one will not be exposed to their persecution, thieving, destructive criticism or ridicule, and, finally, trust that one can rely on both the ego and the non-ego functions and that consequently fantasies will not overrun and drive out all awareness of reality.

Obviously it is quite an achievement to be able to imagine. It is therefore not surprising that as analysts and therapists we may have to help some of our patients to convert fantasy into imagination, while in the case of others it may be a question of helping them to become more accessible to the imaginative process.

Of course, no analyst or therapist, can hope to do his work if he cannot know and experience his own images and imagination. If his capacity to imagine is limited, then he will be limited in his capacity to comprehend the experiences of his patients. For example, an analyst without any auditory imagery is excluded from a vast part of the experienced world of his musician patients.

An analyst who himself possesses a rich imaginal life can help to give impetus to the imaginal development of his patients, since psychotherapy and analysis depend so heavily on the capacity to recall and to re-create persons and situations — real or fantasied — that occupy such an important place in a patient's inner world. Only through image and imagination can these be 'animated' and so brought into relationship with each other, with the person of the

therapist and with the here and now of a patient's actual life situations. Only the 'animation' of people, situations and events, through
the imaginal processes active in both patient and therapist, will bring
to life the patient's inner world, make him aware that he has an inner
world, and at the same time help him to unscramble the past from
the present, the outer world from the inner world and so pursue
further the path of individuation, a concept I will discuss further
towards the end of this chapter.

5. Symbolisation

This function is really the most powerful, the most important and the
most decisive one in the processes of creation and imagination. Its
essential characteristic is the 'as-if' attitude. It helps man to perceive
the links between disparate, separate and individual events, objects
or persons on the one hand and of universals on the other, and so
pay attention to and concern himself with facts, the concrete as well
as with the abstract and the meaningful. Perceptions and images are
but the furniture of the mind. We may delight in their presence and
wish for no more. But when we react to them as tokens of a different
reality, when, like Blake, we 'see a world in a grain of sand', then
imagining has been transformed into symbolic experience.

The ancestors of the symbolic function are:

(1) The direct experience provided by the sensations.
(2) Symbolic equivalence — as described first by Hannah Segal
    (1955) — here two or more separate objects or activities are
    thought of in such a way that the reality of one of them is
    denied and instead becomes identified with the other.
(3) Actual symbolisation, the 'as-if' attitude. Now there can be
    recognition of the similarity of objects together with aware-
    ness of and respect for their separateness.

Jung has made an enormous contribution to our understanding of
the nature and the value of the symbol and the symbolic function for
he believed that it nearly always helps towards the discovery of
something new. It was Jung who first defined it in terms of the 'as-
if' function and saw it as evolving in response to man's great need
to find order and meaning — in the universe, in the world around
him and in his own inner experience.

Jung did not, however, explore the possible roots of the capacity to symbolise in the human person's psychological development, nor did he search out or observe and then describe the psychological conditions necessary and favourable for its development.

It is this gap which Winnicott has filled in formulating the concept of the transitional object, the transitional phenomenon and the 'area of illusion'. In the child's attachment to what he came to call the 'transitional object' — a teddy bear, a blanket, a sucking vest or whatever — Winnicott recognised the earliest expression of man's creative drive, of his capacity to symbolise and of his concern with meaning. The transitional object — triggered into existence when the infant has started to recognise that he and his mother are not really one, are not really fused, but are separate and distinct — is both given to the child and created by the child, and so this is his first attempt to reconcile reality and fantasy, inner world and outer world. Its importance lies neither in its symbolic value only, nor in its actuality, but in the fact that it possesses the quality of a paradox. Hence it would be quite inappropriate to ask: 'Is this real or is it imagined?' In this reconciliation of reality and fantasy lies, so Winnicott explains, the foundation of what he has called 'the third area', or the area of illusion, which then becomes the source of play, imagination, culture, religion and art.

I have recently come to think, and then to believe, that the area of illusion, as proposed and described by Winnicott, may in fact prove to be of particular importance and value to analytical psychology (Gordon, 1985). For it may help us discover that there is an appropriate location in the psyche of the more or less mature person for the experience of archetypal contents — images, themes, personages. I have drawn attention briefly to these archetypal contents earlier in this chapter when I discussed the self. Archetypal contents can be recognised because they possess as their principal characteristics:

(1) universality, across space and time, that is, across different cultures and epochs;

(2) bipolarity, that is, they each carry both positive and negative complementary qualities;

(3) powerful affects, such as fascinations, feeling possessed by something awesome — awesomely terrible or awesomely beautiful, or awesomely significant;

(4) an 'all-or-nothing' quality, which makes whatever is archetypal experienced as stark, powerful and absolute — as absolutely good or absolutely bad, as 'bigger than big', or 'smaller than small', as 'always' or 'never'.

30

Jung has suggested that when archetypal contents and motifs emerge from the unconscious matrix, they can at first be experienced only in and through projection, or else through ego identification. Consequently, at first archetypal contents, fascinating and exciting though they are, distort the individual's perceptions and so, inevitably, vitiate, in the long run, his relationships with the world of objects and persons. This has led many to regard the archetypal as an elemental and archaic force that we need to outgrow and put behind us if we are to move towards an appropriate perception of reality.

There are, however, our very basic and fundamental needs for myths, for poetry, for the fantastic and for every kind of imaginative creation. And archetypal motifs are, after all, splendid, magnificent, inspiring and transporting.

Thus, although psychological maturation does involve the progressive withdrawal of the archetypal themes, images and motifs from actual objects and persons — including one's self — I am sure that they must not be totally superseded, eliminated and got rid of. Rather we must find a way of remaining available to them for the rest of our life, if we are not to impoverish it, render it sterile and meaningless and turn ourselves into dull, grey, even if moderately efficient, robots.

It is Winnicott's 'area of illusion' that offers us now a theoretical model with whose help we can come to understand how and where archetypal experience can be recognised as a valuable and enriching function, even in the adult person. For the third area, the area of illusion, is indeed the crucible where fantasy and reality meet, fuse, defuse and re-fuse. Here sensuous experience meets imaginative invention, cognitive activities are brought into relationship with emotional activities and man's need for meaning finds expression in the discovery and the creation of forms that embody experience.

ART AND ART-MAKING

There are, of course, countless theories and speculations concerning the nature, the purpose and the function of art and art-making. It would be a hopeless task — and in any case not totally relevant to this book — to give a résumé of even some of them. But it is fair, I think, if I try to summarise what I believe are the principal psychological forces inside man that pressure him into art-making, for they obviously guide my thoughts as I write this chapter:

(1) the need in man to externalise internal images;

(2) the need to preserve his sensuous experience by making it get into a form that exists outside and independently of him;

(3) the need to communicate to others — and even to himself — and so validate further his private imagery and experience;

(4) the need to give expression to the fundamental impulse to make, to 'em-body', and to do this in accordance with certain aesthetic rules, be they personal or cultural, many of which may in fact be found to be more or less universal;

(5) the need to communicate with the emotions in their own language;

(6) the need to see, as if projected into some medium outside him — a canvas, a stage, screen, a pattern of words or sounds, or any other object or place — any movement, development or change that might be happening on his own internal landscape, in his own inner and partially secret and hidden world, so that he may follow it, become acquainted with it and know it;

(7) the need to discover — and again and again to re-discover — through the act of symbolisation order and meaning in defiance of the welter of disparate and discrete objects that are all around us, the meaning and purpose of life, the meaning and purpose of one's own birth and existence, the meaning of love and hate, the meaning of death and so on. It is our very consciousness and knowledge of death that makes this particular need so urgent. Arthur Koestler made this point very poetically in a broadcast in 1960:

> Take the word 'death' out of our vocabulary and your great works of literature become meaningless; take that awareness away and your cathedrals collapse, the pyramids vanish into the sand and the great organs become silent.

My summary of the various psychological needs that lead man to make art all involve the translation of the experience of the immaterial into the making of something material. Indeed, all art-making processes require the collaboration of the body and the use of the various functions and skills of the body. The painter needs his eyes to see and his hands to apply the paint. The musician needs his ears to hear, his voice to sing with, his mouth and breath to blow into pipe or a horn, his hands to pluck strings or strike a keyboard. The writer needs his hands to guide his pen, the story-teller needs his mouth, tongue, breath and voice with which to form his words, and the actor needs his whole being to play the role in which he has been cast.

There is, however, one difference that distinguishes one group of art-forms from another group; although all of them need the co-operation of the body, only some of them use the body as the actual instrument for their artistic expression. I am of course thinking here of drama, mime and dance, in contrast to painting, literature and music.

Given this particularly crucial role of the body in those art-forms that use it as the medium of expression, a person's relationship to his body — and to himself inasmuch as he inhabits and possesses it — is obviously of major importance.

When one wants to examine the relationship a person has to his body, three questions — three themes or topics — emerge as particularly relevant, and so of special interest:

The first concerns *identity*; that is to say we need to know with which of the many internal personages the artist identifies, at least at the present time and in the present context. As I have already argued, the sense of 'I' is not permanent, unchanging or totally coherent because we do not have — or are — just one single self, but are inhabited — or possessed and taken over — by quite a number of different selves. I did illustrate this by describing Bob's analysis.

The second question touches on the theme of *narcissism*; that is, the capacity to love oneself. Narcissism has until recently had a rather bad press, in part because it was falsely assumed that we have only a limited amount of libidinal — that is loving — energy, so that whatever amount of it we direct towards ourselves is then withdrawn from our capacity to love another. This assumption has now been challenged and we have come to agree once more with such ancient wisdom as Christ's who, when he said, 'Love thy neighbour as thyself', seemed to imply that unless one loves oneself one cannot love one's neighbour.

However, if one wants to understand the quality and character of a person's narcissism, one must examine:

(a) Who is the 'I' that I love, that is the object of the love of oneself? The love of oneself is healthy and growth-promoting, so we now recognise, but only if the 'I' that I love is in fact truly myself, my own real self, my own authentic self.
(b) Whether this love of oneself is genuine, is primary and is strong enough to extend not only to what is positive and

acceptable to oneself, but also to one's shadow side, to one's weaknesses, deficits and badnesses. In other words, is this a love for one's actual, one's real self, warts and all, or is it a defensive, a compensatory reaction, to a deep, underlying hatred, disgust and rejection of oneself? In that case it is likely to appear as excessive, as exaggerated and phoney and to dominate over all the other personal traits, qualities and affective needs and relationships.

The third question concerns the *body image* — that is the image of his own body a person carries around inside him, usually unbeknown to him. Obviously this is much affected by both identity and narcissism. For if identification has been made with an alien, or 'other' object, then there will almost certainly be incongruity and lack of fit between a person's actual body and his conception of his body. We can see this in an amusing and usually benign form when a little boy walks around in father's suits, or a little girl dons her mother's clothes or puts on her makeup. Of course, we deal here with 'playing at' rather than with actual identification. But the comic quality shown in these games can give some idea of the distortions that an inappropriate and unrealistic body image is likely to produce in the case of an adult.

Here I should say a word about Jung's concept of the 'persona' which he has described (1950) as:

The individual's system of adaptation to or the manner he assumes in dealing with the world. Every calling or profession, for example, has its own persona.

The persona is thought of as that segment of the ego that is concerned with the enactment of social roles and social stereotypes. It is thus a very necessary shield behind which the private, the personal and the vulnerable can shelter without giving offence; it serves to safeguard the true personality and yet facilitates social interaction. Without it a person might not be able to respond appropriately to social pressures; and he would moreover risk unnecessary self-exposure and pain in situations in which intimacy would be out of place.

There is, however, the opposite danger, namely that what is meant to be only a segment of the ego comes to usurp the function and experience of the whole ego. If that happens then a person becomes identified and identical with his persona — a judge who never stops judging, the sergeant-major who turns every situation into a barrack-square, the actor who never stops acting or the therapist who makes every relationship into a therapist–patient relationship and never stops analysing his friends and family. 'Such a person,' Jung writes, 'is unchildlike and artificial and has lost his roots'.

Clearly where the artist uses his own body as the instrument of artistic expression, his relationship to it must be particularly close, favourable and realistic. He must have a good idea of the place it occupies in space; he must carry in his head a pretty good and faithful mirror so that he can know full well what all its parts are up to, how they appear to the onlooker and what emotion, quality or character trait they, each and all, express. And he must also have a specially strong and disciplined control over it, so that he can know not only what it does and expresses, but can also programme it to do and perform whatever he wants and intends. This is, of course, most evident in dance; but it certainly also plays an important part in drama and in mime. This may seem puzzling in view of what I have just said about the psychological danger of identifying with an 'other' person; for the actor's very task is to do just this, to represent, to 'become' some other — or, in fact, many other persons and characters. But, in the case of the actor we are dealing not with fantasy but with imagination in the way I have defined and discussed it earlier in this chapter. In other words, the actor functions in terms of and out of the area of illusion; he is — and he can be — aware of the existence of at least two realities and he can function in both of them. But in order to be able to carry his audience along with him into the character he embodies on the stage, in the dramatic play, which at that time is the dominant illusion, he must be at home in his body and on good terms with it so that it shall serve well both him and his audience.

I think the importance of a good relationship between an individual and his body needs little argument and convincing, if it is the body itself that is the principal vehicle of expression. But I also believe that a good enough relationship must exist between body and person even when the body is only an adjunct, a tool, used to manipulate some other medium through which the artist tries to convey his message and meaning since, as I have already argued, all art-making relies on more or less intricate and complicated body skills.

How important this is even in the non-bodily-incarnating arts, struck me when thinking about Bob. His identification with a mother whom he really wanted to defeat and humiliate, if not murder, was certainly a major factor responsible for the lack of genuine and healthy narcissism. It had in fact lured him into an artistic–creative profession but then tricked him into failing and ridiculing the professional mother-self; hence the expression of triumph whenever he could report to me a new failure, a new humiliation. Yet, he could draw; he did, as far as he consciously knew, want to be a good designer; he wanted to be able to translate his images into perceptual forms and objects. But somehow his imagination kept faltering, and his hand kept blundering, so that what he drew rarely corresponded to what he had visualised inside himself. However, when at last, after the accident, he got on better terms with himself, his work seemed to have improved perceptibly, judging by the approval of his boss and his progress and promotion at work.

Bob's case throws up another factor that one needs to consider when one examines the arts, creativity, mental health and therapy. I am referring to a person's thoughts, beliefs and fantasies about masculinity and femininity and about his own relationship to either and/or both of them. Bob, you will remember, seemed to assume — unconsciously — that all creativity is the monopoly of the woman, the mother. It seemed clear to him that not only could she make babies, but that only she had access to feelings, to imagination and to the capacity and the techniques of expressing them. Masculinity seemed to him to be sterile and so men were destined, were condemned, to be dull, subdued, and more or less impotent. Their role was to stand by, to admire the woman, to be her public and the consumer of her artistry.

It is true that only women can make real, live babies. But they do need a man to make this happen. And the creative process is, so we now recognise, and as has been so well expressed by Marion Milner and Hannah Segal (1955): 'A genital bisexual activity, necessitating a good identification with the father who gives and the mother who receives and bears the child.' Indeed many creative persons have been shown as a result of various psychological tests and through biographical as well as clinical studies to have been — and often to lean overtly towards — more than usual bisexual characteristics.

If a person — or indeed if a whole culture — loses sight of this fact, if he or she attributes the whole creative work and the creative process to either the man only or the woman only, in other words, to either the masculine functions only, or to the feminine function only, then he or she does indeed hobble him- or herself. If it is to his or her own biological gender that he or she attributes the whole 'work' then he or she will probably be unnaturally rigid, static and altogether limited, limited in terms of relating to a sexual partner, limited in general human relationships, and limited in the capacity and freedom to move and develop beyond certain narrow confines. If, on the other hand, as was the case with Bob, all creative power is believed to be invested in the other gender, then he will indeed divest himself of all his — or in the case of a woman of all her — potency. There may then be an attempt to identify with and to assume the other gender; but the reality of one's own actual body is a big obstacle which vitiates and affects adversely those three major enablers and facilitators of the mind–body collaboration; that is, healthy identity, healthy narcissism and a realistic body-image. Moreover, the inevitable and underlying resentment, anger and above all envy present in these persons will absorb and waste much of the energy and effort that might otherwise have gone into the making of a good 'marriage' between the masculine and the feminine, for they are potentially available inside everyone, though their proportion differs from person to person. But a true intrapsychic marriage between the masculine and the feminine would enable conception, gestation and the bringing to birth of one's own 'children', as so many artists quite unselfconsciously tend to refer to their own non-biological creative productions.

It must have become clear by now what might be the relevance to the theme of art-making and the arts therapies of the various questions and psychological conditions that I have discussed so far. For in this study we are concerned primarily to explore those psychological functions that are particularly helpful in translating inner, personal experience into tangible and communicable forms.

DRAMA AND DRAMATHERAPY

To look at last directly at drama and dramatherapy. The recognition — rather later by psychologists and analysts than by artists, writers, poets, dramatists etc. — that there are in each of us a number of different selves, or sub-personalities, must increase our awareness of and sensitivity to the fact that our inner world is also a stage on which are enacted and experienced dramas of various types and of various and varied intensity. For where two or more personalities co-exist — whether outside or inside ourselves — there is almost inevitably conflict, confrontation, argument, dialogue and debate. In other words, we have present inside us on our internal stage some of the very constituents and functions that mark and belong to drama as enacted on the stage outside us — be this the actual stage in the theatre or the mechanically reproduced one on the screen in the cinema or on the television set.

The internal drama — that interaction and interrelationship of our various sub-personalities — does indeed have some of the features that Martin Esslin (1978) has ascribed to drama, such as:

(1) emphasis on action — although the internal drama may be concerned primarily with the preparation and planning of future 'real' actions;

(2) the experience of emotions that belong to several characters;

(3) like drama outside us, the internal drama happens in a 'here and now', in the 'eternal present';

(4) whether enacted inside or outside the psyche, drama is a 'simulation of reality'; it is play; and hence it is reversible, unlike what happens in reality.

This being so, it is not surprising that the art of dramatic enactment, that is drama and theatre, should be one of the earliest and hence one of the oldest forms of art through which man has tried to express his conflicts, fantasies, visions, fears and hopes. Through art, man has tried to make sense and to find meaning in life and in his own personal life. But through dramatic art in particular he has tried, and continues to try, to disentangle the competing, contentious and contradictory perceptions, feelings and demands of the many characters, whether they inhabit the world outside or his inner world. And drama, whether extra-psychic or intra-psychic, is also a means of helping us to understand — through experiencing it — the experience, the 'being' of the other. Drama is thus one of the best, the most direct means of self- and other communication.

But between the happening of the inner dramas and the enactment of the drama outside one lies the field of the operation of creativity. For in order to transport drama from inside to the outside, fantasies must be transformed into imaginations; characters must assume a certain consistency; and identification and empathy must expand from a primitive solipsism to embrace an ever-widening circle of personages, their feelings and experiences, and their maleness as well as their femaleness. One must be on good enough terms with one's own body so that it is available and can be used as an instrument with which to represent a variety of persons; and there must be enough trust that one's public is sufficiently well disposed so that there is little risk that one will become the butt of ridicule or contempt.

By externalising the inner drama and rendering it into a form that is visible both to oneself and to others, one may discover parts of oneself, new sub-personalities, of which one had remained relatively unconscious and unaware. One may then also recognise that there could be different and new ways in which the sub-personalities inside one might co-exist and interact. And one may find that one is really less insulated and isolated, less incomprehensible, idio-syncratic and crazy than one has feared — or in part of oneself also hoped — but that in fact quite a number of people can understand and even share in the experience of one's inner dramas and their protagonists.

When I speak of drama and its protagonists I refer to the opera-tion of two activities: (a) the construction, and the composition, of a drama; and (b) the acting, that is, the portrayal of the protagonists. This leads me to look at, to examine, to compare and differentiate 'acting' in the sense of 'enacting' a part, a role, and what psychoanalysts have termed 'acting out'. By this is meant actions that occur outside the analytic room, the analytic session and the analytic relationships, and which are, or tend to be, counter-productive to the therapeutic work. 'Acting out' has been defined by Rycroft (1968) as 'The replacement of thought by action, and as a substitute for remembering past events'. He suggests that there are three implications: (a) the impulse acted out has never acquired verbal representation; (b) the patient lacks the capacity for inhibi-tion; (c) the impulse is too intense to be discharged in words. Hubback (1984), one of the few Jungians to have dealt in recent years with the concept of acting out, has suggested that

In acting out there is too little thinking, let alone hard thinking, as well as too little appreciation of meaning,

and,

The trouble which leads to acting out: the forces at the instinctual pole of the archetype are activated by powerful emotions, and the other pole, that of meaning, has not yet been reached.

Laplanche and Pontalis (1967) discuss at considerable length the concept of acting out. They suggest there that, according to the most generally accepted definition, 'transference' and 'acting out' are in opposition to one another, 'acting out' being thought of as the unconscious attempt to sever and break off the analytic relationship. They also remind us that 'to act' is really strongly imbued with a theatrical connotation, while the preposition 'out' adds two further shades of meaning, namely: (a) to externalise, to put outside, to show outside what is supposed to belong inside; and/or (b) to accomplish and to accomplish quickly and totally as in 'to carry out' or 'to sell out', etc.

Do we really mean something so very different when we speak of 'acting out' and of 'enacting' in the sense of acting a role on the stage? Is acting out always and necessarily unhealthy and anti-therapeutic? While psychoanalysis was thought of as only a 'talking cure' and while the expression in and through words was believed to be the only way through which unconscious contents could reach consciousness, it was perhaps inevitably that all acting and all enacting should be considered to be an 'acting out'.

But with the more recent developments in psychoanalysis and analytical psychology, with the treatment of sicker and more regressed patients (here Jung and Klein are particularly notable as pioneers of the analytic treatment of such patients) and with the use of the arts as ways of helping the mentally sick, the exclusive reliance on words only has diminished. Instead, making psychic experience both visible and tangible is now recognised as another efficient and valuable way through which consciousness can be helped to expand. Consequently 'acting out' and 'enactment' can no longer be thought of as totally antagonistic and opposed to one another, but rather as being two points on a spectrum along which lie a number of 'actions' that represent and involve a whole register of gradations of conscious–unconscious interactions.

This interplay between enactment and acting out is really further confirmed for us by the fact that in many cultures healing is achieved through dramatic enactment, though admittedly this is usually more or less tightly planned and ritualised.

The interdependence and interaction of drama and healing along a spectrum of consciousness–unconsciousness leads me on to mention and discuss here the technique of 'active imagination'. Jung had been casting around for a method which might enable patients to continue the process of self-development and self-realisation after their regular meetings with their analyst had — very properly and and very appropriately — come to an end. This led him to experiment with and to develop the technique of what he came to name 'active imagination', a technique that seemed to rest on and evolve naturally from his recognition that one of man's most basic needs is to make and to create and that the symbolic function can serve the process of healing. 'Active imagination' can be described as an internalised analysis in which there is an ego that is strong and reliable enough to function as an observing and receptive analyst in the presence of freely flowing themes and fantasies. These may find expression in two or three dimensional images and/or in speech, dialogue, and in the various dramatic and dramatised forms. Jung thought of active imagination as an *intra*-psychic process which one carries on when one is alone, but that like *inter*personal analysis it is usually slow, arduous and at times painful. Like interpersonal analysis, active imagination helps to bring fact-to-face conscious and unconscious experiences so that an effective interchange can take place between them.

Active imagination can remain a purely internal psychic activity, though it may also lead to the making of *actual* pictures, sculptures, or musical, verbal or dramatic forms.

Jung saw two main potential pitfalls to the use of this technique. One he called the 'aesthetic tendency' when a person is carried away and seduced into an idealisation of the unconscious processes and activities. If this happens the ego has relinquished its role of observer and so has ceased to act as a bridge between the conscious and unconscious functions. The second pitfall he saw in the opposite danger, the danger of being in a hurry to 'understand' and to make consciously acceptable sense out of the emergent unconscious material. He thought that this is usually due to an attempt to escape from tension and from the terror of the uncertain, the unknown, and involves an over-valuation of content as opposed to experience.

Michael Fordham has made a distinction, which seems to me to be important, between true 'active imagination', involving the presence and participation of an observing ego, and 'imaginative activity' when imagination remains unobserved, is more primitive and is undirected by any conscious purpose.

Dorothy Davidson (1966) gave a novel and expanded twist to the concept of active imagination. She argued and showed there that the transference–counter-transference relationship between patient and analyst is often an enactment in the 'here and now' of the unconscious drama in which the patient had been caught and held prisoner, and that such an analysis can be viewed as a form of 'lived through active imagination'.

Many have tried to arrive at a definition of drama. Few have succeeded, possibly because it is difficult to keep separate the qualities intrinsic to drama and the means and methods by which these basic and essential qualities are realised and made manifest. But daring to be foolhardy and to rush in where angels fear to tread, I am prepared to risk arguing that all drama involves the enactment through words, mime, gestures and actions of encounters and conflicts engendered by the various clashing and incompatible human needs, longings and pursuits represented on either an external or an internal stage by the different roles or actors.

Given this definition, we can now look at the various functions of drama in the different contexts and settings:

(1) Where drama is an enactment in and through active imagination its setting is a person in solitude. All the actors, the characters, are the personification of exclusively *intra*-personal forms and functions.

(2) In analysis drama is enacted in a two-body relationship. It is thus an *inter*-personal event, although the 'actors' are still predominantly intra-personal forces that issue — if all goes well — from one person only, the patient.

(3) Dramatherapy happens in the context of a multi-body situation. The main purpose is still the translation of essentially personal *intra*-psychic characters and themes, but they are here drawn from not only one, but from several, persons present in the dramatherapy group. Here then are elucidated through drama both *intra*- and *inter*-personal forces and conflicts.

In the three settings described so far, where drama is used primarily as a healing technique, one relies mainly on relatively free improvisations, the principal purpose and function being the externalisation and embodiment of some of the personal unconscious and unknown protagonists inside the psyche, as they reveal themselves in both *intra*- and *inter*-personal situations.

(4) But in drama in the theatre — involving the *active* participation of an unspecified number of actors and the *passive–receptive* presence of an unspecified number of individuals that constitute the audience — improvisation is displaced by a disciplined, ritualised, planned, scripted and structured text, the play, written usually by one person, the author, and brought to an audience through the mediation of a director and a cast of actors. Here the

embodiment of personal *intra-* and *inter-*personal protagonists is complemented by characters that are *trans-*personal; that is to say they are drawn from a people's historic, cultural and collective roots and from personages that represent abstractions and/or supra- or trans-human figures. Here then, we are confronted not only with our personal internal dramas, or with the dramas that belong to our relationships with one another, but we are also put in touch with the whole tragicomedy of the human situation and with our eternal quest for meaning, the meaning of the world, of life and of death in general and of our own life and mode of existence in particular.

Of course, here also we find that the four settings and functions of drama are not cleanly separate and distinct; they inevitably overlap and stray into each other's principal domain. It may be useful to remember, in this context, Jung's distinction of art as being either in the psychological mode — when a work expresses mainly the artist's obsessive personal conflicts — or in the visionary mode, when it has escaped from the limitations of the personal and 'soared beyond the personal conscious of its creator'. Clearly, even the most personal active imagination is likely to contain some general and collective features, and the stage play will carry some of its author's personal preoccupations. But on the whole a good, or great play, will speak to, and for, more individuals than the 'play' that comes out of our very private ruminations and reflections.

My discussions in this chatper have brought me to a point from where I can see that drama is in fact ubiquitous and universal, happening as it does in the world inside all persons, in the world where man relates to universals, to the cosmic, to the good and the bad, to the beautiful and the ugly and where he struggles to discover order and meaningfulness. The presence of multiple and often contradictory forces, both inside us and outside us, creates fields of tension and conflict; our endowment with language, with the disposition to symbolise and with an actual need to make and to create, all this makes the emergence of drama and dramatic forms natural and inevitable.

And then there is man's unquenchable thirst for the development of self, which Jung has discussed, studied and named 'individuation'. Elsewhere I have defined and described the process of individuation as:

a readiness for ever greater awareness of one's own nature, with its positive, as well as negative, tendencies and qualities . . . a growing recognition of one's separateness and one's personal responsibility . . . Individuation aims at the achievement of optimum synthesis of conscious and unconscious processes and phantasies. It leads a person to experience his own individual uniqueness together with the recognition that there are forces both within and without him that transcend his personal and conscious understanding . . . The process of individuation encompasses the process of 'individualisation' though it moves a person beyond this essentially ego-building process towards the search for values, meaning and self-transcendence. (Gordon, 1978, p. 149).

Clearly, drama, whether enacted within or without the psyche, plays a major part in the process of individuation. Drama and the techniques used in dramatherapy — such as role reversals, playing more than one role etc. — must inevitably increase one's range of possible identifications. If one incorporates as one of the goals of individuation the actual experience of 'I', or 'my selves', then the contribution that drama and dramatherapy can make to the process of individuation is clear and evident. For such an expansion must increase the capacity to sympathise and empathise with an ever-growing number of sub-personalities inside oneself and with an ever-enlarging number of individuals outside oneself. Thus will a person be enriched in terms of both the width and of the depth of his knowledge, understanding and compassion.

REFERENCES

Davidson, D. (1966) 'Transference as a form of active imagination'. *Journal of Analytical Psychology*, vol. 11, no. 2

Esselin, M. (1978) *An Anatomy of Drama*. Abacus, London

Fordham, M. (1956) 'Active imagination and imaginative activity. *Journal of Analytical Psychology*, vol. 1, no. 2

―――― (1957) *New Developments in Analytical Psychology*. Routledge and Kegan Paul, London

Freud, A. (1950) Foreword to Marion Milner's *On Not Being Able to Paint*. Heinemann, London

Gordon, R. (1978) *Dying and Creating: A Search for Meaning*. Library of Analytical Psychology, vol. 4, Academic Press, New York and London

―――― (1978) Glossary in *Dying and Creating: A Search for Meaning*. Academic Press, New York and London

———— (1985) 'Losing and Finding: the Location of Archetypal Experience'. *Journal of Analytical Psychology*, vol. 30, no. 2

Hubback, J. (1984) 'Acting out'. *Journal of Analytical Psychology*, vol. 29, no. 3

Jung, C.G. (1916) 'The Transcendent Function'. *Collected Works*, vol. 8

———— (1930) 'Psychology and Literature'. *Collected Works*, vol. 15

———— (1935) 'Tavistock Lectures'. *Collected Works*, vol. 18

———— (1939) 'Concerning Rebirth'. *Collected Works*, vol. 9

———— (1940) 'The Psychology of the Child Archetype'. *Collected Works*, vol. 9

Kernberg, O. (1975) *Borderline Conditions and Pathological Narcissism*. Jacob Aronson, New York

Kohut, H. (1977) *The Restoration of the Self*. International Universities Press, New York

Laplanche, J. and Pontalis, J. (1976) *Vocabulaire de la Psychoanalyse*. Presses Universitaires de France, Paris

Plant, A. (1966) 'Reflections on Not Being Able to Imagine' reprinted in M. Fordham *et al.* (eds) (1980) *Analytical Psychology: A Modern Science*. Karnac, London

Redfearn, J.W.T. (1986) *My Self, My Many Selves*. Library of Analytical Psychology, vol. 6, Academic Press, New York and London

Rycroft, C. (1968) *A Critical Dictionary of Psychoanalysis*. Nelson, London

Segal, H. (1955) 'A psychoanalytical approach to aesthetics'. In *New Directions in Psychoanalysis*. Tavistock, London

Winnicott, D.W. (1971) *Playing and Reality*. Tavistock, London

3

Dramatherapy and Play

Alida Gersie

INTRODUCTION

When we play we loosen our connection with experienced reality,
for it is difficult to play when we are preoccupied with the events
of our daily life. The exploration of alternatives which is inherent
to play demands centred freedom. This is a freedom which comes
from the belief that the world will continue to exist while we absent
ourselves to embark upon a journey of inner and outer discovery.

We can only become half-heartedly involved when there is too
much pain and confusion. The child, who distractedly moves a toy
car along the edge of the carpet, whilst also trying to listen to the
adults' talk, is both here and there, suspended between what is and
what might be, between actual and potential, without a commitment
to either. The child pretends to be involved, but keeps an eye and
ear open to the outside world, so that he or she can respond to what
is happening, ready to obey, to take flight or to defend herself.

In order to play with devotion, we need to feel both safe and safeguarded against unwanted intrusion, secure in the knowledge that we
shall not be attacked, even though the possibility of such an attack
might be the very purpose of our exploration. Thus a frightened,
self-conscious child will find it difficult, if not impossible, to
become involved in play, of whatever kind. Yet it is of crucial
importance to each of us that we gain access to our capacity to play,
for as Piaget (1969) writes:

> it is indispensable to his [the child's] affective and intellectual
> equilibrium that he have made available to him an area of activity
> whose motivation is not adaptation to reality but on the contrary
> assimilation of reality to the self, without coercions or sanctions.

46

Such an area is play, which transforms reality by assimilation to the needs of the self, whereas imitation is accommodation to external models. Intelligence constitutes an equilibration between association and accommodation.

The child who comes into contact with a dramatherapist is likely to experience a whole range of difficulties, which will, amongst others, present themselves as problems surrounding play. These difficulties more often than not severely affect the child's development. The journey towards recovery begins once we are able to help the child to play again.

PLAY AND THE ESTABLISHMENT OF A SUBJECTIVE–OBJECTIVE REALITY

In the course of growing up, most children experience and explore a variety of forms of playing: from early imitative play, via enactive, controlling and repetitive play, to symbolic, expressive play and much later reflective, corrective play. Meanwhile the structures and content of play are likely to develop from the simple to the complex, from low intensity of affect to high intensity of emotions, and from low interaction to high interaction.

The young child has a great deal to learn, to discover and to explore. Initially each child exists in a vast, directionless space where lots of things are happening. During those early years, the moments of external structure are but mere punctuations in a seemingly endless field of time. Slowly and gradually the child develops a relationship with this world beyond the self, where there are people and objects, sounds and sights, smells and tastes. The surrounding unknown is explored. The sense of balance, strength, depth and distance grows. The need to order the information is paramount. Otherwise the child will be swamped by a multitude of chaotic impressions. She needs to create an internal structure which enables her to predict and thereby to expect. When the child masters this complex undertaking the building of her separate identity has begun.

Most children set about the task of conquering and internalising the outside world with an astounding amount of energy and alacrity, with great devotion of exploration and experimentation, trying out what objects feel like in may different positions and what can and cannot be done with them. The examination is thorough. The

47

process of exploration is not merely restricted to objects — people too, are subjected to detailed investigation and scrutiny. The child invents many ways of pushing, pulling and above all relating. What adults call 'play', is often the child's way of seriously attempting to explore variety and possibility and to discover their world.

Where possible, the child will invite an adult to participate in this journey, to become a fellow traveller. The adult is needed for encouragement, as a mirror, initiator and guide. The interaction between adult and child (or between an older and a younger child) may seem rather limited in early imitative play. Yet, this process contains the essence of mutuality. The seed of communication lies in the engrossed copying of perceived actions and interactions.

An outer image has entered the child's consciousness. The entry is acknowledged. Then the child attempts to reproduce the image. Or a possibility has emerged in the child's awareness; she tries it out, and the action is noticed and played back. It is brought forth again, out there, by an other human being. A sign is received. Oneness develops into togetherness. Imitation is self-gratifying. The ability to generate within what was perceived without, or to see echoed without what was developed within, creates a pleasurable sensation.

Initially there is no inner sense of function attached to the new-found motion, just as we may later mouth a word in a foreign language, oblivious to its meaning. When we are then told what the strange collection of sounds stand for, we find it hard to believe that those alien noises truly represent the word which we know so well in our own language. The rational acceptance of ascribed content will occur long before we recognise and transfer the emotional load.

Whenever we copy a movement or sound, a similar process is at work. The other person's knowledge and experience, which informs their gesture or sound, is inaccessible to us unless they let us know about it. We have to develop an associated account of our own, which is only later compared and adjusted to other people's content, so that communication becomes possible and idiosyncracy, which may lead to idiocy, is prevented.

Thus the child not only has to develop a whole range of actions, gestures and sounds, with their associated content, she also needs to learn how far her associations coincide with those of the people around her. In other words she has to find out what is going on 'inside' them and compare this with what is happening inside herself. The frown on a face may remind her internally of crying and discomfort, but is that what the frown on the mother's face conveys?

The child has to try and establish her own subjective–objective reality by noticing how the mother behaves. If she does not smile, or cuddle her as she normally does, then the frown may well acquire the child's inner meaning of distress. If the mother realises that all is not well, the child will have succeeded at matching inside and outside.

But life is not often that simple. Many a time the child will be left bewildered and confused. She cannot get the signals she receives to make sense. Whenever a child cannot achieve a reconciliation between her inside world and the world outside, she will, given the fused and dependant quality of her existence, become tense and show discomfort. As she grows older she may continue to carry the discomfort around inside, never quite knowing whether what she perceives and feels, is indeed what it seems to be. Unable to differentiate between fantasy and reality, between self and other, the child will alter her relationship with people. Depending on temperament, inclination and culture, she will grow at variance with the norm; withdraw, exalt, or oscillate between one and the other. The child is confused as to what's what and unable to understand other people's signs and signals. She may well try to become a sender only, but she does not quite know how to send so that she will be received and therefore her own signals are also confused. The child is labelled hard to read, difficult to know or impossible to get hold of. The muddle continues, until someone expresses concern about this child, and realises that 'something needs to be done about her'. Then contact will be sought with someone who might be able to offer help.

In the book *Dibs in search of self* by Virginia Axline (1971), the writer describes the slow, unfreezing process of a pained young boy. One day, during the session, he bursts into tears. She later records what happened: 'I weep because I feel again the hurt of doors closed and locked against me', he sobbed. I put my arm around him. 'You are feeling again the way you used to feel when you were so alone? I said.'

Gradually the child or adult in therapy is helped to work through their pain and confusion, enabled to rebuild the understanding and experience of human interaction, so that the muddle of conflict and contradiction can be relieved.

THE TRANSFORMATION OF TIME, SPACE AND EXPERIENCE IN PLAY

The ability to create and enter an inner space where we are temporarily freed from a dominant awareness of the events and experiences of our life is of vital importance to each of us. There we can recuperate, regenerate failing energy, and develop new perspectives. Without this capacity we are deprived of the ability to transcend and thereby to transform our situation.

Each human being continuously negotiates the boundaries between self and other, inside and outside, an inward and an outward focus, fantasy and reality. We learn how to maintain the balance of boundaries and discover how they change in accordance with our own development. In this process, the imagination is our greatest gift as well as our greatest danger. When we deny its potential we can easily become shipwrecked upon the shores of the other. Each of us thereby loses our sense of awareness and identity as an individual, separate human being. But when we make imagination our exclusive preoccupation, we become isolated and disconnected from the world and the people who surround us. Ultimately this self too will wither and shrink beyond recognition. The withdrawal into external anonymity leads to inner annihilation of the sense of identity. The outcome remains the same: the sense of self is lost. Then the child or adult cannot but become 'self-conscious', and thus gets caught in a dilemma.

> He may need to be seen and recognized, in order to maintain his sense of realness and identity. Yet, at the same time, the other represents a threat to his identity and reality. One finds extremely subtle efforts expended in order to resolve this dilemma in terms of the secret inner self and the behavioural false-self systems . . .
>
> Laing (1967)

The resolution or treatment of this dilemma might well be attempted through play. For the very characteristics of involved play will enable the child to let go of her painful self-consciousness. The play itself facilitates the establishment of a relationship with experienced reality, which will further her development.

When we are truly involved in play we lose our awareness of quantified time, of time's ordinary rhythm and pulse. When reminded of what the time is, we express surprise at how much or how little time has passed. The inner experience has grown out of phase with the outer actuality, for whenever we become whole-heartedly involved and play with devotion, we leave ordinary, profane time and enter into extra-ordinary, sacred time. Then time has changed into duration. The transition from the time-bound to the timeless resembles the passage from reality to fantasy, from restriction to potential. The one does not exist without the other, yet we are all aware that the return to measured and measurable time is often experienced as a fall from grace.

In his book *Primitive Mythology*, Joseph Campbell (1973) quotes Swami Nikhilanando as saying 'The Play belongs to him to whom Eternity belongs, and eternity to him to whom the Play belongs'. Forgetting how much time has passed, is the beginning of that process. It is due to this special quality of timelessness, the outcome of experienced absorbtion, that the space of play too becomes transformed. The ascribed, alternative reality is the dominant if not the only, experienced reality.

The transformation is made possible by the assignation of alternative functions and roles to various objects and people, and above all by the introduction of the extra-ordinary within the context of the ordinary. Only a relatively known environment can be turned into a play-space. There we approach what was dark and hidden, to make it individually and possibly publicly accessible. A little bit of chaos can be experimented with. We test our strength by relating to formlessness, our skill and confidence through repetition and ongoing experimentation. Here we prepare for adjustment to the external realities and assimilate the outside. The physical space which lends itself best to this type of exploration, rehearsal and ongoing experimentation is likely to be situated at the edge of the ordinary environment. It is marginal space, secluded, yet obviously attached to the 'normal' world.

We play most easily in the fringes of structured time and in the borderland of common space; such as an attic, beneath a table, at the bottom of the garden, on some nearby wasteland. There we explore our choices regarding the private and the public, the personal and the collective. In order to experiment we need an area which in and of itself offers few constraints, thereby generating many possibilities. Such a space needs to allow for easy transformation into apparent seclusion, through the creation of actual boundaries, or into approachability by allowing access of others.

The space of play can only become a space of transformation when there is room to create. Sometimes a child has to make do with very little, actual space. Still we will witness how desperate attempts are made to use whatever is available. The urge to play is not easily repressed. After all, our survival depends upon our ability to become absorbed in play, from time to time.

THE QUALITY OF ABSORBTION — PLAY AS A SELF-AFFIRMATIVE ACTIVITY

Let us take a closer look at the image of a child absorbed in play. We see a person who appears to be inaccessible to outside stimuli, engaged in a private world. If we want to receive her attention we will have to use a strong signal. Whenever we are truly involved, a substantial actual space beyond the self is created. This concentrated space is intruded upon when an attempt is made to draw the playing person into communication. A shift of focus then needs to occur — the flow of energy has to be reversed. Interruptions are experienced as an intense violation of privacy, for they disturb the pattern of inner activity, and child and adult alike therefore prefer to choose the moment of return. This will occur when a point of satiation is reached. We may have enough of our own company, or we may have explored an issue in fantasy in such a way that a temporary or permanent solution is achieved. Or we are simply physically tired. The game is finished, the play has ended. Then the inward-going energy is freed and we are able to relate to the outside world once again.

Play is a self-affirmative activity. It assures us of our existence and the potency of our imagination. This led the psychiatrist Winnicott (1980) to say that 'it is good to remember always that playing is itself a therapy.' For however many external objects and people we incorporate into our play, its conduct and content require our continuous commitment and singularity of focus, without which the play will disintegrate. A self-constructed reality is created with its own boundaries and rules. The child becomes the ruler of the castle. Through participation she directs participation. In the course of time, 'the child must learn to distinguish play from real life, and must develop the ability to suspend play when necessary.' (Kramer, 1971).

The child also needs to acquire the ability to differentiate between the alternative demands and possibilities of play and of reality of which play is a part. However, whether we choose to engage in pre-structured play with others, where the pattern of interaction between the participants is predetermined, or whether we engage in imitative, or symbolic expressive, exploratory play, by ourselves or in a group, one of the outcomes of our playing remains constant: we strengthen our awareness of ourselves whenever we defer our concern with the explicit reality in order to become involved in a fabricated, alternative realm. In this realm the child has the opportunity to experience 'the creation of symbols at will in order to express everything in his or her life experience that cannot be formulated and assimilated by means of language alone'. (Piaget, 1969).

Thus the child exercises her power to act, albeit in fantasy, as well as the ability to make choices, decisions. For action in fantasy precedes action in reality — what cannot be imagined, cannot be done.

Yet, there may come a time when the child grows to prefer the realm of the potential over the realm of the actual. It might be attractive that the imagined powers are substantially untested, precisely because they are not verified. Fear of disappointment in the real world may lure the child into a preference for imaginary activity, whilst she remains actively dormant. The dream of potentiality turns into a nightmare. The gift of imagined and imaginable power becomes a paralysing embrace. Play then ceases to function as a temporary abode for exploration, rehearsal and innovation. Instead it becomes a refuge where the individual is defended against the trials and tribulations of the outside world, whilst simultaneously being deprived of the satisfactions of communication and communion with others. The ability to withdraw and suspend dominant awareness of the environment has developed into an inability to relate and to manifest oneself. The individual's capacity to act, which depends on the ability to exercise choice as well as on the commitment to sustain, is gradually undermined. Submerging a fragile, conscious awareness of self, within an overwhelming, unconscious longing never to have left the womb — the wish to return forever to primordial bliss.

Another person's decision to intervene in this process, then reflects the attempt to establish contact with a human being who appears to be helplessly adrift in a private world. The inner sanctum has turned into a prison. Someone has to try and evoke a response, for every response will be an acknowledgement of a world which exists beyond the self. However well-intended such an effort to establish contact may be, the self-engrossed person might well experience the touching of the private self as a violation of the right to withdraw, whilst only dimly acknowledging an awareness of the need for rescue. A sudden and powerful approach may shell-shock a 'dreaming', withdrawn child out of her protective space, but the acute pain which arises when the child is rawly exposed to input which was previously kept out at substantial cost, may well be too much to handle. The terror a client experiences in the process of change should never be underestimated. Walter, a young adolescent boy admitted to mental hospital following a bizarre suicide attempt put it like this:

> I don't fancy talking, I can't let myself go. Talking's bad, change is bad. Imagine me beginning again. Then everything would start from scratch. I'd also lose my certainty that the world's lousy. If I speak French, then I'll be a Frenchman, I Won't be Walter anymore. If I should change like that, I'd lose my I.
>
> Foudraine (1974)

Change means a letting go of the world as we knew and know it, to enter into the great unknown, without assurances as to what will remain.

The pulling down of resistance 'from the outside in' may therefore not be very useful in the long run. Instead of electing to live without as well as within, the child may in response hastily re-erect another protective, inner dwelling space, out of whatever evidence and material is available. Then the walls will be stronger still and contact is avoided even more forcefully. The determination to cling to the inside has grown. The dramatherapist will have to find other ways and means by which to lure the dweller within outside. Making contact has to become a worthwhile and satisfying experience. Above all, we will have to ensure that the sense of control, which contributes to the experienced safety within, does not have to be abandoned or lost when the child ventures into relating to others. We need to help the child to discover and create defences which protect and which allow expression of the self, and which permit the establishment of satisfying relationships, so that the child who faces darkness might ask: 'Father, the sun has gone down. Where has it gone? Will it come back soon?' And I tell him: 'Yes, son, it will be back soon to warm us.' (Reich, 1975).

THE CREATION AND SAFEGUARDING OF A
DRAMATHERAPEUTIC ENVIRONMENT

Each therapeutic space functions initially as a symbolic womb, the place of conception and growth, the place where something or someone is wholly contained. We can safely assume that by the time a child comes to see a dramatherapist, an unnecessary arrest has occurred in the development of her capacity and capability — unnecessary because the child has the potential to grow further. Whenever growth is stunted, the child and those who share her life often experience discomfort and sometimes acute distress.

In order for a child to be able to play during dramatherapy sessions, and thereby rebuild a healthy relationship with her world, she needs to have her physiological needs fulfilled. It is difficult to embark upon a journey when hungry, thirsty or exhausted. Suppose, however, that the child who comes to a session is fed, not cold and reasonably rested — she may well be rather tired, for a distressed child often means a listless child. Then the next requirement is that the environment and the people the child will be with enable her to feel reasonably safe. In actuality, this means that there should be no interruptions during the session. Privacy must be safeguarded by ensuring that people cannot look in through windows, and that there is not a great deal of noise coming from outside.

During the session the child can then experience the room as entirely hers, or when shared with other children as truly theirs, and learn to trust that the therapist will ensure this. The therapist thus becomes the guardian of explicit therapeutic space, warding off unwanted approaches, modelling to the child how one has the unalienable right to privacy. It is often surprisingly difficult to perform this task, especially when working with young children as other workers, parents and older children tend to presume that they have a right of entry, justified with such words as: 'She won't mind' or 'They wouldn't notice' or 'I just want to peep in, I love to see them play like that'. Maybe the child will welcome the visitor. However, because we cannot predict the response, and because we are often working to redress the balance between inner and outer control, the initiative to establish contact with the outside world has to rest with the child. She will have to learn to make the choice to relate, to share and to initiate contact in such a way that it is a satisfactory experience. The door to the room therefore remains closed to outsiders, yet open to those who are inside.

It also matters that continuity is preserved in the physical environment. Rearranging the furniture or putting new decorations on the wall without involving her threatens the damaged child. Therefore it is wise to ensure that the physical surroundings do not change a great deal for as long as the child needs it. Any necessary changes have to be handled sensitively and carefully so that the child is given time and a chance to adjust.

The type of equipment which will facilitate the child's play will we hope include: paper, crayons and fingerpaints, clay and plasticine, sand and water, various dolls, toy animals, various toy cars, trains, boats, cardboard boxes in different sizes, a box full of pieces of material and clothes, a tape recorder and tapes, and an assortment of musical instruments such as bells, drums, and whistles. These materials are however no more than an asset, not a prerequisite for dramatherapeutic work. It will be helpful if the availability of the materials is made clear to the child at the beginning of the sessions. Also, the rules and expectations regarding use and clearing need to be made explicit because, for many children, a safe environment initially equals a predictable environment.

Expectations and constraints

The need for constancy and predictability in the explicit, therapeutic space applies equally to the dramatherapist's behaviour, which includes style and interventions. The pattern of interaction between the child and the therapist therefore has to be recognisable, as well as at times surprising (though rarely shocking). For not only are we often attempting to help the child to internalise strength; she also may have to relearn or discover the pleasure of change within the constant pulse of the changeless, of the predictable within the context of the unpredictable. Without such awareness, the child may well have come adrift by seeking ever new, but never explored, stimuli or alternatively she may have limited herself to a tight and constrained litle world.

The pattern of expectation with regard to the session will grow out of the ongoing therapeutic contact. Yet it is often helpful to tell a child what she may expect in terms of the structure of the session and the dramatherapist's behaviour; for example, whether or not notes will be taken during the session, whether the dramatherapist will participate in the activities, or tell other people/workers about what has happened. How will the child know that time is nearly up? Will she be given nourishment? What should she do when she needs to go to the toilet? Who will bring her and pick her up to go back home? There might be other questions in the child's mind, such as who will play here afterwards, which she may want to clarify before beginning the therapeutic work. The dramatherapist often forgets that a child can be infinitely reassured simply by being told a few pertinent facts regarding the work.

It is therefore important to talk about these issues at the beginning of the dramatherapy work, and to remind the child whenever she appears to have forgotten. When the child has no choice regarding any of these issues, it matters even more to let her know about the external constraints and boundaries. The sense of safety will be increased and there is less to worry about. Also, boundaries are there to be tried and tested. The child has to be given a change to do so. She can only test, however, when she knows that such boundaries truly exist — whether she can come late, open and close doors, bring in food, sit on your lap to stop you from writing, tear up notes and so on. The struggle around boundaries has to be engaged in. Their initial and ongoing clarity will facilitate this process.

A CHILD COMES FOR HELP

Whenever a child is referred to a dramatherapist, we can presume that something has gone wrong in her life and that she is experiencing trouble which has come to the notice of people around her. The child might have complained about feeling unwell or more likely, has been behaving in such a way that she has been identified as a child in difficulty. By the time therapy is being considered, the child will probably have been in contact with a few other 'caring' professionals: teacher, social worker, youthworker, school nurse or health visitor. Her experience with these people, the kind of questions they asked and above all the response they showed are bound to influence how the child perceives the meeting with the dramatherapist. She will have fantasies about what this new potential helpmate, if indeed a helpmate is wanted, has been told about her predicament and behaviour. Thus the child might enter her first session like a reluctant and frightened animal, or eager and desiring to find someone who might help to alleviate her problems.

The child (or children) and the dramatherapist will, during this first contact, have to establish a range of things:

- a shared understanding of who referred the child and why and when the referral was made;
- a clarification of the purpose of this session;
- a description of the basic ground rules with regard to time, use of the space, and conduct;
- some information about what might happen after this session (specifically if there is an arrangement for an initial assessment session only).

It is above all of paramount importance that the child and the adult create the beginnings of a relationship that the child can use to start on the road to improvement. The child will therefore also need to know something about how the dramatherapist will liaise with the other significant people in her life.

The chances are that not everyone agrees about the nature of the child's problem, and yet whenever we are working with children there are several people who have an investment in the successful outcome. But successful in whose eyes and on whose terms? Thus the child could easily become torn between conflicting expectations, and receive more of the same kind of opposite messages to which she has probably been exposed from a very early age. The dramatherapist therefore has to try to ascertain as early as possible during the referral and assessment stages which kinds of conflicts of perception already exist and which are likely to emerge, so that the child might be helped to deal with these situations.

During the first contact, we should attempt to make it possible for the child to share with us:

- how she knows 'why she is here' and what she knows about her situation and experience;
- how she perceives her situation and what she 'apparently' feels about it;
- what kind of experience has she had previously as a client or patient, and what memory has this experience left her with;
- what her ideas and beliefs are regarding the cause/effect of her situation and which type of solution has she already tried. How she thinks she might solve her predicament;
- what she knows and expects of you as a helper and what kind of things she really wants you to know at this stage.

It has to be made explicit that the contact has been made because there is concern about the child's wellbeing, and also that the contact itself will we hope lead to some kind of change which will help the child.

Some children are only too willing to talk about what is happening to them, others, however, will have decided that it is best never to say anything about what is going on inside them, and the dramatherapist will be left to do most of the talking/explaining and the initiating of contact.

Whether or not the child explicitly communicates about her situation, it is possible and necessary at this stage simply to take note of what is communicated. We have to try and stop ourselves from jumping to conclusions about her. In the first instance we need to get to know her, and to absorb what she does and does not do. Thus we shall try to describe to ourselves (during and after the session):

— how the child presents herself: her physical appearance and how she strikes us when she is by herself or interacting with other children/ourselves
— how she uses space. What her area of movement is
— how she uses time
— how she responds to contact initiated by others
— what her energy level is and how it fluctuates (when?)
— what she actually says and what she appears to be trying to say
— what kind of movement accompanies her words
— how she moves when she isn't talking
— how her eye-contact gestures and expressions relate to the content of the session
— what her tolerance of touch/sound/sight/temperature/smell and taste is like
— when and how she seems to enjoy herself (note: be careful — high-inference observation, as are several of those mentioned above)

If the child has been willing to play a little in our presence, either with an object, with ourselves or with other children, then we can look at the extent and the nature of the child's involvement:

— does she seem to converge or diverge in her interaction
— does she cooperate and/or block, at which stages and around which issues
— what kind of relationship does her playing appear to have to immediate daily life (actual people and animals, story or media people and/or animals)

- what is her concentration like (concentration to be described as her capacity to unfold a relatively organised and extended sequence of activities, without becoming repeatedly dependant on a new, external stimulus)
- what kind of affect or mood does she display

When we try to formulate what we have experienced and noticed, it is important to differentiate between our impressions and our observations. An impression is no more and no less than a statement about a fleeting observation. It is inspired by our hunches as well as our predelictions, our desires as well as our experience. However, an impression is never systematic, constant or distanced. It says as much about the observer as it does about the observed. In our observations *per se*, we will attempt to scrutinise both the observer and the observed. Yet, the fleeting impression is also worth recording, for it is all the more likely to steer our behaviour and intervention if we don't.

Having created an opportunity for the child to become involved in some kind of interactive play, we may then try, either through projective play and/or drawing, to elicit more information from the child about her situation. During this stage of the assessment it might be helpful to bear the following areas of exploration in mind:

- what do you like to play most?
- what do you like to do best when you are all alone?
- do you ever have pictures in your head?
- do you have a make-believe friend?
- could you tell me what you are really frightened of?
- which toy do you like best?
- what's the most horrible thing that anyone has ever said to you?
- what do you do when you feel sad inside?
- what would you like to do?

And above all:
- how do you think I can help you? (Singer, 1973).
The first contact thus centres around:

- the generation of information, which can be related to similar children (age group/sex/background), others in the same predicament and to the child herself in other situations
- the exploration of presentation and interaction, relevant to the

child's situation and experience
— a formulation of a tentative hypothesis regarding the child's
difficulties and a first attempt at describing likely developments with or without professional intervention of one kind or
another
— the initiation of relief
Note: It is of paramount importance that we explore how some
immediate relief might be offered to encourage the child to
sustain the energy needed to overcome her difficulties and to
foster her will to do so!
— a tentative formulation of a proposal for possible treatment and
follow-up.

It is clear that all of the above guidelines for our attention will
continue to matter during our further contact with the child.
Assessment is not something that happens at the beginning of the
therapeutic process, never to be thought of again, but is an approach
which informs the entire relationship. However, it is only at a later
stage, when the child has started to participate in the creation of
(symbolic) enactments, that we shall direct our attention to the
following:

— what is the degree of identification (with the character/s)?
— what did the attitude(s) of the character reveal about the child?
— are there are contextual clues to be found in content, use of
language, organization of the scene, consistency and
originality?
— are there any recurrent themes?
— which wishes, fears and memories emerge from the enactment
which the child does not ordinarily reveal? (Feder & Feder,
1981).

When looking at the interaction-pattern within the enactments we
look out for:

— areas of low . . . high intensity of affect
— areas of action directed towards the other, with no response
expected (passive)
— primitive forms of interaction where responses are immediate
reactions to the other's behaviour (reactive)
— full forms of interaction displaying a back-and-forth response
(full-interactive).

Here it is also important to note where, when and with whom the child initiates interaction, around which issues/themes the interaction tends to occur, and how the child communicates her feelings during the interaction. Her pattern of coping with difficulties and frustrations is likely to be relevant to her experienced trouble.

It is obvious that the child who plays during a therapy session does so in a situation which differs substantially from her playing outside the session. She is not only being observed, but she also receives attention and is being given the permission and encouragement to play. The therapist becomes a participating witness to the child's involvement, a witness who might be variously experienced as accomplice, opponent, mate, rescuer, and so on. In her book *Dibs, In Search of Self*, Virginia Axline describes how Dibs, a young boy, 'walked around the playroom with a smile on his face'.

'I think I will sing', he announced.
'If you want to sing, you sing', I replied. He laughed.
'And if I want to be quiet, I be quiet!', he exclaimed.
'And if I want to think, I just think. And if I want to play, I play, like that, h'mm?'
'Yes, like that', I said.

He was being given permission to be himself, to say what he needed to say. And he laughed! When desire, intention, permission and action coincide, pleasure is the outcome. During any dramatherapeutic programme one of the aims is to enable the client to experience this process. Sometimes that task is not so hard, sometimes it is extremely difficult and more often than not it is a blend.

During our contact with the child, we will always need to be aware of the following:

— the direction and strength of the child's desire, i.e. her longings and wishes
— the strength and durability of the child's intention (which reflects the extent to which she feels she can respond to her desire)
— the power and quality of her internalised permission (her dependency upon internal/external encouragement)
— the capacity to initiate and to sustain action

Let us try to bear some, or all of the above in our mind and heart whenever we meet a child who comes for help, and who in her own way will convey what a Crow Indian once wrote:

If there is someone above
who knows what happens
You
Today I have trouble
give me something to make it
not so.
If there is someone inside the earth
who knows what happens
I have trouble today
give me something
to make it not so

(Rothenberg, 1972)

And may we be able to respond!

THE EARLY SESSIONS

During the sessions which follow our first contact, the child often needs to be allowed to 'fuse and feed'. She is given the permission and encouragement simply to copy movements, to listen to songs and stories and to look at images, whilst being encouraged to participate. But engagement may well be very difficult at this stage, and therefore the dramatherapist has to be relied on to introduce and lead simple sound and movement exercises, which require little initiative apart from the preparedness to join in. The child's decision to participate may well be a monumental step, which requires great courage and determination. It often marks the beginning of a commitment to change.

When the child is able to take some initiative, she will begin to create a variation, or make suggestions for an alternative activity. However, some children are petrified of the mere suggestion of sameness during these early sessions, probably because it has become associated with very unpleasant emotions. Too much togetherness frightens them and they need to be helped to create a separate, physical space where they can engage in a private activity.

It is important that we encourage each child to feel good within her own limits, reassured that we shall not attempt to pull her away from there and encouraged, tempted, and enabled but never forced to explore other areas, where she may find new forms of delight and consolation. The child has to know that she determines her own development by agreeing to participate. The dramatherapist is no more than a helpmate in this process. Through engagement in the early imitation and copying exercises, the child is assured that the adult is a person who is able to offer something, and with whom she can have a clear, possibly pleasant experience. Whenever the adult responds to the child's initiative to change a movement, sound or an entire activity, the child realises that she is being noticed and recognised. That she is 'worthy' of imitation. Thus she is assured that she is welcome and that exploration, which implies change, is encouraged.

Whenever the dramatherapist introduces variety into sameness, the child is exposed to limited otherness. She will bring to this occasion all her specific anxieties about differentiation and separation. During this stage of the work, care has to be taken that the child's longing for 'fused identification' is nourished in such a way that the curiosity, which ultimately enables the child to function as a separate individual, is proportionately stimulated and supported. Many children fear that their options oscillate between a state of fusion and of isolation. Each child has to build, slowly and gradually, sufficient trust to be able to develop autonomy and initiative, without being overwhelmed by shame, doubt or guilt.

At this stage, the dramatherapist's responses to the child's early explorations and attempts at differentiation are therefore of vital importance. It is often moving to see how anxiously a child will watch the dramatherapist's face when she takes the chance to alter a copying game into something else. Will the therapist follow? But above all, will the therapist survive the change, which the child may well imagine to be an attack? When it is obvious to the child that the therapist feels good about the initiative, she may literally heave a sigh of relief. A crucial turning point has been passed. The child is likely to continue the venture towards autonomy, at least within the sessions.

RECOGNISING I AND OTHER

As the sessions progress, the dramatherapist will continue to encourage exploration, whilst helping the child to establish the differences between I and other. This may take a long time, for the child needs to develop an inner sense of being good enough before she is able to recognise another being as someone like herself, and yet different. During these sessions, the dramatherapist, who works with a group of children, will begin to introduce small group- or pair-work, where the children engage in cooperative action. As the child's trust grows, she will begin to ask numerous questions about 'what's going on' inside the therapist. Attempting to check the perceived behaviour, trying to read and understand both text and subtext, she needs to find out how accurate her perceptions are and develop her own subjective–'objective' reality. The therapist's behaviour and responses become a vital testing ground. Emotional availability and clarity are therefore of paramount importance in the therapeutic relationship between adult and child. During this phase of the work, the dramatherapist may, from time to time, have to return to earlier stages of personal — and group — development work by introducing more circular imitation or 'variation on a theme' exercises.

Once the child is able to sustain working with another child or in a small group, we can explore the extent to which she can engage in truly individual work. Can the child keep herself focused on a private task for a while, in the knowledge that others are engaged in the same activity, or will she, through eye-contact and gestures, indicate that this separation has come too soon? Only when a child is able to maintain her own interest and exploration for a little while can we move towards further exploration of differentiation, first in the large group, then in small groups or in pairs: differentiation through movement, sound, action and words. Gradually the child will develop the ability to cope with and contribute to all these different situations at however minimal a level.

When she shows signs of being prepared to allow herself to be influenced by other people's contributions, she can integrate their contributions into a further action; in other words, when interaction and communication happen then we may consider the introduction of enactment — and only then. For each child needs to have a secure enough inner centre, on the basis of which she ventures out on her own into relating with other people.

It is the prime task of the dramatherapist to help the child to say 'I' and to be able to say 'you' or 'we', without simultaneously losing her awareness of what she wants, longs for and likes. The child needs to learn to listen, to share, and to compromise, without any of those activities resulting in an inner sense of annihilation. Above all, the child has to be offered the experience that to contribute results in satisfaction, and that participation offers rewards.

65

The creation of such a 'workable' group may take anything from three to many sessions. It all depends on who is there. In such a group, the participants are in principle aware of one another's space and of their individual right to contribute. The children realise that they have the permission to explore, to invent and to share, that they can elect not to contribute, and that there is power to be derived from non-participation. The child will have experienced the right to say no, to select and to reject, that she can leave and return, and that there is permission to change one's mind or ideas.

BEYOND THE THERAPEUTIC EFFECT

We might well be tempted to say that a child at this stage no longer needs a dramatherapy group. Can we not consider her to be basically healthy and ready to end the therapeutic work? The early stages of dramatherapy may well have a benign effect upon a child, such that the child appears to have recovered from the symptoms for which she was originally referred. However, unless the child experiences the sharing, exploration and resolution of the inner difficulties which contributed to her referral — unless she learns to make some of the private and personal material, which is experienced as 'bad', public, and therefore accessible to other people — she will continue to have substantial difficulties in her life. For we may have helped her to develop some sense of identity, but it is an identity based on simple contribution. The child has learned to trust, but it is trust in a non-threatening and supportive environment. What she now needs to experience is the development of trust and intimacy in relation to disclosure and exploration of experiences, which she herself has considered 'unacceptable, intolerable and overwhelming'. Otherwise, the secret 'bad' self is merely counterbalanced by a public functioning and accepted self and the child is still deprived of real intimacy and a sense of solidarity.

She has to learn how to share 'good, bad and neutral', how to contribute to someone else's experience, how to take care of herself and others, and above all, how to face what is difficult, so that individual despair and loneliness may be transcended into an awareness and experience of communion and care. The creation of a workable group is no more than an introduction to the engagement in this level of work.

CREATING RELEVANT DRAMATISATIONS

How then do we help children to engage in these explorations, and what do we mean by enactment in this context? Enactment here refers to the dramatic representation of symbolic or literal scenes which are charged in an unpleasant way, as well as to the enactment of scenes which have a neutral or pleasant charge, but which have hitherto not been expressed or explored. These dramas are representations of actions and interactions, representations indicating the process of evoking into the present, events and patterns of interactions which have occurred in the past, or which can be imagined to occur. Interaction implies an action which takes place between people, about which there exists a degree of mutual understanding. Without this understanding, the drama cannot develop. Each participant becomes isolated and confused, unable to hold onto the thread which connects the drama into a sufficiently meaningful whole.

The dramatherapist facilitates the structuring of the scenes, by enabling the participants to enter into roles, to develop a variety of patterns of interactions and to explore alternative developments. Real or imagined experiences are thus re-lived, or pre-lived, re-structured and re-presented in direct or metaphoric language, but always within the protection and construct of the role and role-interaction. The child's active engagement in this exploration of 'meaningful' scenes determines the direction of the dramatherapeutic work, the aim of which continues to be to bring about an improvement in her functioning. This improvement will be experienced as such by the child and by the important people around her.

In order for this engagement to occur, the child needs to activate and involve her own inner drama, because the representation of action relies on previously internalised presentations of actions. Whether these actions happened in fantasy or reality is initially irrelevant. Does not our memory through its process of selection and adaptation, contribute to a blending anyway? The dramatisation then allows what is inside to rise to the surface. What has been hidden can, through this method and process, be made to come 'up front' — to become a metaphorical or literal re-presentation of inner stage events.

Whatever role we take on in an improvisation (an enactment which has not been foreseen, which is not pre-planned in detail), we always rely on our inner cast to provide us with a brief, to give us both information and inspiration pertaining to the character. As I have said, that which cannot be imagined, cannot be done. Now we can modify this statement to what cannot be imagined, cannot be played. Therefore, what is played has been imagined and indirectly experienced, whether or not it 'really' happened. We can see why participation in improvised drama is often experienced as revealing, especially when we bear in mind that a group improvisation may well develop in a way which we ourselves would not have chosen. Therefore the dramatherapy group within which the child 'enters into role' has to be safe and secure, for the activity which the child is about to undertake can be profoundly exposing.

The seriousness and the threatening nature of drama for children are sometimes refuted with such arguments as 'children are naturals at plays. They easily slip in and out of role. The role itself does not seem to mean anything very much to them.' Whenever the above points are raised, they tend to flow from the lips of adults, who themselves rarely engage in conscious role-play. Even though few children will rationalise about the importance or effect of a role, few will deny its value or impact. To most children, the role matters, and what happens 'in role' in relation to others cannot simply be dismissed as 'having occured on stage'. Many a child, while still in role, will suddenly respond as if threatened for real, or accused for real. For she still knows that the connection between response in role and response in reality is an intimate one.

The child's apparent slipping in and out of role, is evidence of the proximity of fantasy and reality, and the still-active attempt at establishing connections between the two. Many children openly and freely identify with their roles. The awareness that the stage-character exists in its own right, and is nonetheless created and sustained from the inside, is still prevalent. The child in role knows herself to be the child she is and therefore to be the role which she has taken upon herself. The distancing between role and self which we see at a later stage of development mainly indicates the extent to which we try to deny and suppress aspects of our personality.

What has been said about improvised drama is to some degree true for scripted drama. There the expressed preference for the playing of one established part, rather than another, will be indicative of the child's inner world experiences. The constraint of prescribed language and action development limits the child's opportunity to project herself into the character, as well as to display herself through the role. However, initially the child may experience this prescription of identity, text, action and interaction as pleasantly safe, even though there may be worries about the capacity to read and/or memorise the words.

Most older children like to engage in some limited form of scripted or highly predictable role-play before they are ready to create their own, improvised enactments. In an intermediary stage, we see how the children will make substantial agreements about characters and pre-planned plot, before daring to venture into role. It takes a secure group and child to start an improvisation with only the barest outline of an opening scene. But when these improvisations develop, the chances of personal discovery and revelation are substantial. Then the inner-stage presentations will be clearly expressed in the enacted drama. The intensity is heightened as the events on stage paraphrase the original internalised situation with increasing precision. When the inner drama is associated with profound pain and/or frustration, we witness how the child in role attempts to reduce the inner tension by expressing the knotted-up emotions, by seeking alternative solutions and resolutions, or by an avoidance manoeuvre. Like a caged animal, the child in role may well pace up and down, approaching the issue from a variety of angles, until a satisfactory reduction of tension is achieved. Then, and only then, is the improvisation completed. The character and plot are likely to return over and over again, until their potency is transformed from a constraining into an energising force.

SELECTING A THEME

How then can the dramatherapist help the children to select and construct scenes which will offer useful material for exploration and which will approach and address their inner conflicts? As has been stated earlier 'enactment' during a dramatherapy session refers to the dramatisation of those scenes which are significant. The dramatherapist enables construction and exploration. This means that the dramatherapist has to be a capable translator of explicit reality into metaphoric representative reality, e.g. the weak little girl who is often bullied by her older sister, may need to become involved in role-plays which centre around a dejected slave in the service of a powerful princess, or the young waitress in a busy restaurant, or a sparrow fledgling feeding from the same bird table as a seagull. Then a situation has to be developed which generates tension, leading to interaction and resolution. Role-reversal, doubling and specific role-instructions guide the child's journey in and through the role.

The themes are distilled from the child's behaviour during the sessions, and from her contributions (or the absence of contributions) to the various imitation, free association, exploration and interactive exercises. Several of these relevant themes will recur, more or less independently of the child's specific reasons for referral and/or the individual history and behavioural characteristics. These themes tend to centre around beginnings, change, the unknown, the dark, powerful destructive creatures, abandonment, power, chaos and structure, individuality and togetherness. They are the common human experiences, and the child who is referred for dramatherapy often experiences difficulty with the management of these issues. We can presume that they will at least contribute to the child's predicament. Therefore work around and with these common themes will involve the child in personal exploration. The commonality of the theme is often felt to be reassuring.

The elicitation of themes which are group — and/or child — specific tends to follow the construction and re-construction of these common human theme scenes. The extent to which the dramatherapist is qualified to accompany the child on a specific personalised journey depends substantially upon the therapist's skill, training and understanding of the child's particular difficulties, and the processes by which change can be enabled. The dramatherapist's training in child psychotherapy will set the limits to the work.

Where this training is very limited, the dramatherapist needs to take extra care to operate within appropriate boundaries in order to avoid the magician's–pupil syndrome. These boundaries will generally be characterised by work around the management of themes of common human predicament, rather than the intense exploration of individual difficulties. This is so, even though these specific difficulties will always be directly expressed and worked with in the various roles the child plays, whilst being indirectly addressed in the selected themes. As has been said before, in improvised role-play we always engage and display aspects of ourselves and thereby the child in trouble is encouraged and enabled to resolve her inner conflicts through the participation in these theme-specific constructs.

COMPLETION

The day will come when the child either announces that she is getting ready to stop coming, or that the dramatherapist notices how the enactments are losing their charged content, and are increasingly developing towards the exploration of 'average' emotional and interactive constructs. Completion is around the corner. Child and dramatherapist need to ask themselves whether the goal has been achieved; how the present position differs from the starting one, and what sort of effect the anticipated ending is likely to have upon the child. Once the implicit ending has been made explicit, a regression to earlier modes and styles of behaviour often occurs, but if the acquired strength is real, the child and the group will soon return to their earlier position to explore its implications and possibilities. Throughout, the dramatherapist should evaluate her work, both in the short and long term, in order to draw conclusions and thus improve future practice.

CONCLUSION

This chapter has not addressed issues regarding the specific ways by which a child can be helped to enter into role, to engage in inter-active role-play, to conclude an enactment, and to de-role. Little has been said about the structuring of a dramatherapy session (from introduction, via action and interaction, to sharing, reflection and integration towards a renewed beginning which equals the ending) or about the overall dramatherapeutic process which includes recall or unfreezing, repetition and rephrasing, then through verification and reconciliation to renewal and continuation.

The aim of this chapter has been to reflect upon several considerations for dramatherapeutic practice with children, such as the transformation of time and space, the quality of absorbtion, the need for access to an inner sanctum. Parallels have been drawn between the child's need to internalise a subjective–objective reality, and the phases of the dramatherapeutic process. However, the subtext interwoven into these words has been the hope that the dramatherapist will listen with 'a third ear' and see with 'a third eye' to what is and is not entrusted to others 'like oneself' so that the child in trouble may be helped to make the dream of life come true.

REFERENCES AND FURTHER READING

Axline, V. (1971) *Dibs, In Search of Self*, Pelican, London
Daniel, S. & McGuire, P. (eds) (1972) *The Paint House, Words from an*

71

East End Gang. Penguin, London

Berg, J.H. van den (1958) *Dubieuze liefde in de omgang met het kind*. Nijkerk, Callenbach nv, Holland

Bronfenbrenner, U. *Two Worlds of Childhood*. Penguin, London

Campbell, J. (1973) *Primitive Mythology*. Souvenir Press, London

Erikson, E. (1977) *Toys and Reasons, Stages in the Ritualization of Experience*. W.W. Norton & Company, New York

—— (1980) *Identity and the Life Cycle*. W.W. Norton, New York

Feder, E. & Feder, B. *The Expressive Arts Therapies*. Prentice-Hall, Englewood Cliffs, New Jersey

Figge, P.A.W. (1982) *Dramatherapie bei Kontaktstörungen*. Kosel, München

Foudraine, J. (1974) *Not Made of Wood*. Quartet Books, London

Freire, P. (1972) *Pedagogy of the Oppressed*. Penguin, London

Freud, S. (1962) *Civilization and its Discontents*. W.W. Norton, New York

Hart, O. van der (1978) *Overgang and bestendiging*. van Loghum Slaterus, Deventer

Have, T.T. van (1969) *Klein bestek van de agologie*. Wolters-Noordhoff nv, Groningen

Jennings, S. (ed.) (1975) *Creative Therapy*. Pitman, London

Kramer, E. (1971) *Art as Therapy with Children*. Schocken Books, New York

Laing, R.D. (1967) *The Divided Self*. Penguin, London

McGregor/Tate/Robinson (1977) *Learning through Drama*. Heinemann, London

Petzold, H.G. (1982) *Dramatische Therapie*. Hippokrates Verlag GmbH, Stuttgart

Piaget, J. & Inhelder, B. (1969) *The Psychology of the Child*. Basic Books, Trowbridge

Redl, F. & Winemann, D. (1951) *Children Who Hate*. The Free Press, New York

Reich, W. (1975) *Listen Litten Man!* Penguin, London

Rothenberg, J. (1972) *Shaking the Pumpkin*. Doubleday, New York

Salzberger-Wittenberg (1970) *Isca: Psycho-analytic Insight and Relationships: A Kleinian Approach*. Routledge & Kegan Paul, London

Singer, J. (1973) *The Child's World of Make Believe*. Academic Books, New York

Watzalawick, P. (ed.) (1967) *Pragmatics of Human Communication*. W.W. Norton, New York

Winnicott, D.W. (1971) *Playing and Reality*. Penguin, London

—— (1980) *The Piggle*. Penguin, London

4

Dramatherapy and Drama

David Powley

ONE

To introduce people to the drama in dramatherapy I sometimes do an exercise which I call 'Getting Here'. It has many variant forms, of course, and may develop quite differently according to the nature and needs of the people doing it, but, in outline, what follows is the sequence I most often use.

Stage one

Each student finds a partner. The two of them find their own space and sit facing each other. They close their eyes and everyone spends a minute or two concentrating on the details of the journey here today, from getting out of bed to arrival. Their attention is focused on events — what they did and what happened to and around them.

Each partner then has a turn at telling the other the story of his or her journey. However, the exercise is strictly structured. The narrators have exactly five minutes in which to complete their stories. They do not change over until I say so. Furthermore, the listeners must just listen and the narrators are encouraged to make use of any moments of silence.

When both have had their turn, I ask them to review what they have heard and recall those moments when their interest was most sharply engaged or feelings quickened. Each then must choose one or two such peaks and take turns to explore them further by asking their partners questions about them.

Then they have a short time to share their experience of doing the exercise so far and any thoughts it may have provoked. That may,

73

depending on the circumstances, be formalised by bringing the results of the sharing to the whole group for a short time before beginning stage two.

Stage two

Each pair now selects one of the moments/events examined to reconstruct. The narrator A of the chosen 'story' becomes the director, using the listener B to act the role of A in it. The director may take on subsidiary roles or they may be imagined or, if there are several such roles and they are particularly important, two pairs may amalgamate to provide more actors.

Particular attention is paid at first to accuracy in defining space and where things are in it. Then the focus is shifted to the exact sequence of events, what people did in the space. Then how they did it.

The director is encouraged at first simply to tell the actor(s) what to do, then to show him or her, until satisfied that they have achieved a fair approximation of the event and the actor feel(s) reasonably comfortable with the mechanics. As the sequence being rehearsed is short, the whole process takes no more than half an hour.

Stage three

Now the actor B playing the role of A tries each of the following in turn, while enacting the scene. In role,

(1) Speaking aloud what he/she is doing
(2) Speaking aloud what he/she is thinking
(3) Speaking aloud what he/she is feeling.

In (2) and (3) there is a connection between what is said and what is done and the things and people to which the action relates. He or she risks doing it without help while the director just watches.

Then the actor can check with A how accurate the portrayal has been and A can enter his or her own scene and speak aloud an expanded version of A's feelings for himself.

Stage four

At this point (if not before) I may intervene and focus the whole group's attention on one enactment, partly to clarify the process and partly to involve more people in one person's story.

Rather than addressing his or her feelings to the world at large, A now directs them at the objects or people to which they are attached. To do this, members of the 'audience' enter the scene and 'become' these objects/people. Through a series of role-reversals and interviews, the nature of the feelings and relationships are explored and revealed further.

TWO

In Plato's *Ion* (translation by Rouse, 1970) we catch a glimpse of an ancient Greek poet reciting his poetry to an eager audience. Actually, Ion himself was a professional reciter of Homer's poetry, but poets recited their own verse in much the same way. He dressed up for the occasion and stood on a platform. He tells us: 'Whenever I speak of sad and touching scenes, my eyes are full of tears; when it is something terrible or awful, my hair stands up straight with fear and my heart leaps!' And of his audience: 'I always look down from my platform, and there they are crying and glaring and amazed, according to what I say.'

Fundamentally, there is little difference between our storyteller and the Greek poet, nor between the listener and the Greek audience. The problems of crossing the space between them are the same. Whether they are solved as successfully, depends on how well our storyteller can recreate his or her story and on how well the listener can listen.

THREE

The storyteller and his listener are communicating with each other and are doing so by creating illusions. Out of illusions we build the evanescent bridges across which we meet. And 'if there is no instant of shared illusion, there is no exchange' (Brook, 1972). The story of our 'getting here' is an illusion because we both believe, if only partially and for a moment, that what happened in the past and in other places is actually happening here and now. It is also an illusion because what the listener experiences is at least four-times removed from what actually happened; and further illusory, because he experiences something both less and more than what happened.

What happens is a process of selection and alteration. The event itself will be altered and reduced already by the point of view and nature of the person experiencing it. That experience is further refined by contemplation, the vital moments for the speaker being remembered, the lesser forgotten. Finding the means of telling the story will drastically reduce it to selected images and further transform it with embellishment. It is this edited version, being experienced in fact for the first time by both listener and speaker in this form, which crosses the space between them.

This illusion is then further edited and reshaped by the listener, who, however receptive, has his or her own store of experience of similar events, with meanings attached to the images offered. The illusion shifts and shimmers as it enters the listener's consciousness, stirs the subconscious self and then regrows within him, a new experience, born of an act of communion.

What is remarkable is not only that anyone knows what anyone else is talking about, but also that, knowing perfectly well where and who we are, our desire to enter another's experience enables us to lose enough of the 'who' and 'where' of ourselves to enter the illusion in a willing suspension of belief. Paradoxically, this process of selection is what enables both speaker and listener to experience it together at all. It is through being thus reduced that the experience is able to regrow into something like the event itself, but larger because it carries with it all other similar events and their attached meanings contained in each of the communicants' store.

Equally paradoxically, it is through these illusions that we are able to keep our sense of reality and self intact and, indeed, to grow. Faced with the stony face of incomprehension, we are cast adrift — isolate, unsure — as the edges of our existence shrink and fade.

FOUR

Selecting is what we do naturally a good deal of the time. It is one of the main functions of the eye, to focus on individual objects, and thus to separate them from their context. It is one of our principal tools of survival; through it we can locate, follow, catch, control or avoid the things and creatures of our world. But to do all that, having identified what the thing is, we need to know more about what it will do. We need to be able to predict. Prediction gives us a better chance of control.

We watch what we select to see what it will do next. We really want to know because we need to know. It is at the root of what we call 'curiosity'. It goes on happening well beyond what might be seen as immediate needs or for specific purposes. Some may call it 'idle curiosity'. But curiosity is never 'idle'. It always yields information that might be useful, though we may not yet know how. And it keeps us in practice, on the alert. What we select and how often depends very much on who we are and on our circumstances.

When we single out something and follow its progress, what we are watching for is a pattern of behaviour. We experience life as a series of beginnings and ends. We get up, do things, go to sleep. We start eating, then we stop eating. We reach for an apple off a tree, we pick it; then we start something else. What? So we watch, not just for what happens next but for what will happen in the end. Such patterns of behaviour are the substance of stories. We watch for story patterns.

However, we are not just curious to know what happens next, or in the end, but also whether we will be proved right in our predictions: for we are testing what we see against previous experience. We wonder, in fact, if what we are watching will fit a pattern of behaviour already discerned through previous observations: 'I wonder if he'll . . .' If it does fit, then our power is confirmed and we nod with satisfaction, even if the emotional impact of the event makes us shake our heads in dismay. Part of the excitement in watching, as in listening to the story, is the chance it gives us 'to exercise our skill and judgement', as the advertisements say. And afterwards we exclaim, 'I told you so!' or 'well, that's typical'.

On the other hand, our response may be one of shock: 'Well! That just goes to show! You never can tell!'. What we have seen or heard confirms our knowledge of the ultimate *un*predictability of experience: however well-tried the pattern and however well it seems to fit along the way, *in the end* the event jumps out of life and does not do what we confidently expect it to do. 'Well, there's yer life!', as my grandmother-in-law used to say.

In either case, we are able to share in our recognition and confirmation of patterns of behaviour, and are drawn together through them, thus confirming our sense of connection with each other and satisfying our need for communion. On the one hand we may demonstrate our commonly-held power to predict successfully and are bound more closely together in allegiance to such patterns.

On the other, we draw together for comfort in our common recognition of frailty in the face of a powerfully unreliable universe; and our story even gives us *some* measure of control over it, if only in that it is a vessel in which our feelings of fear may be contained. It will also keep us alert to the dangers that continuously threaten us.

Able thus to share a common pattern, we are better able to enter into each other's specifically different and unique experience of the pattern: a safe validation and expansion of our own individuality.

Already, as we watch the world about us and ourselves in it we are storytellers. How effectively we tell others depends on how well we select, how well we can excite in the listener the desire to know what will happen next, have him or her nodding and shaking the head, to find patterns of experience that can be shared with us.

FIVE

The art of creating effective illusions depends on this process of selection and on our ability to select the most significant moments and features of experience and the most appropriate means of carrying them across the space. Some art takes selectivity to extremes of economy. A Japanese painting may with a few exactly placed and fashioned brush strokes in black evoke a whole world of reeds and dragonflies. So also with words, especially in the haiku form:

> Along the mountain path,
> The scent of plum-blossoms, —
> And, on a sudden, the rising sun!
>
> Basho, in Blyth (1942)

More active but just as economical a mode of expression is mime. All I have to do is manipulate my hand in such a way as to suggest I am opening a door, give weight to my body as I 'push' it open, make a gesture with my hand across my eyes, accompanied by a contortion of the face, then slowly look upward and around the space in front of me, screwing up the eyes a little, and my audience have come with me through a heavy wooden door with huge iron hinges, into a vast, dimly-lit vault, musty, eerie with cobwebs, carrying with them all the other physical and emotional associations they may have with such a scene.

In fact, there will be as many variations of the scene as there are people in the audience but they will all share the same basic pattern of experience and, building on the same few bodily gestures indicating things in space and feelings about them, fill the empty air around them with illusory visions and sounds and smells, and move with me through them.

SIX

All that will depend on how fully we can re-enter our own experience, or experience in the first place.

> Experiencing is penetration into the environment, total organic involvement in it. This means involvement on all levels: intellectual, physical and intuitive.
>
> Spolin (1963)

If we are to involve the audience fully we must involve them physically, through all the senses. We do rely heavily on what the eye can tell us but of course, our other senses tell us just as much. The trouble is, we are far less sensitive to what they tell us than we could be — than are people in non-European cultures or were the ancient Greeks. And what they do tell us is subordinated to and orchestrated by the eye.

Through the eye we gain a sense of being outside the things of the world about us. Through it we may spectate more than participate. Harnessed to the focused eye, our watching may the more easily be uninvolved, clinically detached, much more immediately at the service of our intellect, watching for patterns of behaviour, judging, categorising.

The detachment is more complete when our eye focuses on the written word, which is the sign for an experience rather than the experience itself, a product of the intellect. It may see meanings only, rather than things and action. We may not even visualise them. How many people on reading of 'plum blossoms' or a 'mountain path', actually see them? We are more likely simply to have general ideas of them. For most of us, to visualise them would be very hard work: penetration! If we find it hard to *see* ourselves *walking* 'along the mountain path', how much more difficult it will be to *feel* ourselves walking. Or smell the 'plum-blossoms'.

We can and regularly do translate what we see into an experience of the other senses. When we see something being hit we wince at the impact, or take part with our bodies in the hitting. We can even seem to sense odours if their source is sufficiently evocative; even more so if we see someone else sniffing it. We are, in fact, almost involuntarily, taking part in the action, experiencing it for ourselves. We are doing what Keats says the poet does: 'if a sparrow come before my window, I take part in its existence and peck about in the gravel . . .', which is a 'total organic involvement', and is a natural and human thing to do.

The less we exercise or trust the senses, the less able are we to relate or respond to the world about us, or to learn from them. We narrow the range of experience we can 'take part in', and are less likely to activate the other, 'untrustworthy' senses through the agency of the eye. Even so, however limited our sensual range, we nevertheless experience an immense amount through the senses, thus providing ourselves with an apparently limitless store of information.

Our intellect is involved continuously also, making judgements, predictions, making notes, telling us what to do next, while much of what we experience thus we are, of course, conscious of, if only fleetingly. In that consciousness, through the intellect, we learn far more than we could ever abstract into a catalogue or will ever consciously remember. And even our relatively dull senses can record with far greater sensitivity than can the finest intellect.

We further abstract from some of that experience later, in looking back, and later still are better able thereby to recall it, at least in that abstract form — as a pattern, perhaps. But most of it we will never 'know' in that way at all.

The poet's task is to release in the listener the 'knowledge' locked in the senses, not available in the intellect's catalogue alone, though related to it and being the material from which its ideas have been abstracted. Only by engaging thus the whole person will ideas be filled out, experienced afresh, expanded or bodily changed. A new idea can have its full force only if the body realigns its own experience behind and within it, to carry it forward into what the listener in reality does next. And if that new idea depends for its life on new experience then that experience must engage the whole person of the listener, take its place in the 'bodily store', contribute to the realignment.

The poet must be able both to 'take part in' the world fully and to re-enter the experience, to re-enact it sensually, to unlock his or her own store. Then he or she must re-present that experience sensually so the form it takes enables others (and oneself) to enter and re-enact it. The intellect takes care of the form, the senses of the re-enactment.

The names a poet gives to things — 'plum-blossoms', for example — announce the writer's physical engagement with them, while the sentences he or she sets them in are the journeys from one thing to the next, stories of the relationship with them, defining the nature of the engagement. They are also the patterns of relationship observed and created by the poet. Through them, he or she invites us also to take part and to observe the pattern for ourselves.

Adjectives immediately involve our senses further and more specifically with things and declare more obviously the presence of the poet. To say the 'blossoms' are 'delicate' is to touch them and give them identity through what our hands do to them and what they seem to do in return. We re-enact the poet's act of relationship. In so doing, we identify with the poet but also with the 'blossoms', for in touching them, we physically take upon ourselves their delicacy in our hands. In describing the 'blossoms' we describe ourselves. Verbs, of course, encourage us into particular acts of relationship.

Even the most orderly and impersonal of descriptions is an engagement of at least the eye, looking above, below, moving in an arc, or, with the body leaning forward, brow furrowed, peering into the distance, as layer upon layer is built through the pattern of sentence upon sentence. Even a philosophical treatise roots its ideas in active examples from sensual experience, or at least engages us in the physical movements of logic and balance, taking us step by step, for example, or to the one hand and then to the other, the movement of the sentence giving body to the ideas.

So poetry, narrative, description and even philosophy, in this respect at least, are all drama. They all engage us in a sensual relationship with the physical world, incite us to act within it. In them all the writer struggles to burst through the limits of the written word into action, even if very quietly. And, so bound together are the intellect and the senses that, just as through the words we may enter the action, so through the action we may find the words.

SEVEN

Basho's poem, for all its stark simplicity, is full of drama but, especially in its original, more visually expressive Japanese script, is more a picture to comtemplate than an incitement to action. As a dramatherapist, I admire and try to emulate the way he creates a simple pattern, then leaves people to explore it for themselves, without further prodding. In its quietness and relative lack of involvement, it counterbalances nicely the relative excesses of Ion and his audience. However, it is with the people and drama of ancient Greece that I as a dramatherapist find my roots and more of my active inspiration.

Their 'organic involvement' with the world was 'total' and extraordinarily alive. They thought the world was as active as they were themselves. Their sense of it was elemental and they told tales in a rich, sensual language of action. The 'wheeling sun . . . heats the earth to life' but, 'night looming, breakers lunging in for the kill . . . the black gales come brawling out of the north', leaving 'the Aegean heaving into a great bloom of corpses . . . Greeks, the pick of a generation scattered through the wrecks and broken spars' (Fagles, 1966). Words were primarily still for speaking, tales for telling, not for looking at on a page. They were given the bodily action of speech. Our children could have something of that experience if they were encouraged, for example, to read poetry 'with the ear and the body' (Leavis), instead of being confined so much to silent reading. Perhaps Cratylus was able to tell Plato that to know the word for a thing was to know the thing itself (Guthrie, 1967) because the word was still so physical an activity for him. Certainly, through the word, the Greeks seemed well able to enter into active engagement with the world.

The powers that moved their universe were transformed in the busiest of gods, behaving remarkably like Greeks. What concerned them most was what people *do*. As Aristotle remarks in *Poetics* (Warrington, 1963), 'It is in our actions that we are happy or the reverse'. Little wonder then that they should regard drama so highly and have developed it so fully. The word itself means 'what is going on'.

What was going on was as much a matter for poetry as anything else. Those long speeches that seem so dauntingly static at first glance, in fact seethe with human and elemental activity, leap from event to event, backwards and forwards in time, from place to place, with a cast of people and gods far greater than could ever appear physically in even a ninety-foot circle before the audience, setting the immediate action into a vast context and yoking it to the play's purpose.

For the Greeks, however, drama includes so much more activity. It combines dramatic dialogue, poetry, music and dance. Furthermore, it was the province of the poet. He wrote the words, composed the music, choreographed the dance, trained and directed actors and dancers, designed the set, props and costumes, and even himself acted the main part.

That is what attracts me as a dramatherapist: this all-embracing, eclectic view of the art, in which all these apparently separate arts are but different elements of the one — drama — each and together representing 'men's characters as well as what they do and suffer' (Aristotle). I am excited by their 'sense of the wholeness of things . . . perhaps the most typical feature of the Greek mind' (Kitto, 1960).

EIGHT

The ancient Greeks were also given splendidly to extremes. They experienced life in themselves and in the universe as a continuing conflict between extreme, opposing forces, as they flew or were flung from one to the other. Knowing the extremes so well they were constantly faced with the problem of control. They sought balance and harmony in nature and in their own behaviour, because they *needed* them, and their desire found moral expression in the doctrine of the Mean. The Mean was essential to the achievement of all-round excellence, for otherwise, through specialisation, they might have been too good at one thing to the detriment of the others. The same was more obviously true of human qualities such as pride, an excess of which could be disastrous. This conflict of extremes and people's attempt to find balance found its most exciting form of expression in the Greek drama. Through it we are involved in the attempt and in what happens if we fail.

Without conflict, we are often enough told, there is no drama. What is 'going on' is a pattern of conflict, the story of struggle between opposing forces. A common assumption is that this simply means people disagreeing with each other in varying degrees of violence. That is a rich enough source of drama, certainly, but conflict and its resolution are more fundamental to the drama process than that suggests. Just as all art seeks to reveal pattern, so it depends for its success on the presence of conflict, which provides the poles between which pattern forms, and is how we experience life. To understand how drama works as an art, we must understand both how conflict is experienced in life and what is special about the way drama reveals this experience.

To the Greeks, life itself was a product of conflict. Empedocles, for example, saw it as a struggle between Strife and Love, the former influencing elements to disassociate themselves from each other, the latter mingling one element with another to create composite creatures. Heraclitus saw life as a battle between fire and air, water and earth. However, what is most important is that this struggle is itself the basis of equilibrium and the source of life, and therefore not only necessary but good. It is a harmony of opposites, an attunement of opposite tensions, like that in a bow (Heraclitus), from which life flows.

Empedocles and Heraclitus were early Greek philosophers. They were in the thick of a particularly Greek and world-changing conflict. There emerged among them the conviction that beneath the complex, changing surfaces of the world as we know it through the senses, with all its active variety, there exists 'a fundamental simplicity and stability, a hidden permanence' (Guthrie, 1967), that there are unchanging and unchangeable laws, over which even the gods have no power. However, humans do have the power, through reason, the exercise of the intellect, to discover and articulate that simple permanence and law.

Perhaps as a result of their vivid sensual awareness of things they began to examine and talk about things rather than gods. Perhaps it was also a consequence of their powerful interest in things human and of their remarkable self-confidence. In any event, it was a declaration of individual human independence against the power of communal tradition and the gods. It marks the emergence of a society of individual, free-thinking people, taking hold of the painful responsibility of being individual, from a society dominated by communal pressures, traditions and myths, in which individuation was avoided in favour of merging with the group.

Ironically — and as such of particular appeal to Greek sensibilities — while enormously expanding human potential, faith in the products of pure reason was at times excessive and, unchecked by observation, led to the imposition of patterns where they did not fit. Worse, it led to the belief that intellect is more reliable than the senses and therefore superior to them; and that led eventually to what we simplistically call the mind/body split, a conflict we still experience acutely.

It is not surprising that this should happen. After all, if the world of the senses is so active and changeable, how can we predict with any certainty what will happen next? And we must be able to predict. If the intellect really can provide us with more reliable patterns, from which we can predict more successfully, than the senses, gods or oracles can provide, then, naturally, we will prize it highly. We are easily led thus to take leave of our senses, through the language of logic to that most intellectual of activities, mathematics, in whose cycles we may always be certain.

NINE

Drama itself, however, arises from a still deeper conflict in nature: between life and death. The earth dies in winter and is born again in spring. It has to happen thus or we humans will also die. The rituals devised to encourage it to happen and then to celebrate it were among the most vital to survival everywhere, not just in Greece. Following the pattern of earth's journey into death, the god of fertility, consort to Mother Earth, must be killed to be born again. This was given bodily existence, acted out in earnest, once upon a time, with human sacrifice, the ritual killing of the god in human form, the king or king-substitute; then, later, of the god in animal form: in Greece most commonly the bull or the goat. The drama, in its Greek tragic form, was born of the god's passion in death and rebirth, the Passion of Dionysus, much as the English drama was reborn in medieval times out of ritual celebrations of the Passion of Christ.

So also, however well we strive for and achieve excellence in all things, we have to die. From this is born the 'passionate tension' of the Greek tragic sense (Kitto, 1960). We may live on only in our children, who even while we live, supplant us. Ironically, we may suppress their rise to delay our own decline or from fear that they will supplant us too soon, the consequences of which are well documented in Greek myth and drama.

So also day dies in night and is reborn with the rising sun. As Jung discovered in Africa, 'the *moment* in which light comes *is* God. That moment brings redemption, release.' (Jung, 1983). Though the god at that moment may be identified as the sun, it is 'the archetypal experience of that moment', the release from the dark that matters.

The dark, night, death retreat into the tomb of the earth, the underworld, and is full of evil, danger, fear. It contains the violence and passion that are often the cause of death, as well as the avenging spirits of the dead. It is full of the uncertainty of shadows and the caprice of death itself, which may strike at any time without, as we say, rhyme or reason. Yet the earth's darkness is ambiguous, for it is also the womb of mother earth from whom all new growth springs, passionately but with joy. It is a nurturing, fruitful source.

Within the earth itself is a conflict. This is the unreliable world of the senses, of primitive earth-goddess religion, matrilineal society, the female principle in which the individual loses itself in the group, against which is opposed the bright clarity of the sunlit sky, of certainty, intellect, individuality, the sky god, the male:

> . . . within the soul from its primordial beginnings there has been a desire for light and an irrepressible urge to rise out of the primal darkness . . . The longing for light is the longing for consciousness (Jung, 1983)

TEN

The conflict of light and dark is little more than a game of Peekaboo! Now you see me, now you don't! The urgent mission of the eye is to separate out, identify, control: tell where we are, by knowing where the other is. If the object of its attention disappears, merges with its background, we wait anxiously, or excitedly for it to reappear. Each time it reappears, it comes as a minor revelation, shocking us with a sort of pleasure. We are constantly engaged in the conflict between what we see and what we do not see, and in seeking the shock and release of revelation.

Such a revelation may be of something quite unexpected, and thus a genuine surprise but it may also be a confirmation of what we expect. In Aeschylus' *Agamemnon* there is a scene in front of the palace where dire warnings are being uttered by Cassandra, the prophetess whom no-one will ever believe, that the king who has just entered the palace is about to be murdered and that she, too, when she enters, will be killed. No-one believes her and she enters. The chorus of old men dithers and debates the meaning of her prophecies. A blood-curdling cry is heard from within. Still the men dither. After all, is it really the king? Another cry from within! Even if it is the king, what can *we* do? At last they decide to see for themselves and rush up the steps to the great double doors — which, as they reach them, swing open to reveal two blood-stained corpses and, standing triumphantly over them, sword in hand, the blood-drenched murderess, the queen.

Even if we did not know what was going to happen beforehand — and the Greeks *did* know the story, in detail — the play arouses in us every expectation that the king has been killed. Having our predictions confirmed may give us a grim satisfaction: 'I told you so!' But it is not the confirmation of that fact that makes what is revealed a revelation: it is, rather, how that moment is reached, when precisely it comes in the pattern of movement towards it, and what exactly is then shown. Our frustration with the old men, exacerbated by not being able to use our knowledge to influence them in their lack of it, as they move towards and away from the door, until at last, released from their inaction, they act, at that moment, when the door opens, our frustration blooms into recognition of, yes, that is how we do not prevent crimes that could be prevented, and, yes, the *irony* that though we know what will happen we still seem unable to act! — And the queen! What sort of person is she, standing over her victims? What may we expect now from her? Her power is overwhelming. But will the blood of the dead king fertilise the soil of the state and bring about the hoped-for rebirth? Her words are well placed, the first to break the silence: 'Words, endless words I've said to serve the moment — now it makes me proud to tell the truth.' (Aeschylus)

What is most exciting about this relevation is that for the whole scene the most 'dramatic' events have been happening out of sight. The drama is not simply in what we see happen, nor even in what we do not see, but in the denial of our desire to see what we cannot see, in the conflict between here and there, the suspense of anticipation. While the foreground of our attention is taken with Cassandra and the old men, in the background we yearn forward into the house, and in the yearning we imagine, create, the events going on there and take part in them. We are in two places at once with a movement in us to and fro. When the doors open and we see the blood-drenched queen, what has been happening at the back of our minds leaps forward into her presence and in her is given flesh, flooding us with the full horror of what she has been *doing* behind closed doors.

ELEVEN

Though the impact of revelation may be used quite legitimately by dramatists predominantly to excite and amuse, most really satisfying plays also use it to teach us something; or, rather, manipulate revelation in such a way that our experience of it will excite us to learn and thus in some way change, just as, for example, change is both acknowledged and brought about by the initiation dramas of Australian Aborigines (Campbell, 1976).

Aeschylus may confirm and celebrate such communally respected moral qualities as courage, integrity, justice and moderation but his plays involve his audience in an *experience* of those values in action or of what happens if they are not respected. The *ideas*, easy enough to talk about 'to serve the moment', are given flesh in not only the actors but also in the audience, in so far as they 'take part', and are realigned, relearned, experienced afresh, expanded and perhaps even harnessed to the forward-moving energy of desire.

That is in essence what happens, for example, in Gestalt Therapy. A client may feel genuinely 'miserable' and thus far be really experiencing what the word means. However, the word, the idea, may be used more to obscure and avoid the precise nature of the misery than to reveal and deal with it. Having found the word, it is easy to assume that that is all there is to it. The client may now rock him or herself into numbness using the word as a kind of incantation. That perhaps is *all* he or she can do sometimes and for a time it may 'work'. But what if it keeps happening, this pattern of behaviour?

The gestalt therapist, as dramatist and teacher, knowingly or not, follows Aristotle's dictum that 'it is in our actions that we are happy or the reverse', and focuses the client's attention on what he or she is doing in his or her misery, at this moment, thus re-awakening the body into a finer awareness of its own action and feeling. What in its action, then, is the body — or this or that small part of it — *saying*? (Fagan and Shepherd, 1972). The therapist helps the client to 'take part' in his or her own experience. Little by little the client lifts himself or herself thus from the 'primal darkness' into consciousness and further, possibly remedial action.

Aristophanes in 405 BC in his comedy, *The Frogs*, gives Aeschylus the line: '. . . from the very earliest times the really great poet has been one who had a useful lesson to teach'. Fortunately, as Aristotle a few years later says: 'To be learning something is the greatest of pleasures not only to philosophers but also the rest of mankind . . .' That is doubly fortunate, considering how essential to survival learning is.

However, *how* to provoke learning and *what* that learning should be are always themselves matters for conflict. Our desire to know where we stand, for permanence, leads us to get used to, then to expect certain patterns of both content and representation. But as life as we experience it is changeable so our needs either change in themselves or must find new means of expression and satisfaction.

Aeschylus, according to Aristophanes, says poets '. . . have a duty to see that what we teach them is right and proper'. Euripedes, however, fifty years his junior, says what he did '. . . was to teach the audience to use its brains, introduce a bit of logic into drama. The public have learnt from me how to think . . .'. Euripedes '. . . wrote about familiar things, things the audience knew about, and could take me up on if necessary . . .' and gave his characters language and clothes — rags if necessary — to fit. Aeschylus, however, dressed his characters to look larger and more splendid than in life, while in *The Frogs*, Euripedes accuses him of trying to 'bludgeon' the audience 'into unconsciousness with long words', with 'great galumphing phrases, fearsome things with crests and shaggy eyebrows'. Aeschylus attacks Euripedes for being an 'enemy of the gods' and encouraging 'pimps and profligates'. These are things, he says, 'the poet should keep quiet about . . . not put on the stage for everyone to copy'.

Though these statements are made by the two poets as characters in Aristophanes' comedy, in which he makes fun of them both, the play's intention is serious, debating issues of great concern to a city at war and in political turmoil and in need of advice it can rely on. Which of the two great poets should Dionysus bring back from the dead to save the city? In the end he favours the older Aeschylus with his old-fashioned views; not before setting out for us, however, the main arguments of the realism–fantasy debate that continues to this day, though in different forms.

'The strongest, most influential and most radical theatre man of our time', (Brook, 1972) Bertolt Brecht, in 1933 says of his kind of drama — 'Anxious to teach the spectator a quite definite practical attitude, directed towards changing the world, it must begin by making him adopt in the theatre a quite different attitude from what he is used to.' (Willett, 1964) However, when we hear that he '. . . began working at a time when most German stages were dominated either *by naturalism or by great total-theatre onslaughts of an operatic nature* designed to sweep up the spectator by his emotions so that he forgot himself completely', (Brook, 1972), we see him attack the 'naturalism' Euripedes espoused as well as the 'bludgeoning' identified in Aeschylus.

He was trying to prevent the spectator 'losing himself' in the drama, whether it was 'true to life' or not. Just as his drama '. . . refrains from handing its hero over to the world as if it were his inescapable fate, so it would not dream of handing the spectator over to an inspiring experience,' (Willett, 1964) or to the crippling thrill of witnessing on stage action so remarkably lifelike in its surface detail that all we can do is nod and shake our heads and say, yes, that *is* how life is.

This led him to attack what he calls 'Aristotelian' drama, that creates an empathy in the audience with the characters on stage, the very involvement I have suggested is essential to the drama process and to any act of communication. Brecht was worried that the audience would not take part also with their intellect, would not think about and learn from their experience. Not only was the life, such as it was, on-stage 'offset by the passivity it demanded of the audience', (Brook, 1972) but the audience itself was less active in its approach, perhaps, than a Greek audience would be, or, anyway, had grown to *expect* a thrilling experience or to remain a spectator. Brecht with his 'non-Aristotelian' drama was at heart closer to the Greek poet/teacher than his German audience was to the Greek people.

Brecht did as much as he could to break the spell and to shock people into thought. He called on the looser structure of the Aristotelian 'epic' to make his plays more episodic, separated scenes with placards and film, broke the action itself with songs and bits of narrative and had his actors step in and out of role. He went out of his way to call his audience's attention to the fact that it was really in a *theatre*, rather than to persuade it otherwise. He called this process 'alienation': one that shocks people out of the experience into thinking about what is happening and what can be done about it. That in their own way is what both Aeschylus and Euripedes tried to do, and Aristophanes.

In fact, Brecht modified his own theories himself. He recognised that we can have empathy and think at the same time:

> . . . a sister lamenting that her brother is off to war; and it is a peasant war: he is a peasant off to join the peasants. Are we to lose ourselves in her agony? Or not at all? We must be able to lose ourselves in her agony and at the same time not to. Our actual emotion will come from recognising and feeling the double process. (Willett, 1964).

A double process that sounds remarkably like the 'attunement of opposite tensions' out of which life is born.

TWELVE

Brecht in his concern for the peasant class notices that 'lofty speech is bound up with the individual problems of the upper class'.

Aeschylus, in *The Frogs*, links the 'concatenation of commonplaces' of Euripedes' poetry, 'as threadbare as the tattered characters who utter them', to the idea that that is really all one can 'expect from a person of (his) rustic ancestry'.

Both Brecht and Euripedes in their rebellion express the same kind of anarchic energy that gives such rumbustious life to that other great early form of drama, Comedy. Its origins are the same as those of Tragedy: the Spring Festival of Dionysus; but, whereas Tragedy came to be associated with the interests of the ruling classes in its celebration of the Passion of the god in the form of the community's Priest-king, Comedy belonged primarily to the peasant classes, an earthy expression of the rising sap.

It is an outspoken celebration of sex, with its grotesque masks and large phalluses, both rigid and floppy, and its full-frontal humour. This same energy was also given freedom at this time to flout the rules, to burst out of the bonds of accepted and expected patterns of behaviour. As part of their processional improvisation from earliest times, people hurled insults at all and sundry, mocked and parodied, turned the world upside down. Comedy developed both these anarchies and gave them form and directive force in a regenerative conflict.

Peter Brook gives an example of how Brecht's alienation effect works:

A girl, raped, walks on to a stage in tears — and if her acting touches us sufficiently, we automatically accept the implied conclusion that she is a victim and an unfortunate one. But suppose a clown were to follow her, mimicking her tears, and suppose by his talent he succeeds in making us laugh. His mockery destroys our first response. Then where do our sympathies go? The truth of her character, the validity of her position, are both put into question by the clown, and at the same time our own easy sentimentality is exposed. If carried far enough, such a series of events can suddenly make us confront our shifting views of right and wrong.

That is what Greek Comedy does. Indeed, at the Festival, the Tragedies would be followed closely by Comedies, in which the extremes of suffering revealed by the Tragedies, arousing such strong sympathies in the audience, and even the characters and the poets themselves, were parodied and mocked mercilessly.

In the centre of all this is the ambiguous god, the same god that suffers and dies, Dionysus himself. Indeed, in *The Frogs*, he is on-stage in the flesh, egging on and judging Aeschylus and Euripedes in their conflict, himself a scurrilous Lord of Misrule, making jokes which Aeschylus describes as 'in the worst of taste'. With his energy, when at last the old men in *Agamemnon* rush up to the doors of the palace and they swing open, revealing the corpses and the queen, Monty Python might have her say: 'Has anyone got a Band-aid?.'

Eugene Ionesco (1964), a playwright of our own time, tries to:

> confront comedy and tragedy in order to link them in a new dramatic synthesis. But it is not a true synthesis, for these elements do not coalesce, they co-exist: one constantly repels the other, they show each other up, criticise and deny one another and, thanks to their opposition, thus succeed dynamically in maintaining a balance and creating tension.

He goes on to say:

> The tragic and the farcical, the prosaic and the poetic, the realistic and the fantastic, the strange and the ordinary, perhaps these are the contradictory principles that may serve as a basis for a new dramatic structure.

Revelation may be a matter of seeing through the hole made in the one through collision with the other.

THIRTEEN

> Dionysus is the spirit of unthinking, physical enjoyment, of the instinctive Group-personality, of anti-intellectual energy. In him, as E.R. Dodds says in his 'The Greeks and the Irrational', are mingled joy and horror, insight and madness, innocent gaiety and dark cruelty. We ignore at our peril the demand of the human spirit for Dionysiac experience. (Grant, 1962)

Euripedes in *The Bacchae* shows us what happens if we do. Pentheus, intellectually arrogant, suppresses it and pays by being torn to pieces by its female initiates. His own mother leads the frenzied procession on-stage, brandishing his head.

The Greek valued the Mean so highly because he knew the

extremes of passion, not because he was, as Kitto (1960) puts it, 'a safe, anaesthetic, middle-of-the-road man'. Inasmuch as we are anaesthetised, safe, passive we need rather to stretch ourselves nearer the extremes, to meet our needs and explore our potential. Free of the confines of surface reality, the extremes of dramatic form give us a means through which to take the risks of discovery in relative safety, provide us with a vessel of unreality into which our real feelings may the more easily flow. The Greeks provide models of the extreme in both experience and form.

Of the many oppositions possible, those ranged *against* the individual, the intellect, the ordered, may, in fact, be the ones we most need to experience. We do need to sink our individuality in the group; be sustained by it and to revel in it; we need to give ourselves up to the senses; we need to experience our madness and our cruelty; need our primal darkness. The Greeks in their drama balanced individual, intellect, order with the ground-stamping rhythms of communal dance, the ritual chant, the flickering half-light of torches burning in the dark, the keening of pipe-music, all deriving from the rituals of Dionysiac religion. Through the drama they are given a new form, an experience from which we may learn. To use it thus may save us from being swept destructively under its spell, as millions were, for example, when manipulated to that end by Hitler.

FOURTEEN

There is a male character in Aristophanes' play *The Poet and the Women*, who has gained admittance to a women-only festival by dressing up as a woman. Much of the play is devoted to how he succeeds in hiding and how the women eventually succeed in revealing his masculinity. The climax comes with him being undressed to reveal, at last, yes, a long, floppy phallus. Much fun is had on the road to revelation and heave-ho hilarity released at the end of it.

Who are you? How can we be sure in this shape-shifting world that you are the person we think you are? Who, for that matter, are we? Oedipus spends a whole play discovering his identity in a series of relevations and ends his journey of enlightenment by stabbing out his eyes with a brooch pin, eyes that while they were open saw nothing.

One way of knowing our identity is through recognising the roles we play. The word 'role' is a theatrical term referring to the part an actor plays in a drama. We use it metaphorically to describe a similar process of 'playing' in life off-stage. In either case, we recognise the nature of a role through action: what we do sufficiently often for a pattern to emerge. A 'role', in fact, is the name we give to a pattern of behaviour. And as what we do always relates to something or someone, our roles will actively manifest themselves in how we negotiate those relationships.

We can describe who we are by making lists of sentences starting, 'I am the sort of person who . . .', and call them 'roles' we play. For convenience we can categorise the actions that produce these patterns with nouns. For example, if I am the sort of person who judges people, then I play the role of 'judge'. If I walk a lot, then I am a 'walker'. We may analyse the roles more specifically by adding, for example, adjectives: a 'severe' judge; an 'energetic' walker. Or we may find more general categories that include a whole cluster of such 'roles'. My role as 'father', for example, will include my role as 'judge'.

Many of these roles may be quite compatible with each other, take over freely from each other or even be played together. The role of 'walker' may walk quite happily, for example, with the sort of person who is keen to keep fit, or who collects things, or, even, who judges. However, even this happy family of roles may come into conflict. The 'collector' may potter about too long, leaving the 'walker' and 'fitness freak' impatiently stamping their feet. My 'father' as 'severe judge' may struggle with my 'father' as 'friend' or 'counsellor'. My 'father' as 'fair judge' and 'friend' may struggle with my 'loyal husband' when my wife chastises my daughter. My 'student' may battle with my 'walker' on my way to drama class on a sunny morning and as I yield to the 'walker' my 'chastiser' may tell me off thoroughly, the argument having disastrous effects on my 'careful driver'.

Each of these struggles, if we observe carefully, will manifest themselves in bodily action. The drama, of course, refines and heightens that action to make the conflict clearer. Our journeys from event to event are stories of how these roles negotiate with each other, work together, clash or give in to each other. When we talk of fulfilling ourselves we mean giving each of these roles the chance to complete its pattern. Having fulfilled the role of 'student', how much freer I feel as 'walker', and vice versa. When we talk of being at ease with the world, we may mean being able to slip into the appropriate role to negotiate each new experience. That means being at ease with a lot of roles and having role flexibility. The drama enables us, in clarifying conflicts, to see which roles need more exercise if they are to function more fluently and which need to be diverted from over-dominant activity.

Because in reality our various roles keep blurring or bumping into each other, causing confusion, our ability through drama to stop the world long enough to isolate, exaggerate and inhabit a single role fully is essential to our survival. We do it in drama to stylised extremes with clothing, paint, masks and contortions of language, or, less obviously, in a slice-of-life setting, simply by confining a character to one pattern of behaviour: for example, 'the sort of person who keeps falling asleep'. Indeed, all the characters in a play may only embody the most significant of only one person's roles; or may represent roles fundamental to all human beings, which each of us must somehow satisfy and keep productively co-operative.

Nothing is barred in the theatre: characters may be brought to life, but the unseen presence of our inner fears can also be materialised. So the author is not only allowed, but recommended to make actors of his props, to bring objects to life, to animate scenery and give symbols concrete form.

Ionesco (1964)

The Greeks gave form to inner fear — the Furies, for example, in *The Oresteia* — filled the acting-space with talking creatures — in Aristophanes' *The Frogs*, for example. Things and creatures of this world are anyway full of people: ourselves and others. We readily respond to the other people we sense in them or give them those of our feelings and thoughts that best fit their form and function. In mimicking them and giving a thing words and movement we may convey a delicate mixture of the nature of the thing itself and that part of our humanity best fitted to its form. The more intimate is our relationship with it, the more it can tell us about ourselves.

The fun and absurdity involved in being or seeing, for example, an animated chest-of-drawers, allows us in the gap opened up by laughter to enter freely and more fully the life contained within it, and to discover the tragedy it may conceal. The fun derives from the conflict between animate and inanimate, human and non-human, reality and fantasy. Playing a chest-of-drawers is no less playing a role than playing Hamlet.

The word 'role', of course, may also apply to a character in a play clearly exhibiting a variety of often contrasting patterns of behaviour, where all the 'roles' are contained in the one person. It is this that leads to some confusion about the word's meaning. Such

95

a 'role' we think of as 'rounded' and in so far as we demand characters in a play be recognisably like people we meet in reality, so we consider the 'rounded' character to be 'better' than the 'one-dimensional' because 'more convincing'.

Ironically, the way we relate to most people in reality suggests that we do not see 'real' people as at all 'rounded'. Being 'rounded' means being ambiguous and that arouses in us uncertainty, discomfort, even in relation to our *own* roundedness. It is easier and forever fascinating to come across it in a play, though many people find even that more upsetting than they can bear. In our constant quest for predictability we type-cast people and ourselves. Then we complain about being thus confined and bored.

All the time we carry with us rough approximations of the world in general, and hope, like the poet, we have chosen the most significant bits to serve our purpose. In particular and not surprisingly, given their importance to us, we spend the bulk of that time, consciously or unconsciously, discovering and selecting patterns of behaviour in other people: media through which to relate to them. To know what to do ourselves we need to know what others will do. Perhaps because it is so exhausting to be constantly alert, and perhaps because we too badly need to know where we are, we settle for some very rough and limited approximations of each other. Furthermore, we so readily expect ourselves and others to fit them, in reality, that we often force ourselves and others into roles we would rather not play.

If our patterns of expectation in relationships are broken, we get a shock. How we respond to the shock is crucial to our survival. Can we adapt our behaviour appropriately, find the right role? If we are too inflexible, too fixed in our role, unless we are also very powerful, then we may break. We may also be too flexible, of course, but we do have, all the time, to learn new roles or adapt old ones. Of course, most of us do, a lot of the time, unconsciously and consciously. And we spend a lot of energy being dramatists on our private stages in the attempt: talking to ourselves, telling ourselves stories, in alternative versions, going over the past and rehearsing the future. On the more public stage drama keeps us on our toes, shocks us into greater flexibility, perhaps, through revelation or insight, in endless variations of pattern and response — if, that is, we can fully 'take part'.

FIFTEEN

What the poet/dramatist/actor does and the problems he has to solve
are in their various ways only specialised and heightened versions
of what we all do and have to solve. It is partly a legacy of the past,
when the poet/dramatist/actor was also the priest/king, specially
charged by the Gods, part of an elite order guarding the mysteries,
that we so frequently suppose ourselves unable to do what they do,
and in so thinking, make it so. That is not to deny that some people
have special qualities that make them better able to do these things,
nor that to become skilled does not take a lot of work. However, as
Viola Spolin (1963), herself a leading influence on modern attitudes
to actor-training, says: 'everyone can act'. She suggests that talented
behaviour may be 'simply a greater individual capacity for experiencing'. Thus, 'it is in the increasing of the individual capacity for
experiencing that the untold potentiality of a personality can be
evoked'. One of the problems, as Stanislavski (1937) sees it is:
'How can we teach unobservant people to notice what nature and life
are trying to show them?' The exercises they both devised for the
training of actors are equally valuable to us all.

The first stage of my 'Getting Here' exercise may be recognised
by training counsellors as a listening exercise. From an actor's point
of view it is also an exercise for recall and communication; and a
role-training exercise. At first, many people feel uncomfortable
doing it. 'It feels unnatural,' they say, 'false. People wouldn't
behave like this.' But, of course, it is no more unnatural than what
we have to do, for example, when we start a radically new job. A
whole new set of roles must be learned. We naturally find what we
are unused to uncomfortable, as when we call on unused muscles.
Furthermore, changing habits of behaviour, however cramping they
may be, is more painful than giving ourselves up to them.

The 'listener', for example, keeps wanting to speak, play 'storyteller' or 'commentator'. What he hears triggers his own thoughts
and feelings, whose increasing demands for expression throw him
into a fidget. Or he may mould the teller's tale by approving or dis-
approving, agreeing or disagreeing, or judging, thus encouraging or
discouraging particular lines of development. Or he feels an
irrepressible need to be 'helpful' when the speaker has difficulties
in remembering or finding words or quite simply stops speaking. So
half the time he is not listening at all.

Similarly for the speaker: he may feel a failure if he falls silent,
or have so little respect for his own life as to believe he has nothing

to relate, or so need approval or fear disapproval he dare not begin. So half the story remains untold. The speaker is no more attending to his story than the listener. The roles they try to play are blocked by other roles, by other patterns of behaviour.

Another influential actor/director/teacher of our time, Jerzy Grotowski (1975), says of his company's work: 'Ours . . . is a *via negativa* — not a collection of skills but an eradication of blocks.' The problem is: how to eradicate them? Partly it is a matter of recognising them and devising strategies for stepping round them. It is, however, also a matter of learning to concentrate our attention on what we want to do.

Stanislavski (1937) makes 'Attention' one of the 'elements' of the 'system' of exercises he devised for the actors' training. It is an essential ingredient of all the other 'elements' and exercises. Some exercises concentrate on encouraging 'Attention', while most others are structured so that attention is concentrated on whatever else is being developed. Stage One of the 'Getting Here' exercise is thus structured and has the development of attention as one of its objectives. However, all this on its own and for its own sake would be an arid, tense affair, mere mechanics.

The Greeks originally thought of poet/actors when in full song as being possessed by a god. The god sang through them. And that accounted for the effect their songs had on themselves and their audiences. Stanislavski thinks of this godly power as 'creativity', 'inspiration', and locates it firmly in the actor's own 'subconscious', a word he uses in a more general sense than would a psychologist. In creating a character an actor must be able to tap his own subconscious, draw forth his creativity, in order to create from his own inner life an inner life for his character. External technique on its own, however perfect, remains mechanical and dead. Thus, whatever 'role' he plays, he is always 'playing' himself. Unfortunately we cannot activate the subconscious directly or control it. Stanislavski (1968) developed his 'so-called system' of 'external technique' and 'psycho-technique' to approach it indirectly. He likened it to stalking an animal: he used his 'techniques' to 'lure' creativity from the subconscious. We catch what we cannot control through what we can control. As these techniques are very much the product of the conscious mind and encourage the use of reason as a starting-point they illustrate well his motto, 'the subconscious through the conscious'.

It is in the 'subconscious' that feelings are engendered. It is by engaging the subconscious and releasing creativity that an actor, or our storyteller and listener, or any of us in response to the world around us, are able to feel something new each time we enter an experience through our selected approximations of the world. We do not directly, and would be unwise to try to, create the feelings, or *re*create each time feelings we had before, for what Stanislavski (1968) says of the actor (quoting Pushkin) is true for us all: '. . . the work of the actor is not to create feelings but only to produce the given circumstances in which true feelings will *spontaneously* be engendered. It is this creative flow of energy from the 'subconscious', animating our various selves, that gives us a central sense of a single self far greater than the sum of the parts, even as we concentrate our attention on only one.

The actual nature of this energy, or the 'subconscious', remains a mystery. We may as well call it 'god-within-us', for we cannot otherwise properly anatomise it. However, as Stanislavski clearly demonstrates, we can analyse what happens when it is or is not flowing and can analyse and thus create the conditions that cause it to flow. None of these strategies would work, however, if we were not *whole*. That is to say, mind and feelings are interdependent, belong to the same body. Stimulate one and the other is immediately activated. Stanislavski adds 'will' — the 'I want to' desire — to the other two, and the three together are the interdependent triumvirate on which the whole of his 'system' is based: 'mind–will–feeling'.

Another word associated with the 'subconscious' by both Stanislavski and Spolin, is 'intuition'. Spolin's 'experiencing' means 'involvement at all levels: intellectual, physical and intuitive'. She, too, seeks to engage the 'intuitive': in her view, the most neglected of the three. It 'comes bearing its gifts in the moment of spontaneity, the moment when we are freed to relate and act involving ourselves in the moving, changing world around us'.

Spolin calls her drama exercises, 'games'. The game is a natural group activity, familiar to all and giving the group its purpose: a problem to be solved; while the rules are its governing structure. She makes Stanislavski's 'Attention' central to these games, directing it at the problem to be solved and renaming it the 'point of concentration'. The rules and objectives, furthermore, are agreed on by the players.

The mass of problems facing the actor may be thus broken into clearly defined, manageable units, graded in difficulty according to the skills and needs of the 'players'. The actor is thus encouraged to learn artistic control over himself and his material, but, beyond keeping to the rules and the point of concentration, has complete freedom as to how he reaches the objective.

> The energy released to solve the problem, being restricted by the rules of the game and bound by the group decision, creates an explosion — spontaneity — and as is the nature of explosions, everything is torn apart, rearranged, unblocked. The ear alerts the feet, the eye throws the ball.

It is vital to the success of games that the players are freed from feeling they must be 'right' or 'wrong', there being many possible solutions to each problem. The shared responsibility for the game, furthermore, shifts the focus of their answerability from the director to each other and themselves. Evaluation is also a shared process in which judgemental and prejudiced responses are discouraged, objectivity encouraged: did they solve the problem? What did they *do*? What was communicated? In this way, what Spolin sees as the heaviest blocks to our creativity, our need of approval or fear of disapproval, are blown away.

The 'explosion' she describes is, in fact, cathartic. Catharsis, since Aristotle's time has been defined as a kind of emotional purgation, as, by sympathetic involvement with the action and excitation through suspense, the hitherto suppressed feelings of the audience burst their bonds and overflow. It may be experienced by all *participants*, be they an *involved* audience or the players themselves. What feelings are creatively released will depend, of course, on us but also on the nature of the game. Comedy is as cathartic in laughter as Tragedy in tears. It is also essentially a *shared* experience possible only through an act of communion, and transcendence of the self in the group.

In the players the flow it releases creates the action itself, which then enables the audience to 'take part'. In both it is to be hoped that the release of feelings will not only be a welcome relief, enabling us to get along better with things as they are, but also establish a creative engagement with life, enabling us to cope with and bring about change.

SIXTEEN

I end my 'Getting Here' journey with four 'scenes' from the 'Getting Here' exercise.

Scene one

We watch as one of us has a morning bath. The water is deep and very warm. She has looked forward to this moment, prepared for it with care. Now, with precision and anticipation she mimes undressing. We smile and glance at each other, sharply aware of the shared intimacy. She tests the water with her toe. It *is* warm! But not too warm, for now she steps carefully into the bath. She pauses then, holding the sides of the bath for support, slowly lowers herself into it. Just as her bottom touches the water she stops: the heat! We stop with her and hold our breath. Then she sinks with a sigh into the water, smiling blissfully, scooping up her hair above the neck as she leans finally back, almost totally submerged. We sink and sigh with her, looking at each other and laughing but coming with her remarkably to rest. We stand quietly enjoying the cleansing relief. We share the experience and her creativity, delight in her mastery of the medium and, through it, momentarily, of our world.

Scene two

A pair of jeans mocks its owner as she struggles to pull them over her hips. 'You'll never do it! You'll have to get bigger ones. The trouble with you is, you won't admit it, you're too *fat*! Hey! You're splitting my seams! Oh, you're hopeless! You keep *saying* you'll slim but you don't. You've got no will power! You're pathetically *weak*!'

Meanwhile, a young man steps furtively on to a rosewood dining table to change the light bulb suspended above it. 'Ouch!' shouts the table, 'get off! And take your *shoes* off! Just look at my polish!' And out of the grain emerges his mother: 'David! Look what you've done! You've no respect. No matter how hard I . . . Everything I do! Everything!'

'Oh shut up! You never give me credit for anything!' shouts a woman to her car/husband. 'I *can* drive!' 'It's about time you started helping in this house, instead of leaving it all to me!' another tells her pile-of-dirty-washing-left-for-her-to-do-on-the-way-to-work/family. 'In fact, I shall leave you to get on with it — they're all *your* clothes!' Exit left, slamming the door.

Scene three

His journey to the front door is a series of conflicts: a drawer does not open, then pulls right out, depositing clothes in a heap on the floor; he trips over the cat; cuts his finger cutting the bread; the car won't start, and it's raining. One of those days. Is it a joke or all too much?

She amazes us all with the frenetic speed, the juggler's skill, with which she dashes from one job to the next on her way to work: dressing, waking the children, cooking the breakfast, feeding the cat, mending the toaster, doing the washing, putting out the milk bottles, spraying the spark plugs with cold-start and weaving through the traffic, to arrive at her drama session just on time, and with her hair just in place, smiling. Selected, exaggerated, full of voices calling at her, switches of role, when she watches others acting it she wonders, 'Why do I do it?! All that energy!'.

Scene four

'Getting Here' starts with getting up: a story of resurrection. How do we make the transition from night to day, dark to light? As we watch the story re-enacted, or act or re-enact it ourselves, the silence, left long enough, grows pregnant with sounds, stillness with movement, the suspense of anticipation: the alarm clock rings! What happens next is the story of a man's battle with gravity, his attempt to rise from horizontal (the earth) to vertical (the sky) and to walk. How it develops depends on how much night is a tomb to him or womb, whether birth or death is welcomed or resisted. How he responds to the first revelation of the day is the first revelation of the sort of person he is, as he lifts himself from the pillow and then subsides. Or perhaps he lifts himself, then, in an exaggerated burst of energy, thrusts himself back under the blankets: a moment of natural drama which in giving heightened form to the feeling releases it and makes the opposite movement of rebirth that much more decisive . . .

REFERENCES

Aeschylus *see* Fagles
Aristophanes *see* Barrett

Aristotle *see* Warrington

Barrett, D. (1964) Trans. *The Frogs* by Aristophanes. Penguin, London

———— (1964) Trans. *The Poet and the Women* by Aristophanes. Penguin, London

Blyth, R.H. (1942) *Zen in English Literature and Oriental Classics*. He gives a quite different translation in Haiku Vol. 2. Hokuseido Press, Tokyo

Brecht, B. *see* Willett

Brook, P. (1972) *The Empty Space*. Penguin, London

Buxton-Formans, M. (1952) *The Letters of John Keats*, 4th edn., Oxford University Press, Oxford

Campbell, J. (1976) *The Masks of God, Vol. 1: Primitive Mythology*, quoting Baldwin Spencer and F.J. Gillen, *The Native Tribes of Central Australia*. Penguin, London

Fagan, J. and Shepherd, I.L. (eds) (1972) *Gestalt Therapy Now*. Penguin, London

Fagles, R. (1966) Trans. *Agamemnon* by Aeschylus. Penguin, London

Grant, M. (1962) *Myths of the Greeks and Romans*. Weidenfeld & Nicholson, London

Grotowski, J. (1975) *Towards a Poor Theatre*. Penguin, London

Guthrie, E. (1967) *The Greek Philosophers from Thales to Aristotle*. Methuen, London

Ionesco, E. (1964) *Notes and Counternotes*. Grove Press, London

Jung, C.G. (1983) *Memories, Dreams, Reflections*. Fontana, London

Kitto, H.D. (1960) *The Greeks*. Penguin, London

Plato *see* Rouse

Rouse, W.H.D. (1970) Trans. 'Ion' in *Great Dialogues of Plato*. New American Library, New York

Spolin, V. (1963) *Improvisation for the Theatre*. North Western University Press, Illinois

Stanislavski, C. (1937, 1980) *An Actor Prepares*. Methuen, London

———— (1968) *Building a Character*. Methuen, London

Warrington, J. (1963) Trans. *Poetics* by Aristotle. Dent, London

Willett, J. (1964) *The Theatre of Bertolt Brecht*. Methuen, London

5

Dramatherapy and Psychodrama

Martin H. Davies

INTRODUCTION

Psychodrama has often been confused with dramatherapy, not only by the uninitiated but regrettably, by some trained workers who encourage their clients to participate in supervised exercises through which they might helpfully rehearse various roles and personal interactions. This confusion has been the greater because both approaches evolved rapidly from the relatively straightforward use of drama as a source of creative self-expression into more deliberate and ambitious attempts to facilitate social learning and even to resolve deep-seated emotional conflicts.

Creative therapists do not, of course, slavishly reproduce the techniques of their teachers. They experiment, often imitating, elaborating or reinventing what others have used previously in different contexts. It was almost inevitable, therefore, that these two therapies, which share a common aim of facilitating spontaneity and creativity, have begun to overlap and at times appear superficially indistinguishable.

Herein lies a real danger. Unless the theoretical basis of therapists' actions is made clear, the novice is likely to acquire only a 'bag of tricks' which, used indiscriminately, will confuse or hurt those he or she tries to aid. A similar situation can be observed among the analytically oriented psychotherapies. Psychoanalysis is not the only effective method of verbal psychotherapy. Other schools have borrowed freely from its concepts, but it remains a distinct coherent system of ideas concerning human emotional experience and behaviour, for which it affords a specific method of investigation. Although it is obviously not the last word in our deepening knowledge of ourselves, a proper understanding of its language and techniques still provides an essential yardstick for the evaluation of other theoretical models and their clinical use.

Psychodrama represents the first organised application of dramatic action to the solution of interpersonal problems and the growth of individual — or group — awareness. It was developed in the 1920s and 1930s by Jacob Levy Moreno (1892–1974), and it is remarkable how many of his original ideas and methods anticipated similar later developments by more than a quarter of a century. Before embarking on a detailed comparison with dramatherapy, an account of the history of psychodrama, its techniques and, most important, the model of personality and social philosophy which it embraces is required.

HOW PSYCHODRAMA BEGAN: ENCOUNTER, SPONTANEITY, CREATIVITY, SOCIOMETRY AND CATHARSIS

For Moreno, the conception and birth of psychodrama was inextricably bound up with his overall view of the human condition. From the outset he was deeply concerned with the philosophical and spiritual roots of our social being. In his earliest writings, he emphasised that as individuals we depend primarily on others to provide the source of purpose and value which sustains our sense of personal identity. If we are truly to meet and know other people, we need to learn to see ourselves through their eyes and they to see themselves through ours. He suggested that although we remain embedded in a social matrix which influences and guides our actions and self-perceptions, we also possess a profound and powerful urge towards self-expression, play and experimentation — that spontaneity from which our creative life draws its energy and which makes us collectively into our own deity, co-responsible for the future well being of our planet. Works of art, customs, formal roles and rituals represent the cultural conserve distilled from this ferment as we respond afresh to the challenges of our physical and social environment. These in turn may either inspire further acts of creation or become increasingly petrified, restricting spontaneity and new growth.

A balance between these two forces — the spontaneous and the institutionalising — exists at every level of human organisation and is crucial to their continuation and healthy progress. Excessive spontaneity and too many novel responses which are not adequate or appropriate to our needs can lead to personal or social disintegration.

But equally, a pathological suppression of spontaneity can cause damage by its inflexibility and dehumanising rejection of all that is most sensitive, creative and adaptive in us. Modern society has been leaning perilously nearer to the overcontrolled. People are at risk either of becoming robots surrounded by their robot servants or of revolting against this trend into an equally dangerous chaos of disorganised and even violent self-assertion. Only by fostering spontaneity responsibly, with much more mutuality and openness, can we hope to survive.

With these serious thoughts in mind, Moreno soon began to seek ways of measuring the form and structure of relationships in groups. The techniques of sociometry which he invented have since been widely and successfully adopted by his successors, becoming an accepted field of social research in their own right. At its simplest, this approach relies on asking members of the social grouping under investigation to indicate their relationship to each other so that, for example, a pattern of dominance (vertical structure) or affinity (horizontal structure) can be discerned. These measures may be committed to paper in diagrammatic form (a sociogram) or expressed by the individuals arranging themselves in positions symbolising their relationships (an action sociogram). More complicated interconnections and patterns can be demonstrated and the group asked to explore alternatives in order to recognise sources of conflict and misunderstanding and to modify them. Moreno foresaw a new discipline for which he coined the name 'sociatry' in which the social organisation rather than the individual is the object of the healer's endeavours, a truly 'group' psychotherapy.

The third strand in Moreno's conception of psychodrama was his use of improvisation in the theatre. While working with children, he had already been impressed by the ingenuity and originality with which they could act out the themes of stories they had been told. In his 'Theatre of Spontaneity' in Vienna, he persuaded adult actors to play scenes without prepared scripts or rehearsals. Freed from these constraints, they began to act as themselves in their chosen roles. This was the 'eureka' experience out of which psychodrama crystallised in 1921.

For centuries, drama had offered the audience a means of experiencing their own inhibited or unexpressed emotions through the actors, with whose portrayals they could identify themselves. This therapeutic release of pent-up feelings was part of the ritual process by which the community could come to terms with the frustrations and struggles of its fight to survive in a mystifying and often hostile world, with its losses and gains, joys and sorrows, disasters and triumphs. Aristotle had called this vicarious relief of tension 'catharsis of the emotions'. Now suddenly, the actors were experiencing their own catharsis and the audience were drawn into an even more gripping reality than the contrived emotions of the conventional staged production.

Psychodrama was a leap forward via the experimental theatre into the 'reality' of the protagonist's own unique life experiences, from the comparative safety of the prescribed role to the sensitive core of needs, fears, frustrations and expectations at the centre of his or her being. The intensity of feeling, the quantity of spontaneity generated by it, was so great that it could not be anything less than a major new route to personal growth, psychotherapy and better social integration and collaboration. Or so it seemed. For spontaneity is largely locked in by group and individual psychological barriers. Like atomic energy, once released, it may appear to threaten a chain reaction which will rush out of control. To expose oneself to others in this way requires the help of a skilled therapist in whose hands one can feel safe to move into action, an opportunity to warm up to the task at one's own pace and a strong confidence in the understanding and sensitivity of those who will portray the important others in one's 'cultural atom' or share this intimate experience as spectators. Can such conditions be created regularly and predictably? Moreno was convinced that they could.

CLASSICAL PSYCHODRAMA. THE 'THERAPEUTIC THEATRE'

Classical psychodrama requires five instruments, the stage, the subject, the director, the auxiliary egos and the audience. Although Moreno frequently stated that psychodrama could take place in many natural settings, he advocated the use of a stage of his own design, circular, 12–15 feet in diameter, 1–2 feet high with two surrounding stepped lower levels, seating for the audience, a 'Juliet' gallery and equipment for varying the colour and brightness of the lighting. This format was aimed at providing a space and generating an atmosphere in which the subject could rise up to move and act with increased freedom and imagination.

The locus of a psychodrama, if necessary, may be designated everywhere, wherever the patients are, the field of battle, the class-room or the private home. But the ultimate resolution of

deep mental conflicts requires an objective setting, the therapeutic theatre. Like in religion, although the devout may pray to
his God in his own chamber, it is in the church where the
community of believers attain the most complete confirmation of
their faith.

(Moreno)

The second instrument, the subject, the patient or protagonist, is
asked simply to be him or herself. At first, the protagonist walks
with the director who quietly prompts him or her to talk openly
about the self, its world and its concerns. Warming to the task he
or she is led gently to the top level to enact a scene, to recreate some
part of daily life, an incident from the past or some future unfulfilled
possibility. Only the simplest of stage properties are provided so that
the imagination may be used to the full to enter into the action with
the protagonist's own vivid picture of the circumstances uncon-
taminated by elaborate scenery or furnishings.

The director has three functions to perform: to produce the
psychodrama, to facilitate the protagonist's efforts of expression and
to analyse what he or she sees and hears. The director does not make
verbal interpretations but uses his or her understanding of the
subject's predicament to help confused or inhibited impulses and
feelings to emerge into the open through the spontaneous actions
which are initiated in the psychodrama.

The auxiliary egos in classical psychodrama are trained
therapeutic aides. Our 'cultural atom', the external expression of the
ego, is that cluster of roles which we play in our lives, some brief
and superficial, others more permanent and central to our sense of
personal identity, worth, and capacity to cope and live up to expectations. Nearly every role we play influences and is influenced by the
counterpart roles of the 'others' with whom we interact. Our roles
can be fulfilling, varied and expansive, or they can be frustrating,
stereotyped and restrictive. Often we force each other into distorted
and limited self-portrayals. Only if we can open up to experiencing
ourselves more fully and seeing ourselves from the outside can we
release the spontaneity which these fearful, repetitive, automatic
responses imprison within us.

The auxiliary egos play these reciprocal roles or antagonists
according to the instructions of the subject, helping him or her to
create personal 'reality' on the stage. But this is not their only task.
At the director's instigation they can vary their behaviour, exaggerating, repeating, reversing roles with the protagonist, doubling

thoughts, words and gestures, mirroring the performance. In stretching the boundaries of the protagonist's perception, his or her experience of the self and cultural atom is extended, stimulating a cathartic release of feelings and a greater understanding, tolerance or even resolution of the conflicting emotional needs and assumptions which characterise it.

The fifth instrument of psychodrama, the audience, share in the feelings and actions of the protagonist and auxiliary egos. Sometimes the director calls upon members of the audience to participate actively, speaking for the crowd, the public or in some other role, but their chief function is to recognise their own needs and problems, beliefs and experiences, through those of the protagonist.

The psychodrama session begins with a warming-up phase in which the discussion leads gradually to the selection of the subject and the production of the psychodrama. This in turn is followed by a further discussion in which the audience can reflect their own experiences back to the protagonist, sharing their emotions. Interpretation and theorising are actively discouraged by the director but real feelings and genuine spontaneous reactions to the psychodrama help the protagonist to consolidate what has been achieved. They also reinforce the group's capacity to acknowledge their own feelings more honestly and those of the protagonist more completely.

So brief an account cannot do justice to all the possibilities of this rich therapeutic medium. But it would be beyond the scope of this chapter to pursue them further. Interested readers are recommended to the bibliography, or better still, to obtain some practical experience of psychodrama. Many have testified to its powerful impact upon them and the real positive changes it has wrought in their lives.

PSYCHODRAMA, GROUP THERAPY AND PSYCHOANALYSIS

In 1925 Moreno left Vienna for New York where he began to apply his psychodramatic methods to mental illness, delinquency and socially deprived or damaged people. He set up an 'Impromptu Theatre' in which others could gain experience of his techniques. He worked with adolescents in a residential treatment centre and in his seminal work *Who Shall Survive? Foundations of Sociometry, Group Psychotherapy and Sociodrama* (1934) he presented his most important findings and theories to the public. In 1936, he established the Moreno Sanitorium at Beacon, New York, including the first purpose-built psychodrama theatre and the following year founded the journal 'Sociometry'. As more of his students progressed with experience and practice, from protagonists to auxiliaries and auxiliaries to directors, there were soon enough 'psychodramatists' to form a national organisation, from which emerged the present-day American Society of Group Psychotherapy and Psychodrama. Psychodrama theatres were built in a number of hospitals and institutions and by the 1950s, psychodrama was, in the USA, an established and even respectable movement! Moreno's gift of innovation was so prolific that many of his ideas germinated and have grown to fruition in the hands of others, to produce gestalt therapy, encounter groups, personal construct theory, family systems and therapy and perhaps also, dramatherapy.

Such intense activity and creative fertility has led to what Eric Berne, the founder of Transactional Analysis, called the 'Moreno Problem'. Reviewing Fritz Perl's book *Gestalt Therapy* in 1970 he wrote in the *American Journal of Psychiatry*:

> In his selection of specific techniques he shares with other active therapists the 'Moreno Problem', the fact that nearly all known active techniques were first tried by Dr. J.L. Moreno in psychodrama so that it is difficult to come up with an original idea in this regard.

Psychodrama was clearly not intended by its creator to be a limited activity, a highly specialised therapy available only to selected groups in certain conditions. He plainly stated that it should be something of universal application used in many ways and in many situations to help humanity to test out its 'surplus reality', the untried and incompletely acknowledged inner world of the imagination, in the enlarged living space of psychodramatic action. Psychodrama in its ultimate sense is life itself, and its object the whole of mankind.

But this kind of universality, exciting though it is, causes some problems. If psychodrama is a concept of such wide application, it becomes almost impossible to consider it critically, to establish its limits and the qualifications to its use. Yet without at least an attempt to do this, its undoubted historic importance will be diminished and its influence incompletely acknowledged.

I will concentrate first on what seem to be the important distinguishing features of the psychodramatic and psychoanalytical approaches to individual and group dynamics. Incidentally, it is also worth noting that Moreno used the term 'group psychotherapy' in several senses, including (1) the treatment of the natural group, using sociometry and *in vivo* psychodrama, (2) the recreation of the protagonists' natural groups through the auxiliary egos and (3) the group experience of the audience in psychodrama. Although none of these corresponds exactly to analytically oriented group psychotherapy, they all convey Moreno's insistence that the individual and the group are never truly separable except by artificially ignoring the one or the other.

In psychodrama, the psychoanalytic understanding of the psyche is not rejected but amplified. The individual conscious and unconscious are considered to have emerged in social evolution from the co-conscious and co-unconscious of the group. The life of the personalised mind belongs as much to the 'external' surrounding 'social atoms' as it does to the 'internal' ego of its possessor. The fantasied possibilities which have not been tested in action are also considered as genuinely part of our 'reality' but surplus to our immediate present requirements rather than as primitive, childish or pretentious illusions. That many barriers to the testing and sharing of the different realities of the group, its members or subgroups, can be traced to the repressed residues of earlier experience, or to the group's own resistance to undergoing change, is not disputed. But it is through active exploration of the underlying, desired or feared, emotional events and their consequences and not through their interpretation that they are surmounted in psychodrama.

We are here close to the nub of the matter. The two best known schools of group psychotherapy derived their methods from individual psychoanalysis. Badly shaken by the unexpected emotional impact of his only exposure to the Impromptu Theatre, Sam Slavson decried psychodrama and set about organising a rival group-therapy association (Moreno 1974). The aim was instead to be the analysis of the individual in and by the group. The British School of Group Analysis was formed a little later out of the experience of psychotherapists working together during and just after the Second World War. Foulkes, Bion and their colleagues focused on the group as a whole, its resistance and dynamics, the analysis of the group process providing the 'container' in which individual process could in time come to be understood.

Both these schools, with some variation in emphasis on the individual or the group, inherit the Freudian belief that the inactive, undisclosing therapist, the 'highly polished mirror' will best help the patients to project the contents of their unconscious psyches on to him or her, and each other, undiluted by the actualities and accidentals of the therapist's own feelings and attitudes, so that transference will be more clearly developed, identified and interpreted.

Psychodrama takes the opposite view. Since it is in practice impossible to conceal oneself totally behind a blank therapeutic mask it is preferable to maximise the positive elements of one's interaction with the subjects. The projections and distortions will still be present but an open, warm, respecting, empathising attitude, modelling a confident acceptance that conflict and ambivalence in human relations are normal and manageable, is likely to make it easier to acknowledge them. These conditions (familiar to students of Carl Roger's 'client-centred' counselling) help create the 'therapeutic alliance', that trusting commitment to self-disclosure and risk-taking necessary to effective psychotherapy. In psychodrama, the patient is being asked to act, not merely describe, his or her world. So the strength of the alliance must be the greater. Since a group is also involved, similar conditions of trust, caring, honesty and respect must be established among them if this is to be achieved. But if it is achieved movement can be rapid.

Catharsis is effective because it completes the uncompleted act. The imagined worst has been met and survived, releasing for other purposes the mental energy tied up in unresolved conflicts, traumata of the past, fears of rejection or humiliation and other avoided emotions. Resistance and transference are transcended through the same route, acted through rather than being commented upon. The psychodrama will often operate at several simultaneous symbolic levels in which the individual's experience, that of his auxiliaries, if selected from the audience, and the present dynamics of the group are all playing a part.

Are the critics of psychodrama mistaken then? Not entirely. This model of working has two obvious consequences. The first and more serious is the temptation to seduce the subject (or the whole group) into premature self-revelation or if there is no dramatic catharsis, to confront or pressure them too vigorously. Moreno's confidence in his ability to judge the capacity of the protagonist to move into sensitive areas successfully allowed him to work at depth, often with little previous knowledge of the individuals involved and even in public sessions. However, in his clinic, the psychodrama was almost always part of a larger programme of psychotherapy with skilled staff available to support the protagonist and other group members, helping to build on the experiences and insights gained in the psychodrama. It is in this context or that of the extended psychodrama workshop that classical psychodrama continues to produce the best results and the fewest problems. But there was also the 'one off' demonstration, the psychodrama 'road show'. All too often with a less experienced or sensitive director the need to produce a performance, to force the subject through an important life transition as quickly as possible can become an end in itself. Or a participant may be left 'high and dry' with an incomplete cathartic experience which arouses high levels of anxiety without the consequent emotional relief or insight.

Of course, these criticisms can all too easily be attributed to defensive fear of the medium and the consequences of bad therapy are not as uniformly fatal as might be suggested! In the hands of relatively less skilled and supportive encounter-group leaders, the subjects experiencing bad abreactions only occasionally appeared to suffer any long-lasting emotional damage. But they cannot be dismissed lightly. Pressing a person beyond the point he or she and the group are ready to reach is insensitivity not therapy. Judging just when and where they are ready to move requires a high level of skill and responsibility for which careful selection of trainee therapists and a good grounding in individual and group dynamics are essential.

The second consequence is that it becomes the more important to distinguish between the intensive therapeutic psychodrama and the occurrence of catharsis in other therapies and forms of human relations training. So before looking more specifically at drama-therapy, perhaps a brief consideration of Moreno's social theory in the light of more recent theories of social psychology and personality might be worth while.

ROLE AND CATHARSIS IN THE LIGHT OF PERSONAL CONSTRUCT AND SYSTEMS THEORY

I think we can now begin to see some links between psychodrama and theories which have appeared in social psychology and psycho-therapy in the last twenty or thirty years. My first observation is that while the practice of psychodrama has survived and is currently enjoying a resurgence of interest, Moreno's general theories have remained much as he first conceived them. To find any real elabora-tion of them we must look further afield.

Personal construct theory was devised by George Kelly in 1955. This model of personality sees the individual person as constantly striving to make sense of his or her world, actively creating criteria by which to evaluate his or her own and other peoples' attitudes and acts. These 'constructs' are necessary to maintain a working understanding of events, which, while always changing, has sufficient stability to allow an effective response to them. The 'repertory-grid' technique has provided a valuable tool for measuring the individual's constructs as they are employed in given situations and the changes which they show from moment to moment. Moreno's 'role' is defined as the functioning form which is assumed as a person reacts to a specific situation involving other persons. Role is the unit of culture. The 'cultural atom' is the external expression of the self, the totality of roles played in a particular individual's life situation.

Now Kelly's theory also includes the concept of role. 'To the extent that one person construes the construction process of another, he may play a role in a social process involving the other person (Kelly, 1955). This appears at first to imply a more passive view of personality. But it is evident that the process of construing is inseparable from the interaction with the other person which confirms, questions or qualifies the construct.

Roles are the products of the individual's own constructs together with those of the antagonist. As they interact, their respective actions influence each other's subsequent actions, sometimes confirming their respective positions more fully and accurately and at other times forcing upon them a rigid and even distorted pattern of relationship. The more direct and real the appreciation of the other's perception, the closer they move towards Moreno's ideal personal encounter in which they see each 'with the other's eyes'. Kelly's self-creating person seems to embody the same capacity for spontaneous and creative development as Moreno's 'homo socius'. The theory of personal constructs provides a valuable approach to understanding more fully the cognitive aspects of role and personality.

Moreno was also concerned with the way in which groups of human individuals spontaneously structure themselves so that the individual's roles are determined by the composition and activity of the group as a whole. In his book *Self and Social Context* (1977), Holland has suggested that the concept of role has been restricted by the role limitations of those who have made it the object of their research. Each specialised professional approach has tended to work within rigid theoretical and methodological boundaries. The student of personality has tended to focus on the individual and one's freedom to express oneself through one's roles. The sociologist has emphasised the prescription of roles by the social order in which he or she lives. The anthropologist has described the function of roles in the different cultures and traditions which sustain and are sustained by them. Holland argues strongly for a more trans-disciplinary study of role in which the limitations of the separate methods of investigation may be overcome by the removal of the self-imposed boundaries which exist between them.

Systems theory seems to go some way towards this goal. Moreno's 'cultural atom' could be interpreted as an open system of roles through which the individual participates in larger open systems, the family, the working group, the recreational group, etc. Systems theory postulates that every system tends towards an equilibrium which determines and is determined by its constituent parts whose function within it serve the goals of the system as a whole. The system itself must respond to its environment, which is another open system and so on. This picture of social networks of ascending order might be described as a kind of social molecular structure composed of Moreno's 'cultural atoms'.

Some systems in which the individual has a place provide an opportunity for close involvement and must contribute greatly to the maintenance of a consistent and effective self image — what Kelly called the 'core constructs'. Other systems may have a more super-ficial impact. The family, especially for the child whose freedom of action is limited, represents an important system and it is perhaps not surprising that 'family therapy' has come to rely heavily on systems theory in its analysis of interpersonal behaviour.

If we examine Moreno's views on emotional and social dis-turbance, I believe we can see much that foreshadows this theory of social systems. A person's own system, or 'cultural atom', may be disrupted by a variety of changes in the higher order system to which he or she belongs. Displacement from an existing role, loss of another member of the system, the acquisition of new roles and perhaps, most important, the pressure of a social system on him or her to sustain a role which is at variance with attempts to play a more satisfactory part in it or prevent him or her from becoming involved in other systems to which he or she may gain entry. The stereotyped, excessively dominant, submissive or dependent relationships observed in social groupings are recognised examples of the system's tendency to force its members into over-specialised and inflexible roles.

Moreno's concept of role is thus confirmed and expanded both by construct theory as an expression of the active structuring of the meaning of relationships and by systems theory in its dependence on the dynamic social networks within which we strive for understanding and self-esteem.

Spontaneity, one of Moreno's fundamental concepts, is subjectively the freedom experienced in interacting with others and objectively the tendency to exhibit or elicit new and adequate responses within social systems. Creativity, spontaneity's twin, can be interpreted as the activity in which constructs are loosened and re-formed in new and more productive patterns, often catalysing change in the surrounding system towards more satisfying and effective individual roles.

Psychodrama is an approach which allows the protagonist to achieve several goals: one completes social transactions whose outcomes are fearfully avoided since they threaten one's self-image — rightly or wrongly. The social systems in which one lives are reconstructed with the possibility of exploring roles and those of other members more fully and also testing, in a safe situation, the effect of changes in these roles. Through the aid of a sensitive double, competing alternative but inhibited roles may be evaluated. By role-reversal and mirroring, the roles and personal constructs of others can be recognised and accommodated more successfully. All these activities will tend to free the protagonist to choose from a more flexible and less anxiety-provoking range of roles.

Catharsis, a difficult concept to define, might be represented as the undergoing of emotionally evocative interactions previously avoided because the feelings aroused might be intolerable within the existing pattern of role-expectations or personal constructs. When met and survived, the emotions excited by such situations even if unpleasant are associated with a sense of release, and an altered expectation of future events. Catharsis is the moment in which the existing structure of roles finally yields to reform itself. Internally, this means a change of constructs and an altered perceptual gestalt of one's own and others' activity. Before it occurs, there is inevitably a build up of tension as the system strives to maintain the existing equilibrium and it is often associated with powerful but contradictory emotions — anger, grief and elation — all the affects of the avoided interaction and the relief of the effort required to avoid it.

It is not something which belongs only to psychotherapy or theatre. It is a universal phenomenon, the process by which excessive development of culturally conserved roles is periodically overthrown by a surge of spontaneity to be followed inevitably by a further consolidation. It is the same phenomenon which manifests itself in the life crisis of the individual through every level of social organisation to the political upheavals of nations. As Moreno recognised, people's only hope of survival is in learning to understand and live on better terms with their social natures.

REMEDIAL DRAMA, DRAMATHERAPY AND THE DRAMATHERAPY CLOSED GROUP

Dramatherapy grew up in Britain in the 1960s and 70s. Pioneers in the field included Sue Jennings, whose own background of social anthropology and group analysis has had an obvious influence on its character. It began with remedial drama, as much in the sphere of the educational as the health professions. Games, exercises to increase body awareness and non-verbal communication, the use of masks and puppets, creative fantasy work, dance, music, and painting, storytelling, mime and role-playing all came to be included in the repertoire of remedial drama. Reading Jennings's (1983) account of the underlying principles and goals, one cannot but be struck by many similarities to Moreno's ideas and interests of nearly half a century before: the primacy of the act compared with the word; the heritage of ritual and tradition which pervades all human cultures and provides an important vehicle for the symbolic resolution of crises and conflicts in our life as communities as well as individuals; the playfulness and curiosity which distinguishes humans from other creatures just as significantly as their upright stance and problem-solving skills; the inseparability of therapy and education from the larger process of social interaction and day-to-day living; the importance of the group and our need to be self-aware and trusting in the roles which establish our personal identity within it; but (*pace* Moreno) with a less 'Messianic' intensity and universality of vision than that of the old master.

Not surprisingly, remedial drama developed into dramatherapy, a change of name which indicated among other things the growing confidence of the movement and accompanied a gradual shift into more specifically psychotherapeutic areas. Though little classical psychodrama was practised in the United Kingdom, there was naturally an interest among dramatherapists and when opportunities arose to participate, they were keen to seize them (in contrast with the bulk of nurses, psychologists and doctors in psychiatric

117

institutions who in typical British fashion were suspicious and hesitant in trying out these 'transatlantic histrionics', with their apparent lack of academic standing and rigorous evaluation). But despite this expected initial enthusiasm, dramatherapists were not completely at ease with it and there is still a gap between the two movements, whatever their obvious rapport and similarity of orientation might suggest. Why is this so?

For a long time this puzzled me greatly. I have gradually come to see that it is a reflection of the innate diversity of both activities. If the first experience of psychodrama is a brief but effective demonstration of 'classical psychodrama', by a technically able exponent, the exploration of highly emotive themes and the exposure of much personal and sensitive material among relative strangers can leave the observer thoroughly bemused. Is it all as simple as that? Are the doubts and warnings of experienced, carefully trained and thoughtful therapists to be dismissed as merely the fussing of 'elderly parents' who cannot keep in touch with a new generation of ideas? Is this a magic formula, a door into a new country in which we can become powerful healers with a few hours of simple lessons; or is it a dangerous dramatic illusion? Were we all carried along on a tide of theatrical excitement, group pressures and seductive, suggestive techniques?

One reaction has been to continue a kind of ambivalent courtship between dramatherapy and psychodrama, which is seen perhaps as too clever, too powerful to include among the skills of the average dramatherapist. But of which he or she should nevertheless have proper knowledge and at least some direct personal experience, even aspiring later to becoming trained in it, as if it were a kind of 'top grade' dramatherapy. Another reaction is to exclude it entirely from dramatherapy, regarding it, like gestalt therapy, as a specialised type of intensive individual psychotherapy, of interest but of no direct relevance to the dramatherapy student. In fact it is neither.

Moreno was perhaps not so much the 'father' of psychodrama as its 'midwife'. It can occur anywhere at any time, wherever and whenever the level of spontaneity is sufficient to release it. What Moreno did was to define those conditions which catalyse its occurrence and harness it to positive therapeutic goals. It can happen in real life. It can certainly happen when a therapist creates an ambience conducive to spontaneity and active self-expression through drama and role-play. It had its origin in improvised drama and is always potentially present in it. Thus every dramatherapist must understand it and have the self-knowledge, skill and sensitivity to handle it, to judge how far to encourage catharsis or to move the session back to a 'safer' level and take more time to look at the emerging emotions. If psychodrama is this kind of phenomenon, it is something we should all learn about whatever brand of therapy we practise.

On the other hand, if we are deliberately encouraging our patients or clients to look more deeply into themselves and we are working with groups, which is likely, then are we not obliged to obtain also an appropriate experience of psychodynamic mechanisms and more specifically of group process which will allow us to use 'catharsis through action' beneficially and avoid its more countertherapeutic effects?

If we trace the development of dramatherapy, we see that there has been a progressive extension from remedial drama towards intensive psychotherapy. Jennings's model of creative–expressive learning and therapeutic dramatherapy can be seen to operate at increasing degrees of depth which are paralleled by the equivalent forms of psychodrama (Table 5.1).

This three-tiered system has at its surface the creative–expressive dramatic action in which the subject can usually safely distance the self from the role as far as he or she wishes. At the educational level, there is less freedom to avoid personal feelings but the subject can stay within the 'common denominators' of the group with which he or she identifies, but at the therapeutic level, the subject attempts to work through roles to which a great deal of personal and possibly threatening or discomforting emotion is attached. Here we are close to classical psychodrama. Though the full range of dramatherapy techniques may be employed the thrust is towards a 'closed group'

Table 5.1: Parallel levels of dramatherapy and psychodrama

	Dramatherapy	Psychodrama
First level	Creative-expressive	Improvisation of 'safe' characters and themes
'Symbolic distance' greatest		
Second level	Learning	Guided role-playing, sociodrama, spontaneity training
'Symbolic distance' smaller		
Third level	Therapeutic	Classical psychodrama, sociatry
'Symbolic distance' minimal		

with many of the characteristics of an analytical group approach and all the consequent attention to the conditions of the therapeutic alliance, to resistance and transference and group dynamics which I have already mentioned. Thus dramatherapy seems to have followed a parallel evolution to that of psychodrama from a general attempt to encourage spontaneity and creativity to a more intensively structured and carefully controlled system for exploring and solving important emotional issues through personalised dramatic action.

PSYCHODRAMA GROUP THERAPY.
'HYBRID' PSYCHODRAMA

I have earlier distinguished between 'classical psychodrama' as developed by Moreno and the 'psychodrama' which occurs whenever sufficient spontaneity is available for the enactment of a part of some surplus reality hitherto unexpressed. Perhaps an example of the latter might make this clearer.

An eighteen year old girl had developed agoraphobic symptoms. Her father had died in hospital of cancer over a year before. Prior to his death there had been severe emotional difficulties between the two parents, in the course of which the mother took the patient, her daughter, into her confidence seeking her sympathy and support but binding her not to reveal her secrets to the father. Thus she had been drawn into an insoluble conflict of loyalties. She was not present at her father's death and did not appear to have grieved it. In the course of therapy at a Day Unit, she began to express openly and vehemently her disbelief in the death of her father, demanding to see the ward in which he died. She was not given an interpretation but accompanied there by a therapist and with the cooperation of the nurses searched high and low, even checking adjacent wards. After an hour of futile and increasingly frantic efforts she asked to be returned to the psychiatric clinic where she wept profusely and at last began to acknowledge more openly the importance of her father to her and her difficulty accepting his loss in the middle of such problems. From this point she improved rapidly with almost complete remission of her agoraphobia.

This was catharsis. This was her spontaneous psychodrama. But if the staff had not been ready to help and support her, this therapeutic opening might have been missed.

Now if we compare classical psychodrama to a cultivated flower, grown under glass with ideal soil conditions, humidity, etc, then natural psychodrama might be more akin to the wild specimen, with less exotic blooms but a hardier plant, cropping up all over the place often in the least expected site. If we pursue this horticultural analogy further, there is a third possibility, the 'hybrid' psycho-drama, strains which combine some of the luxuriance of the cultured species with the capacity to flourish in a greater range of conditions, of slower growth but of greater durability.

These hybrid approaches have been developed independently by various therapists. My own training was in one of Dean Elefthery's Psychodrama Group Therapy programmes (Elefthery, 1975). All the selected members had to have received some form of psychotherapy training and were working in recognised professions in the mental health field. The class of up to twelve participants met for periods of three to five days every three to four months over a three-year period. The group was a closed one. The group process, while not analysed, emerged fairly clearly in the psychodramatic action. There was never any pressure to achieve catharsis or even psychodrama. The leader's model and direction was always to take our time, to work as a group and allow the group process to be worked through spontaneously and with as much discussion and non-dramatic interaction as necessary. Since we all had differing psychotherapeutic backgrounds, orientations and training, this provided a varied and stimulating experience.

The French Triadic Psychodrama of Ann Ancelin Schutzenberger seems to be a similar hybrid (Schutzenberger, 1975). Again the group is small, meeting weekly usually for two years with occasional longer sessions. The therapist attempts to create a warm non-directive atmosphere using classical psychodrama techniques to examine the group dynamics and often spending several consecutive sessions processing a single psychodrama. This method makes a clear distinction between the psychodrama of the individual *within* the group and psychodrama *by* the group. Gestalt therapy and some public sessions of classical psychodrama are dominated by the former. The group are moved by the action but do not have a real personal connection with each other except through their common focus on the protagonist. In contrast, when the theme and its protagonist arises out of a group which has already begun to cohere and take shape, the content and process displayed are of much more profound and therapeutic relevance to its members. The subject of the psychodrama is more fully supported and respected by the others. The dynamic status of the group emerges more clearly and effectively. They are 'sharing' at a much deeper level than the *ad*

121

hoc audiences would ever be capable of doing. Issues of transference between members and particularly with the leader of the group are more honestly and easily examined in this way, also de-mystifying and strengthening the insights gained through the action.

Roy Shuttleworth has adopted a similar group analytical approach in his work with adolescents and families, advocating training in group analysis as a prerequisite (Shuttleworth, 1975). There are probably a number of others who have cultivated their own hybrids (eg. Marrone's analytic psychodrama — Marrone, 1979) and I would venture that the dramatherapy 'closed' group has moved close to this position too. It seems a more realistic kind of growth and, who knows, one which Moreno could not have followed himself without at the same time losing much of the initial impact and 'shock' which was his personal trade mark and without which the psychodrama might never have been recognised at all.

All the psychotherapies seem to include three common ingredients, the establishment of the therapeutic alliance, the re-experiencing of suppressed feelings and fantasies, and the gradual working through of these to establish a more harmonious and realistic equilibrium in present relationships. Psychodrama has provided us with methods and skills which help to accelerate the first and second but without the third, emphasised by all the analytical therapies, permanent benefits may not be achieved.

REFERENCES AND FURTHER READING

Berne, E. (1970) *American Journal of Psychiatry*, vol. 126, no. 10, pp. 163–4

Blatner, M.A. (1973) *Acting In: Practical Applications of Psychodrama Methods*. Springer Publishing Company, New York

Davies, M.H. (1976) 'The Origins and Practice of Psychodrama'. *British Journal of Psychiatry*, vol. 129, pp. 201–6 (Reprinted in *Dramatherapy*, October 1978, vol. 2)

———— (1979) 'Moreno's Social Theories Now'. *Dramatherapy*, vol. 3, no. 1, pp. 16–20

———— (1982) 'Psychodrama and Other Therapies'. *Dramatherapy*, vol. 6, no. 1, pp. 40–3

———— (1983) 'Role Play and Psychodrama with an Out-patient Group'. *Dramatherapy*, vol. 7, no. 1, pp. 20–2

Elefthery, D. (1975) 'Psychodrama'. In G.M. Gazda (ed.), *Basic Approaches to Group Psychotherapy and Group Counselling*, Charles C. Thomas, Springfield, Illinois

Holland, R. (1977) *Self and Social Context*. Macmillan, London

Jennings, S. (1973) *Remedial Drama*. Pitman, London
────── (ed.) (1975) *Creative Therapy*. Kemble Press, Banbury
────── (1983) 'Models of Practice in Dramatherapy'. *Dramatherapy*, vol. 7, no. 1, pp. 3–6
Kelly, G.A. (1955) *The Psychology of Personal Constructs*, vols. 1 & 2, Norton, New York
Marrone, M. (1979) 'An Approach to Analytic Psychodrama'. *Dramatherapy*, vol. 3, no. 1, pp. 21–3
Moreno, J.L. (1934) *Who Shall Survive?*. Beacon House, New York (New York Edition 1953)
────── (1941) *The Words of the Father*. Beacon House, New York
────── (1945) *Group Psychotherapy*. Beacon House, New York
────── (1946) *Psychodrama*. Vol. 1, Beacon House, New York
────── (1951) *Sociometry, Experimental Method and the Science of Society*. Beacon House, New York
────── (1970) 'Psychodrama and Group Psychotherapy'. Pamphlet published by Moreno Institute, Beacon House, New York
────── (1974). In I.A. Greenberg (ed.), *Psychodrama Theory and Therapy*. Behavioural Publications, New York
Schutzenberger, A.A. (1975) 'Psychodrama, Creativity and Group Process'. In S. Jennings (ed.), *Creative Therapy*, pp. 131–56, Pitman, London
Shuttleworth, R. (1973) 'Some Clinical Aspects of Psychodrama'. (Paper read to Social Psychology Section of the British Psychological Society, Loughborough, March 1973)
────── (1975) 'Psychodrama with disturbed adolescents'. In S. Jennings (ed.) *Creative Therapy*, pp. 157–80, Pitman, London

6

A Systems Approach to Dramatherapy

Roy Shuttleworth

During a recent dramatherapy group, Sue, a 32-year old professional woman, asked if she could do some therapeutic work on her problematic relationship with her partner Bill. She said that she had lived with Bill, 38, for ten years and while they vaguely thought from time to time of marrying, neither had seriously pushed to make this happen. She explained that they had drifted into the relationship and couldn't even remember how it was decided that they would live together. The relationship was described as passionless, with neither working very hard to make it more interesting.

Sue was asked to select people from the group to play herself and Bill and then to make a sculpture of a typical evening. She placed the two role-players in chairs about 10 feet apart and placed another chair in front of them representing a television set. The couple stared intently at the television paying no attention to each other. When Sue doubled for Bill, she put much of the blame for the poor relationship on him, saying that he was lazy, off-handed and only interested in his own needs. When she doubled for herself, she presented herself as the victim, who while longing for attention and affection, was stuck with a man who was incapable of giving her these things. When asked what she had done to make him more interested in her, she replied 'Not much, it is a waste of time'. When she returned to double Bill, 'He' was asked whether 'He' ever tried to make the relationship more interesting. 'He' replied that while this rarely happened, when 'He' did try, Sue always seemed to find a way of sabotaging his attempts by saying such things as 'I would like to go out but not to the place that you have suggested', or 'How can you expect me to do something enjoyable with you when you have been so awful to me recently?' As the exercise proceeded, Sue started to get some understanding that the difficulties in their relationship

124

could be seen in interactional terms with each sharing the responsibility for what was happening. If anything therapeutic was to be gained in looking for 'Who is the persecutor?' or 'Who is the victim?', then we could punctuate the situation in two ways. From Bill's side we could say 'Of course the poor man is not going to make more effort to be sociable because whenever he tries, Sue always sabotages his attempts'. Or we could punctuate it from Sue's side 'Of course Sue isn't going to respond to Bill on the odd occasion when he attempts to be sociable, because most of the time he is so dreary'. Neither punctuation is going to be of very much value when it comes to therapy because at the very least, the person labelled the persecutor will see the therapy as hostile to him/herself and therefore something to resist. Despite Bill's absence from the group, were we to collude with Sue's negative attributions about him then it is possible he will sense this when he is in her company.

It would be my assumption that while Sue was genuinely unhappy about her relationship, there would be many important reasons to be found in her wider family system for selecting a distant partner like Bill. I would also assume that as she was now more strongly complaining about their interaction that something had changed significantly in their wider family system. In order to investigate these hypotheses, I asked her to extend the sculpture to include her own family members. She said that she was an only child and that her parents, now in their late 60s, were both alive. She chose two group members to play them and placed her father in a chair very close to her so that he could put his arms around her. With her father present, she no longer watched the television because she was looking warmly into his eyes. Her mother was placed well away behind the chairs. While doubling for the father 'He' said that Sue had always been very close to 'Him' and that she was the main reason why 'He' had stayed in the marriage when she was a teenager. Sue was then asked to double herself to explain what he meant by this, and she related that when she was about 13, her parents' relationship, which up until then had been reasonable, had deteriorated and that finally, one night after hearing a particularly vicious row, she had heard her father say that he was packing his bags and leaving. She had run to him and begged him to stay and he had finally agreed to her request. When she returned to double her father and later her mother, she described her parents present relationship as being much more satisfactory. While doubling her mother 'She' was asked what it was like being placed on the outskirts and 'She' replied that 'She' had always felt that 'She' came second in her husband's

125

affection but had done nothing to try and change the position.

Sue was then asked to include Bill's family in the sculpt and she placed his mother kneeling at Bill's feet, looking up to him for support. We discovered that Bill was the eldest of 6 children and he had taken on many of the paternal aspects in the family after his father had died when Bill was 15. He had regular contact with his mother who is now in her 60s and has never re-married.

Now that the sculpture was complete, I was able to develop hypotheses as to why this couple had got together in the first place, why their relationship had developed as it had and why the relationship was becoming more problematic.

It would seem that both Bill and Sue had powerful alliances with a parental figure. In Sue's case, an already strong alliance with her father in childhood had been exacerbated when she was 13 by the belief that she needed to continue in a strong relationship with him in order for him to stay. While this belief had some substance when she was 13, it now had no reality. However, she continued to behave as if this loyalty was still important. In Bill's case, an existing close alliance with his mother, which is quite common with elder sons, was also exacerbated by the death of Bill's father, which led to him becoming almost a husband to his mother. This situation still continued in reality as Bill's mother very much relied upon him to give her emotional and physical support. If my hypothesis that Sue and Bill were still strongly aligned to their important parental figures had validity, then we can start to see why they selected each other in the first place. Primarily unconsciously, each recognised that they must select someone who would be emotionally aligned elsewhere and therefore not want a close relationship so that their strong emotional ties to their parents would not be threatened.

We are then faced with the question as to why Sue is now not only saying that she wants greater closeness to Bill but is actively seeking help. We also discovered that for 8 years she had had little contact with her parents but for the last 6 months they had been seeing a lot more of each other. She said that she was surprised to see how well they were getting on as she had always fantasised over the years that their relationship was pretty disastrous. We could therefore hypothesise that her belief that she was the one who kept her father in the family had been modified and therefore her close emotional linkage with her father had been loosened. As a consequence, she had the emotional room to move closer to her partner. The dilemma for this system however is that while her needs for closeness have changed, her partner's needs have stayed the same as his mother's

126

circumstances have not changed and therefore any attempt by Sue or by a therapist to help them get closer, may be unconsciously resisted. Consequently, straightforward advice as to how Sue might more effectively have a closer relationship with Bill by, for example, responding positively to his attempts to be more sociable or taking a lead herself, may be sabotaged. The therapist in this case may describe a paradoxical injunction *against* change because of the potential dangers to the wider system. This was the suggestion made to Sue at the end of her session. A paradoxical injunction can sometimes have a very powerful therapeutic effect particularly when straightforward methods have failed (see Cade, 1984).

The reader will be aware that often the more the therapist attempts to push for closeness, the more this will be resisted by the client. It could also be hypothesised that any changes in Sue and Bill's relationship will have repercussions in the rest of the system. If Bill was to move closer to Sue, then his mother will have emotionally less of him; she may unconsciously try and get him back by producing a symptom, e.g. she may become depressed or find some other way of behaving incompetently so that he is tempted to be pulled back into his old supportive role. Alternatively at a more positive level, she may respond by using her greater independence and perhaps becoming more involved with the community or even making a new relationship. This indicates that the relationship between Bil and his mother is also a mutual interaction with perhaps Bill's mother unconsciously believing that it is very important to allow Bill to support her because he may be disappointed were she to allow others to have this role. By Bill moving closer to Sue, she could be freed from this belief. If Sue gets closer to Bill, this will also have potential repercussions on her family system. As her father realises she is less aligned to him he may start to get even closer to his wife. While this may also be a positive step, it is always possible that they may produce symptoms to prevent greater closeness because there may be an unconscious resistance to father letting go of his closeness to Sue or other alignments may be threatened e.g. to his own close parent figure. Also Sue's mother's unconscious alignments will also be potentially threatened. Consequently, to resist this change a symptom such as sexual difficulties may arise as a distancing manoeuvre. The systems model therefore suggests that changes in one part of the family system will potentially have a ricocheting effect throughout the rest of the system. As a result, in order to maintain the *status quo* or homeostasis, either change will not occur or a symptom will arise somewhere in the system in order

127

to re-establish homeostasis. Thus a problem should never be looked at in isolation. While individuals may, through their general physical make-up, have certain propensities to behave in particular ways, e.g. a neurological predisposition to act in an extroverted way, the best way we can understand an individual's behaviour is within the specific context of his or her interactional system. Consequently, a person who has an extroverted disposition, will not behave in extroverted ways in all contexts, e.g. a man may be the life and soul of the office party or the bar room of a pub, but when he is at home with his wife and children may be quiet and uninvolved.

Particular patterns of behavioural interaction develop in social contexts which may eventually become very rigid and difficult to change. These rigid patterns may be seen in a negative light by the participants but, because they have value to the individual's wider system, will persist, despite the fact that the participants know consciously how they can be changed. Sue and Bill, as two intelligent and mature people, knew how they could improve the quality of their relationship without any intervention by a therapist, but this knowledge was not used because they unconsciously believed, rightly or wrongly, that there would be potential dangers to their wider family system if they were to get closer.

While each family system will have its own rules for the inter-actional games, I believe there are some universal rules which arguably apply to all human beings. From my personal and clinical experience, it seems to me that individuals are continually struggling to 'leave home'. No one ever seems to achieve the complete separation from parental figures and the alliances with these figures will have a profound influence throughout life on the nature of other relationships, in particular with partners and children.

The rules that seem to apply are:

(1) The closer the emotional relationship between the child and its most important parent, the more distant is the optimal relationship between that person and a partner. So, the person who has a very close emotional alliance with a parent will have an optimally distant relationship with a partner and conversely the more distant the relationship between the person and their most important parent, the closer will be their optimum distance to a partner.

(2) These alliances to parental figures will often be very unconscious and therefore the person has little or no understanding of how it is influencing his or her relationship with a partner.

(3) The patterns of the intensity of alliance between one

128

generation and another will be passed on from generation to generation. Consequently, if there is a tradition of a very close alliance between parent and child, then one or more of the children of that child will also have a close alliance with them.

(4) The family system will attempt to achieve some form of homeostasis or balance so, for example, a man who has a very close alliance with his mother, will unconsciously select for his partner, a person who has a similar strong closeness to their important parental figure so that neither will have their parental alliance threatened. However, this homeostasis will be threatened by life transitions, both natural, such as engagements, marriage, the birth of a child, a child going to school, a child becoming an adolescent, a child growing into adulthood and leaving home, retirement and death, as well as the less predictable transitions such as being made redundant from work and illness. These transitions can alter the balance of the family system and consequently put it into a state of flux. The system may resolve this dilemma by accepting the changes, or one or more members of the system may produce symptoms as a way of regaining the homeostatic balance e.g. a couple where each is very aligned to a parent, may be attracted to each other because each unconsciously recognises that the other has an optimum need for a distant relationship. At the beginning of their relationship while they are relatively uncommitted, they will be able to have an apparently close relationship with good sex, communication, a desire to be in each other's company and faithfulness. The life transition of marriage may have the effect of bringing them emotionally closer together and therefore put their alliances with the parents under threat. Consequently, the system will attempt to adjust to the change. For example, the couple could bring in distancing mechanisms such as lack of communication, poor sexuality, finding ways of being apart and unfaithfulness. Alternatively, symptoms may appear within the parental subsystem such as a parent becoming depressed, which may have the effect of pulling their child back to the depressed parent and away from their partner.

(5) The alliances between parent and child may be based on reality, i.e. the mother may very overtly make it clear that she expects her son to be more loyal to her than his wife, or the alliance could be based on a belief system which is well out of date, e.g. a person's relationship with his or her partner may still be influenced by an alliance with a dead parent which is no longer tenable in reality.

129

As I have discussed elsewhere (Shuttleworth, 1983, 1984, 1985), I have found Watzlawick's (1978) notions of the way we understand our world very useful. Briefly, he suggests that while much of our intellectual understanding of the world is centred in the dominant hemisphere or 'left' brain, much of our more irrational and often unconscious behaviour is determined by the non-dominant hemisphere or 'right' brain. In particular, he has a model of 'world image' as part of 'right'-brain functioning. My understanding of the 'world image' is that it is a very inefficient but powerful aspect of brain-functioning. I perceive it as an element which from our early years is storing information about our world and continues to do so throughout life but despite new information being received, the old information is often not updated and consequently still has a powerful effect on our behaviour. One important feature of our 'world image' is the belief about alliances to parents. For example, as a child there may have been messages between father and daughter which said 'You must have a close relationship with me'. Forty years later, the newer information that this father is now dead will have been fed into the 'world image' but still the woman will have a relationship with her partner determined by the very 'old' information. Consequently, one of the major functions of therapy is to try and find a way of allowing the 'new' information to determine a person's behaviour. Clinical experience suggests that attempting to give a person intellectual or 'left' brain understanding is often not effective. Therefore, effective therapy often requires communications which can bypass the intellectual 'left' brain and finds its way into the more unconscious 'right' brain.

In recent years, therapists have been developing what might be called indirect techniques which serve this function. These techniques include the use of Strategies (Hayley 1977), Paradox (Cade 1984), Palazzolli Boscolo, Cecchin & Prata (1978) and Metaphor (Shuttleworth (1984) and Cade (1982)). These techniques are usually used in very brief therapy often of no more than six sessions. Dramatherapy also offers many opportunities for communicating with the 'right' brain despite the belief of many dramatherapists that the active ingredient of dramatherapy is in 'left' brain cognitive understanding.

Assuming that it is best to see an individual's symptom within the context of that person's wider system, then it is logical that the best way to understand that system is to have as many members of that system present in therapy. This allows us to understand how the system is operating and also creates the circumstances where the eventual intervention will have the widest impact. This is the rationale behind the increasing use of family therapy over the last 20 years.

Dramatherapy groups are usually made up of a collection of individuals. However, because of the nature of some of its techniques, we can develop an excellent understanding of how a particular individual's family system operates. In my earlier description of Sue's session, we saw that by getting her to use various members of the group to play members of her family, we had a proxy family-therapy session. We are however faced with the dilemma that the therapeutic intervention is only acting directly upon her. However, if she were to change as a result of the session, then this must have an effect on the system she returns to. If she interacts with Bill in a different way, then this could lead to them getting closer. This greater closeness will then lead to a 'rippling' effect throughout both their family systems with potential changes for their parents and others in the system. Another possibility is that her changed interaction with Bill in attempting to get closer, will put too much pressure on his loyalty to his mother and if he should choose to remain more loyal to his mother than Sue, then he may unconsciously introduce some countermeasures which will distance them again. So for example, it may be that after a short period of greater closeness, they will suddenly find that their relationship becomes far more argumentative or one of them may develop a sexual difficulty. Alternatively, Bill's mother may produce symptoms such as depression which will serve the function of pulling Bill back.

I subsequently discovered that events more akin to the latter took place. Sue reported that she did get closer to Bill for a few weeks but they then started arguing over petty things and within a month had decided to split. Sue has now found herself a partner who better matches her new closeness needs. While therapy could have been seen to fail because their relationship finished, I believe that it was a success because it helped them to dig their way out of an uncomfortable rut. It may be that Bill will be able to find a relationship more consistent with his requirements. While Sue may have benefited from some 'left' brain conscious understanding of her dilemmas from the sculpting, I would assume that the major active ingredients would have been the less conscious 'right' brain perceptions arising from the exercise in conjunction with the paradoxical 'no change' prescription.

When an individual presents a difficulty to a dramatherapy group,

131

my first question will be 'Why does this person's system require a symptom'. I will make the assumption that the individual already knows the solution to their difficulties. If the reader doubts that this is a reasonable assumption, then you should try an experiment. Role-reverse with your client and ask them what they think is the solution to the difficulty. You will find they usually have the answer. This would suggest that it is nonsense to devote a lot of time in therapy providing the client with *your* solution. Therapy should therefore become orientated towards attempting to free the client from what they usually unconsciously perceive as their system's requirements. In a dramatherapy group I will use techniques to explore the individual's system, but the group will not be encouraged to push for changes, indeed great emphasis may be placed on not changing because of the wider ramifications to that person's system if change was to occur. I therefore use dramatherapy primarily as a vehicle to help change the individual's 'world image'. If this is successful, then the individual will find his or her own salvation.

Let us now look at how a dramatherapy group can be run to take into account the systemic model. Many of the techniques used will be similar to those used by therapists who work with a different therapeutic model, however my reasons for using a particular technique and the actual procedures followed will often be quite different.

I will take as an example a recent intensive weekend which involved about 16 hours of therapy. The same principles would apply if the group were to meet for shorter periods of time over a number of weeks. This particular group was made up of 16 people all involved in the helping professions. The group had been meeting for one day a week over the previous 20 weeks and I had been invited as a guest therapist both to show them my approach and also help continue the process of personal growth. For the sake of brevity, I will concentrate on the specific details of 3 group members although it should be understood that all 16 had some aspects of their own systems explored.

The group began with physical warm-up and trust exercises so that they could be more receptive to working intensively. Because the group had been together for some time, I next used an exercise which could quickly tell me something about the way in which the individuals in the group interacted. My assumption was that their interactions with each other in the group system would reflect their interactions with their own personal systems outside. I therefore used the 'swimming pool sculpture' developed by Sue Jennings. In this exercise, I asked the group to imagine that the room had become a swimming pool and pointed out the areas which represented the deep end, the shallow end, the changing rooms, the area around the pool and the ticket office. Initially a group member was selected to place her colleagues in the position and activity which metaphorically represented their involvement in the group. She placed our 3 illustrative representatives in the following way. Gary, a single man in his late 40s, was placed leaning against the ticket box in a position which suggested that while he had entered the pool and paid his money he was unsure as to whether he would now get changed and swim or go home. Phil, a married man with 2 young children in his early 30s, was placed in the deep end, swimming around happily splashing those women who were near him. Jan, a divorced woman in her early 50s with grown up children, was placed holding onto the side of the pool at a point midway between the deep and shallow end. When the group were invited to place themselves according to their own perception of their position in the group, there were some minor changes but our three representatives stayed where they had originally been placed. As the exercise proceeded, Jan became very agitated with John, another member of the group, who had placed himself in the shallow end, lying on his back and frequently spending long periods with his head under the water. She could not restrain herself from attempting to pull him up and responded angrily when he told her he was enjoying it as he continued to sink to the bottom.

This simple exercise had already provided me with a few clues to construct some preliminary hypotheses about each individual's role in their outside systems. My preliminary hypothesis for Gary was that he was a man who would find it very difficult to commit himself to a peer relationship and he would therefore have some very powerful family alliances restraining him. Jan appeared to be a woman whose primary role outside the group was in rescuing people. This is not an uncommon role among people who choose a professional career helping others, and my hunch was that this was a substitute for a more intimate peer relationship and served the function of protecting other relationships in her family system. Phil seemed to be the one who could most let himself get into peer relationships, but at this stage, it was hard to tell whether they would be of a more permanent nature or transitory.

The next stage was to move on to more intensive personal work. I used the 'puppet mask and strings' exercise which involved each member of the group imagining themselves as a puppet and then deciding who most in their lives acts as the puppeteer who pulls their strings. They were asked to draw masks of both the puppet and puppeteer and then this material was explored by role-reversing with a partner (see Shuttleworth, 1985 for a fuller description of this exercise). After working in pairs, each group member then presented his or her puppet material to the group. This was done by each person playing their own puppeteer while their partner role-reverses as the puppet. The puppeteer having attached strings to each of the puppet's arms, took a position in the room holding these strings.

After Gary had attached the strings to his puppet's wrists, he placed himself as the puppeteer a long way from the puppet, standing in the same position in the room as he had been placed when doing the swimming pool exercise. The puppeteer held one string loosely while the other string lay in front of the puppeteer. Gary then spoke for the puppeteer, saying that he represented two women who were important in his (Gary's) life. One was a girl friend who had been his first love and had let him down badly when she finished the relationship. The second was the only other woman in Gary's life. Their relationship had also finished when she had become pregnant with Gary's baby. She had refused to marry him and had ended the relationship at the insistence of her father. Gary cried as he said that since then, he had never trusted anyone. His role-reversed puppet described itself as a very lonely figure and pointed to the puppet mask which showed a small boyish face tucked at the bottom of the paper. The puppet said that it had drawn an 'iron skin' around itself so that it would never be hurt again.

When Jan played her puppeteer, she identified it as her ex-husband from whom she had been divorced for 5 years. The puppeteer knelt in front of the puppet holding two short and tight strings. Jan's puppet had a mask suggesting compassion and concern. The puppet said that the puppeteer had spent most of his time in this position and even now they were divorced, the puppeteer had not shifted his position. Jan was asked at the end of the exercise to continue playing her puppeteer and to place him where she would like him to be in relationship to the puppet. She hesitated and said that whereas she would like to detach the strings, she felt too obligated to her ex-husband to do this. The group encouraged her to at least try and after she had let the strings go, she looked very lost and also started to cry.

Phil's puppeteer was an ex-girlfriend whom he had recently met again after no contact for some years. As the puppeteer, he placed himself quite close to the puppet with fairly loose strings linking them. The puppet said that it would quite like the puppeteer to pull the strings tighter as its relationship with its wife was no longer a very happy one. The major obstacle to this happening was their young children. When Phil the puppeteer was asked to move her where Phil himself would like her to be, she moved into a position sitting close to the puppet with the strings tightly and mutually held.

This exercise provided some additional information to build on my original hypotheses. Each of the three representatives had aspects of their lives which caused them concern, Gary in his lonely isolation, Jan in her role as rescuer/mother and Phil in an unhappy marital relationship. At this stage in the group, I advanced my hypotheses and asked myself the following questions. Why did Gary's family system require him to unconsciously select two women as partners who were 'lost causes' and once having lost them, while understandably initially feeling a lot of pain at their loss, continued to mourn them many years on? What positive advantages for Jan's family system were there in selecting for her partner a man who behaved in a childishly dependent way and to continue with this role even though they were divorced? Finally, who in Phil's system was protected by his distant relationship with his wife, a relationship which at one time had been close.

While this exercise provides a lot of specific information about group members, its most valuable function is therapeutic. The metaphoric nature of the task triggers a lot of 'right' brain activity for each individual not only through their own puppet work, but also through observing the presentations of other group members. This is shown through the powerful group process where each individual shares often non-specific feelings of particularly, sadness and confusion. This process is especially difficult to describe and can only really be experienced. When the group shares this process, it is very important for the group leader not to be seduced into lightening the atmosphere with a lot of activity. These often painful feelings are an important part of the potential healing process.

The next stage was to develop this process further by using a 'community exercise where initially, all verbal communication is banned and later allowed in a limited form. (See Shuttleworth, 1977.) The group was first asked to imagine themselves as a family and then choose the family role most appropriate to them.

Gary chose to be a distant uncle of the family, Jan, a very caring aunt who lived with the family and took a lot of responsibility for them and Phil became a 16-year-old adolescent boy who was close to his mother. The overall group family was fatherless and rather disintegrated. After presenting themselves as a family sculpture, the group were asked to arrange themselves in the room in a position most appropriate to their family role. For the next half hour they were asked without words to do whatever they felt like doing within their role.

The overall theme which emerged in this exercise was one of the group members attempting to find whether their place in life was within the family circle, with a partner, with friends or in isolation. These elements were naturally developed by the group in the room as the exercise proceeded with, for example, the family area being represented by a circle of chairs where people could get sustenance and support and the 'couple' area represented by a set of cushions arranged like a bed where a form of simulated intimacy could take place.

During the exercise, Gary moved uncomfortably between the family area, where he attempted unsuccessfully to make a relationship with the maternal figure, to the 'couple' area where he would behave very comfortably, finally ending up in his place of isolation in the area of the room which had been his position during the swimming-pool exercise. Jan spent a lot of time in the family area being particularly supportive towards the maternal figure. Phil moved between the family area, the friends' area where he played like a little boy and the 'couple' area, from which, after a few minutes of simulated sexuality with one of the women, he moved back to the family area.

The behaviour of our 3 representatives added further data to my hypotheses about how they related to their family systems and overall suggested that my earlier perceptions were on the right tracks. All 3 appeared to be still negotiating some aspects of leaving home.

After half an hour with no verbal communication, the group were asked to express their feelings about themselves and others in the group by crystallising their thoughts into a series of one word statements. The exercise then lost its playful element and became serious with a group process emerging consisting of sadness, confusion and anger. The anger was particularly directed at the parental figures. Gradually the process changed to one more orientated towards feelings of loss.

Whenever I use the community exercise, I find the same four elements emerge in the group. These elements consist of areas representing the family, the couple, non-sexual friends, usually playing and the individual, either in a state of isolation or comfortable separation. This appears to mirror the dilemmas that we face in life of first dealing with being an integral part of the family, then leaving home and deciding which of the potential positions we want to primarily adopt away from the family. This usually consists of closeness to an intimate or a variety of friends or choosing isolation. In my experience, few people find the 'couple area' a comfortable place to be in the group and the greatest energy is exerted dealing with the strong pull of the original family. Even those who find an 'individual' position still behave in such a way that indicates that the family is exerting a strong pull.

During the community exercise, group members behave most strongly under the influence of their 'right' brain because the loss of language to a large extent cuts off the more cognitive 'left' brain. Consequently, participation in this exercise is a powerful therapeutic manoeuvre.

This exercise completed the first day's activities and the group were instructed *not* to talk about their experience so that they would stay with the group process and not cut across it by attempting to intellectualise the experience.

On the second day, I recreated the natural sculpture of the community exercise with a particular reference to the four elements. Chairs were therefore placed to represent the family, couple, individual and friends areas. The chairs were placed in a position in the room which most represented those areas on the previous day. As the feeling of loss had been the most powerful process in the groups, I instructed the group to move around the room and, without consciously thinking too much about it, to see which person in their own lives came to mind who most represented the sense of loss and to decide where they would be positioned in the room. When they had found that 'person', they were to imagine how they were sitting and then to have an imaginary discussion with them. After the group had had about five minutes to do this, each group member in turn was invited to allow us to listen to their conversation. This was a very powerful experience for the whole group. Gary chose the couple area and his conversation involved a very tearful attempt to find out why his second lover decided to accept her father's wishes in preference to his. Phil chose the family area and was having a conversation with his mother with whom he had been very close. She had recently died and it was clear that he was still very much involved in the mourning process. Jan also chose the family area and was speaking to her father. It emerged that in her early teens, her mother had died and that she, as the eldest daughter, had taken over much of the maternal role in the family. She expressed many angry feelings to her father because he had never really appreciated what she had done for the family and indeed had always shown strong disapproval for all her actions. This disapproval had included her marriage to her husband.

One of the major dilemmas for a group leader when he or she has so much potential material to develop into a full-scale psychodrama is to choose someone who could best represent the process for all group members. On this occasion, because there had been so much empathy, I left it to the group to decide and they chose Gary. This both surprised and pleased me because I was aware that up until this weekend, he had been very much a group outsider, which was consistent with his general role in life. Gary role-played his lover and it emerged that she was living with her parents and the 10-year-old daughter of her liaison with Gary. She said that she saw Gary about twice a year and realised how much he loved her and their child but that she was happy living with her parents. She said that Gary had never really put any pressure on her to marry him and that she was not sure what she would do if he were to become more insistent. Another group member then took over the lover's role and Gary, playing himself, was directed to become more insistent in declaring why he wanted her. He told her that he could not get her out of his mind and that he had gone into a form of self-imposed exile while he waited for her. I asked Gary to tell her how long he intended to wait for her to make up her mind and he became very confused and said he was unsure whether she was worth waiting for. When asked what would be the signs that he had given her up, he said that the major one would be that he would start making relationships with other people, both male and female. As the psychodrama proceeded, it became clear to both Gary and the group that the chances of wresting his lover away from her family were slim. No attempt was made to urge him to do this. That decision would have to be his.

In order to understand why he had systematically first chosen and then clung on to this relationship, I extended the psychodrama to his wider family in a similar way to that described for Bill and Sue earlier in the chapter. The most important parental figure he produced was his mother whom he placed in a chair behind him. When role-playing her, he presented her as a very cold demanding woman who had been unhappily married. The most significant thing he said for her was a statement that she had made when he had been a young boy. She told him that she always expected him to stand by her and demanded that he promised to do this. Another group member was asked to play the mother's role and to repeat this demand. Gary promised to do this and then crying, he said that this promise seemed to be very unfair. As he was crying, Gail another group member who had shared Gary's isolated position in the group, became very angry at Gary's passivity. Gary said he couldn't be angry and so Gail was invited to do it for him. After initially telling Gary's mother that she should free him from his promise, she then turned her anger on Gary. I got both to stand and place their hands on each others shoulders and push each other with Gail saying 'Yes' and Gary 'No'. Gail put enormous energy into this task, sobbing as she did it. Gary was much less certain, mainly fielding Gail's pushes. Gail eventually collapsed into Gary's arms exhausted and the rest of the group surrounded them in a tearful hug.

It became clear during the group-sharing which followed this session that the work that Gary had done had great significance for the rest of the group and therefore he had been working for them as much as himself. While the specific details of Gary's psychodrama involved his personal life, the more general issues tackled in the psychodrama of this struggle to cope with the demands of the family system and its consequent effects on other relationships was generally shared. Because the psychodrama was done after a group process had been established, each group member's 'right brain' had been activated and the potential therapeutic impact was enhanced. A psychodrama which is done cold, without first establishing a shared group process, may be of benefit to the protagonist but may do little for the rest of the group while they play a game of 'cure a patient'. (See Bion (1961) for a wider discussion of the ways individuals protect themselves in groups from change.)

In the sharing, Jan said that she would have liked to have spoken to her father and expressed similar angry feelings for him as Gary had for his mother. She was allowed to do this for ten minutes as a form of brief psychodrama, using one of the men in the group to play her father. After initially expressing some angry feelings about his treatment of her as a child, she then went on to say that she felt very responsible for him. I suggested that by holding on to her ex-husband, she allowed herself to continue to feel responsible for her father even though he was now dead. This was not said in a direct way that would suggest she should immediately stop doing this. It seemed clear that at some level of unconscious understanding, she

139

appreciated how much of her life had been devoted to maintaining the close link with her widowed father, to the point of selecting and maintaining a relationship with a man who could never threaten that alliance and not allowing herself to get into a relationship which would threaten it. She now had the potential to re-assess her 'world image' and perhaps change the course of her life.

Phil said that he felt enormous sadness about the way his marriage had deteriorated. Again we did a short ten-minute psychodrama looking at the way he interacted with his wife. It emerged that a major difference of opinion was around her lack of sexual desire. In the brief psychodrama, it became apparent that he always approached her in such a brutish way that there was a high probability she would refuse him. Again the group experience enhanced the potential for his 'world image' to be modified, particularly with regard to his close link with his mother, which required him and his wife to be distant. It was pointed out that any attempt to change things would have potential ramifications not only for his alliances but also his wife's. In other words, he knew how to approach his wife in an affectionate way and could avoid the potential affair but both of these distances served a useful function to their present system.

As the group-sharing proceeded, it was noticeable that while the group members remained thoughtful, the mood started to lighten with a lot of genuine warmth and closeness. The group ended as a closely knit circle and I asked them to think first of all of the things they would like to change in their lives and then to decide how they would most effectively sabotage that change.

While I have not been able to systemically look at the subsequent effects of these groups on the participants, more informal feedback is often very encouraging. I learnt recently that the effects on Gary had been very positive. Not only had he become a much more integrated member of his group but was also actively and positively courting the mother of his child.

I have concentrated in this chapter on the effects of the family system. However, therapists themselves can also become a very important part of an individual's system. As I have explained elsewhere (see Shuttleworth, 1983), a therapist, while initially acting as a solution to an individual's problem, can eventually become the problem. If the therapist encourages clients, either consciously or unconsciously to become dependent, then he or she can become a very important stabilising effect in preventing change. If we take as an example a man who has sought therapy because of his poor relationship with his partner, then we may find there are important systemic reasons for him not getting close to his partner. Unless the therapist is very careful, he or she can enter into a 'therapeutic marriage' with that man which can eventually prevent change with his partner, because while he is communicating and expressing warmth to the therapist he does not have to express these things to his partner and consequently, the original distance is reinforced.

While there is less chance of this happening in a group than in individual therapy, anyone who has attended groups will be aware of individuals who have undergone a lot of therapy, who know the solutions to their problems and can express warmth and closeness to other group members and the therapist but seem incapable of doing it in their home setting. These group 'season ticket holders' are often very difficult to help as they usually know all the tricks to avoid being genuinely affected. I recently attended a psychodrama group where a young woman very easily had a cathartic reaction while talking to her mother. This was greeted with relief by the group leader because he thought he was doing some useful work, but was eventually flattened when during the feedback the young woman said 'I really got something out of this, the last time I did it, it wasn't nearly as useful'. The more people use therapy as a 'way of life' the less likely they are to change, because by changing they will lose the benefit of the closeness engendered by the therapy. This is a major dilemma for anyone working in the caring professions. The solution, which is more simply said than done, is to not encourage dependency. The more neutrally a therapist works, the more likely this aim will be achieved. To an extent, neutrality seems to be at odds with some of the humanistic principles upon which a lot of dramatherapy practice is based.

SUMMARY

I have attempted in this chapter to explain why an individual's difficulties can be perceived within the context of his or her inter-action within systems, in particular, the family system. An understanding of these principles can help us appreciate why a lot of good therapy seems to be ineffective and also provides guidelines showing how we can be more effective. I have emphasised the importance of finding ways of communicating with the basically unconscious 'world image', a phenomenon which can explain much

141

of our irrational behaviour. We are still very much in the early stages of understanding how we can quickly and effectively help people modify their 'world image'. I hope I have shown that drama-therapy offers techniques for helping us achieve this aim. In particular, the techniques should in themselves provide the most powerful pathway to change by emphasising action, visual stimulation and metaphor and giving less emphasis to intellectual processes. The signs in the group that some form of unconscious reassessment is taking place will not be in what is said but in the engendered shared group process.

REFERENCES

Bion, W.R. (1962) *Experiences in Groups*. Tavistock Publications, London

Cade, B.W. (1982) *Some Uses of Metaphor Australian Journal of Family Therapy*, vol. 3, no. 3, p. 135–40

———— (1984) *Paradoxical Techniques In Therapy*, Journal of Child Psychology & Psychiatry. Vol. 25 no. 4 October, p. 509–16

Hayley, J. (1977) *Problem Solving Therapy*. Jossey Bass, New York

Palazzoli, M.S., Boscolo, L., Cecchin, G., & Prata, G. (1978) *Paradox & Counter Paradox*. Jason Aaronson, New York

Shuttleworth, R. (1977) 'Dramatherapy in Professional Training Groups', *Dramatherapy*, vol. 1, no. 1

———— (1983) 'Wheels Within Wheels: A Systems Approach to Mal-adjustment', *Journal of Maladjustment & Therapeutic Education*, vol. 1, no. 2

———— (1984) 'Dramatherapy in Northern Ireland A Compartive Look at Group Process'. *British Journal of Dramatherapy*, vol. 7, no. 2, pp. 24–30

———— (1985) 'Metaphor in Therapy'. *Dramatherapy* vol. 8, no. 1

Watzlawick, P. (1978) *The Language of Change*. Basic Books, New York

Dramatherapy and the Teacher

Richard Courtney

PROLOGUE

Drama as spontaneous improvisation was frowned upon when I began teaching in 1948, while 'therapy' was a dirty seven-letter word. Drama was a playscript ('a good play') read around the class with the rest of the children silent. Anyone in therapy was called 'a lunatic' who should be locked up in an asylum.

I was told so by the vicar. He had cycled up the hill, puffing and blowing, to the tiny, two-room village school where I taught the older children (aged 7 to 11). My classroom was a chilly stone-walled room warmed weakly by a smoking black coke stove that made us all cough. The vicar was the chairman of the school board and he had heard (he heard about everything in that village — even the sexton called him 'Big Ears') that I had done about fifteen minutes of creative drama with my class the day before. And in history, of all things!

'Whatever for', he asked, unctuously rubbing his soft white hands together and still catching his breath. Then, presenting me with the fixed, sickly smile with which he usually finished his sermons, he asked, 'Just what good can it do for your 'Little People' to pretend that they are Queen Elizabeth or Sir Walter Raleigh?'

I was young and innocent of the ways of education. I talked enthusiastically about the children 'living' their history — I had read Caldwell Cook (1917) and Joseph Lee (1915) a week or so before. Both books had been written over thirty years ago — surely they were respectable? I became quite voluble and said, 'dramatic action creates meaning', and other such phrases.

The vicar sat smiling wanly, smoothing his white hands over each other. He obviously thought I was a victim of my youth. And then

I made a grave mistake — I told him that drama could help the self-concept, motivation and emotional development of the children. 'It helps them psychologically', I went on, not noticing that he now sat very still. 'It's a kind of natural therapy.'

There was a long silence. The smile had gone and he sat motionless, his face as white as his hands. Then he cleared his throat. Twice. 'I want you to understand', he said, his voice quavering, 'that NONE of the children in my parish are MAD! If they were, they'd be locked away!'

That incident took place almost forty years ago in rural England — it could not happen today. Or could it?

A funny thing happened to me only a few weeks ago. At a teachers' meeting in a major Canadian city, I was having coffee in the interval with the two drama teachers, both graduate students of mine. The younger MA student was telling the other older teacher who was studying for his PhD, about some recently published research. Apparently, improvisation had been shown to improve the self-concept, self-esteem and self-confidence of children and so, by making them feel better about themselves, their normal school work improved. 'You see!' he cried enthusiastically, 'spontaneous drama provides a natural therapy!'

'Hrumph!' said a voice behind us. We turned to find the Director of Education glowering at us over his glasses. He had clearly been listening. 'You drama people are all the same', he growled. 'Therapy has no place in my schools. The kids aren't nuts, you know! They're there to learn through hard WORK — not to play around with drama and such stuff!'

Hasn't the world changed in forty years? Or is it that the pendulum has swung backwards?

ACT ONE

Scene one

After getting my degree and teaching diploma and doing some work in the theatre, I returned to teaching. This time it was in the bowels of a great industrial city — Leeds. It was with some trepidation that I walked through the bustling streets, past the smoking factory chimneys, and found my way to the school.

It was 1952 and the school was Harehills Secondary School for

Boys, a huge nineteenth-century building where the sound of students' shoes could be heard clattering on the stone steps and reverberating up the stairwells for floor after floor. The boys were tough — very tough. One was on probation for stabbing a man in Roundhay Park and the same boy in another incident knocked a teacher down a stairwell and broke his jaw!

At first I taught general subjects but gradually, over the years, managed to teach more and more drama. I did so in a surreptitious way by simply not mentioning it. After all, the headmaster made himself clear at the interview. And who was I to argue the point? 'You're the drama man, I hear!' he snapped. 'Well, I . . .' 'Ah!' he said with a snort. 'Well, we don't do no drama here. Not in schooltime, that is. After school, with the school play, yes. But none in the classrooms.' 'But . . .', I began. 'Is that quite clear?', he thundered.

It was! So I worked undercover. The students did all they were supposed to do in English, foreign languages, history and geography, but wherever possible, we worked dramatically. My purpose in using improvisation was two-fold — for learning and for therapy. It allowed them to learn through drama, create their own meanings and thus, motivate their learning and give it permanence. But drama was also a 'helping' instrument so that each of them could develop their personal and social potential. One example will serve.

Larry was classified as educationally subnormal, physically handicapped and emotionally disturbed. His left arm was partially paralysed, his left leg was twisted and he had a severe speech impediment. Teased by the others (he was smaller than them), he would occasionally flail about him in a fury when his frustration became too great. His school work was dreadful; he could hardly write his name. My job, as his teacher, was to educate him, unaided by social workers or therapists.

Larry loved drama. Not that this helped him to begin with. He was isolated by his peers — none of them wanted him in their improvisational groups. So, at the start, I chose the members of the groups and placed Larry in a different one each time. Slowly he came to be more accepted, but only to a certain extent.

When, after the drama, we wrote about what we had done, Larry's writing improved. Not that he was ever fluent, but he began to enjoy his writing — and then reading — and then looking things up in books to help with his drama work. Because he worked more amenably with others, they teased him less and his aggression subsided. His furious outbreaks decreased. He even began to chatter,

145

forgetting his speech impediment. Although it was still difficult to hear him clearly, he could usually make himself understood. Sometimes after school, he and I would talk about his drama work and, even, discuss his problems.

Towards the end of my first year at Harehills, Larry's class worked on the Renaissance voyages of discovery during their history periods. They had progressed so much that these stories became improvisations in which the whole class joined. We could not clear the desks to the sides of the room as they were bolted down to the floor so they improvised in the five-foot wide space in front of the blackboard. There, in that long and narrow space, the voyages of Vasco da Gama, Magellan, Columbus and the rest became broad, sweeping dramatizations where the boys lived through the historical events, facing the crises of each voyage as if they themselves were there.

From the outset, the class faced up to the problem of Larry. And so did he; he had pointed out straight away that, with his physical disabilities, he could not be a sailor. Almost all his improvisation was of himself in a fictional situation and only rarely did he take on a separate role.

So he decided to be 'the fish'! Under every ship that sailed on a voyage of discovery, Larry swam. He swam below the ships of Philip of Portugal, he swam round the Cape of Good Hope all the way to India, and he struggled hard to cross the Atlantic. Not only was he now taking a role, but the others supported him. Before they reached the Cape of Good Hope, they had decided that 'their lucky fish was with them again!' Indeed, they became proud of his efforts and continued their support of him outside the drama. But it was as the sailors were leaving America for home, followed closely by 'the fish', that the headmaster walked through the door.

'Here!' he said in a loud stage whisper, drawing me to one side and clutching my arm in a vice-like grip. 'I thought I told you that we didn't do no drama here?'

'Well, yes', I confessed, 'but what we're really doing is history. You see, we . . .'

'Look here!' he exclaimed with anger, pointing at Larry swimming across the floor. 'Don't tell me that's not drama. I know drama when I see it. And that — well damn it — that's drama, that is!'

But the explosion was defused when I suggested that he should question the class about what they had learned in history. From his questioning, it was clear that the students knew and loved their history. He was, in fact, a wise gentleman and he knew that this group of boys was not the brightest. And when Larry, instead of being silent to hide his speech impediment as he had in the past, bubbled over with excitement to tell what had happened on those voyages that he himself had witnessed, the headmaster even ventured a smile.

In our interview afterwards, the headmaster handsomely acknowledged that the students had learned well through improvisation. But I did not mention the drama therapy Larry had undergone. One thing at a time, I thought.

Scene two

The following year, the headmaster rewarded me for my good work by giving me the 'Hut class'. This was a temporary wooden hut sitting on the asphalt in a corner of the school yard against the iron railings that separated it from a street of back-to-back houses. It was as though the hut had been placed as far away as possible from the main school building.

This hut was the home of 'the dodos' — as they were affectionately known by the other students. They were some 28 students, aged 11 to 14, all classified as educationally subnormal. They were of all shapes and sizes and with a multitude of physical, emotional and learning disabilities. And it was to be my job to teach them all day, every day!

I had no training of any kind in dealing with 'special' students, and said so to the headmaster. 'Now, don't worry, lad', he said with a warmth that I distrusted. 'Just look what you did for that group in their history last year. I know that the Hut class is not quite as bright as those boys were' . . . (dear God, I thought) . . . 'but the thing is, you're a teacher. And a teacher's a teacher, after all!'

That platitude rang in my ears as I struggled onwards through the long weeks. The first month was a kind of purgatory but slowly, very slowly, things improved. I learned, first, that normal school discipline was useless. Not only was such rigidity a great strain on me, but the students learned very little under such conditions: their individual disabilities remained constant; they retained virtually nothing of what they were supposed to have learned; and they were perpetually rowdy and 'naughty.'

But when I did a little drama, things worked better. They were still noisy but their noise was for a purpose, and they were no longer 'naughty'. Quite the reverse. Once I accepted their natural noise

147

level and relaxed with it, I found them keen and eager. Often they would draw me into the discussion when preparing an improvisation. On odd occasions, I was suddenly incorporated as a participant. I learned, by experience, that I could take on a role and be immediately accepted within their dramatisations. But in the mathematics or English classes, things remained quite as difficult as before.

At the end of the first term, I was worn out. At the beginning of the Christmas holidays, I slept a great deal and my wife was quite worried about my health. Yet, surprisingly, I was reasonably well recovered by the opening of the new term.

I began with a new strategy. Whenever and wherever there was a story-line to anything on the syllabus, we dramatised it. When there were things to learn by rote (such as multiplication tables), we made games of them. Slowly, I weaned them from the whole-class games to small-group games. Then I could begin individual work with single students while the others were in group activities. I still had to ignore the noise!

Quite soon I discovered that, despite their disabilities, I could trust most of them to complete a simple task without being watched. They had learned to trust me and so I could trust them. This began when one group worked on their own in the hut's small foyer, and a second group worked in the walk-in cupboard with the door closed. Thus the noise in the classroom was reduced and those of us who remained could get more work done. I alternated the groups between the three spaces and soon discovered those who could be trusted more, and those who could be trusted less. Then I placed leaders with the more unco-ordinated students. Soon I could allow some small groups to work in the school yard — at least, in the few fine days of an early Yorkshire spring. At various times over a month, they engaged in map-making by measuring and plotting the whole exterior of the school. Most of the time, they did so without me.

By the beginning of the summer term, things were working with reasonable smoothness. They were learning things slowly, it is true, but they were learning. And that was what I was paid to do. Through mutual trust, we had managed to set up a framework within which we could all work without too much disruption.

What has this to do with dramatherapy? At the centre of all we did was the drama. Most of the time we used group improvisation, the students choosing their own topics, practising them, and then performing them; sometimes to other groups, sometimes not, much depending on the needs of a group at any particular time. But we also did the activities that have more recently become more common in educational drama. We did dramatic exercises: individually, in pairs, in small groups or as an entire class. The latter were least successful because of the variety of handicaps in the class. We dramatised stories, either ones I read or ones they created, or the students improvised events in their own lives. And we did a lot of physical work: physical education, creative dance and gestalt-type activity. I had to invent most of these things on the spot as there were no relevant books or courses. But these the students enjoyed immensely and also absorbed the right attitudes for learning.

By January of that particular school year, I had learned to base all classroom activities in special education on the needs of the participants. I had learned to be sensitive to at least three things: firstly of the personal and social needs of the individuals, secondly, those of the group and thirdly, of their needs as learners.

A specific student with a unique handicap required a very particular approach — at that moment — in the 'here and now' — which is the nub of dramatic action. An another time, perhaps, a different approach was necessary. Yet simultaneously the class itself had its own dynamic; it required a specific attitude and response from me as the teacher. The most difficult thing, I found, was to keep a balance between the two demands — of the individual(s) and of the class as a whole.

I had also learned that, with 28 students, all with different types of handicap, the balancing act I was attempting was impossible much of the time. About seven was the maximum number I could work with effectively at any given moment. So, with 28, groupwork was essential. Moreover, if it came to a choice between the individual and the group, I had to answer the needs of the individual.

The headmaster hardly bothered me that year. 'Out of sight, out of mind!' as one of my colleagues said. From brief conversations in the staffroom, it was clear that the head had given up hope of the 'Hut class' learning anything. So he was very surprised, when he visited the Hut late in the summer, to find lots of good writing, model-making, and even books full of sums with bright blue ticks beside them.

I was rewarded by being given the 'Hut class' the following year!

FIRST INTERLUDE

When my time at Harehills Secondary School drew to a close, using drama in schools was still not easy. Schools regarded their only purpose was to improve the students' learning. There were specific things to learn (which usually meant 'remember') on each year's syllabus or programme and, if the children did not learn them, both parents and administrators thought that the teacher was unsuccessful. Back in the early 1950s, I was facing two battles against the use of conventional teaching methods, one involving the use of educational drama for learning and the other, the use of drama as a therapeutic tool. These were inter-linked. The 'trick' was to combine learning and therapy through dramatic action — to allow students to function better as human beings and, thereby, learn better. The other trick, too often, was not to get caught at it!

There were few books or articles to help the teacher. Jacob Moreno's work on psychodrama (1946, 1959) dealt largely with disturbed adults and so his techniques were only marginally useful in a school. However, I gleaned his material very carefully, changed his methods around, and adapted them for classroom purposes. More helpful were the writings of play therapists — Margaret Lowenfeld in particular (see Lowenfeld, 1935). Books about play therapy were useful for two things: they provided a background of emotional development with young children that was helpful; and the therapists conveyed an attitude of mind that, adapted for schools, gave a new flavour to teaching — one of 'helping' rather than of direct instruction.

Teachers' books for drama hardly existed. Cook and Lee had been out of print for years. E.J. Burton's *Teaching English Through Self-Expression* (1948) was the only secondary teacher's book then available; it was (and remains) full of useful ideas. The appearance of Peter Slade's *Child Drama* in 1954 was very important. It was a mine of information for drama as both a learning and 'helping' tool. Yet it was more of an indirect aid to my teaching at Harehills because it was largely concerned with younger children. In the subject-based work of a secondary school, I found that I had to adapt Slade (as I did with Moreno and Burton) for work in my own context.

Only later was I to understand that here lies a key to good drama practice: the adaptation of many ideas to a specific set of circumstances.

ACT TWO

Scene one

I was appointed drama master at the new Colne Valley High School, near Huddersfield, in 1956. This was one of the first British comprehensive schools: a huge concrete-and-glass battleship that sat on the crest of the Pennines over-looking the chimneys of the Crowthers of Bankdam. I taught nothing but drama, assisted by two other teachers who, amongst other subjects, also taught dramatic dance and creative speech. I faced 40 different classes each week, mostly in a normal classroom which I adapted as a drama studio. There was also a small gymnasium for dance and movement activities that, after school, could be used for small shows. There was also a large and rather splendid new theatre, which I myself had designed, for major school plays.

With a humane headmaster and a progressive board of governors, I was encouraged to develop drama in many ways throughout the school. One was with small classes in special education. It was still called 'Drama'. I had learned my lesson. I did not use the term 'dramatherapy'. But that was what I was engaged in.

One of these classes occupied me a great deal over the years. In 1956, there were seventeen boys and girls aged between eleven and twelve with their own regular teacher. Their IQ's were between about 75–85. Many were physically uncoordinated, about half would be classified these days being as 'hyperactive', some were emotionally disturbed and many were socially deprived.

One of the most difficult students was Sarah. She was 11 and a very large girl for her years. She had an overly large head, unpleasant features and was a complete loner. Her teacher said that on many days she refused to come into the classroom; she stood in the corridor, looking in from time to time. After a while, he managed to get her into the room and even into a desk. Rarely did she do any work. As far as he could tell, she could neither read nor write. As she had come from outside the catchment area into the new school, he had no information on her background.

When I began drama activity with this class in September, Sarah stood against the wall and did nothing. I tried various methods of encouragement, friendliness and cajolement but nothing worked. A few weeks later, her classroom teacher told me that the social worker had called at Sarah's house but could get no reply. None of the neighbours knew anything about the newly arrived family.

151

Early in October, a group of her class were improvising a family theme: a father and his young son were sitting at home with an uncle and an aunt, talking about how they were going to be able to eat when there was no money in the house. Sarah was standing at the side, saying nothing as usual.

Suddenly, however, she walked into the scene pulling a smallish boy by the arm. 'Come on!' she said, and walked with him through the room and out the other side. There she and the surprised boy stood in silence. After a shocked pause, the improvisers continued, not deflected from their dramatisation at all. A few minutes later, Sarah moved into the scene once more, again pulling the boy by the arm. She took him to the front door, planted a kiss on his cheek, and said, 'Good night! See you next week!' She then pushed him out of the door and came back into the scene to sit down. During the rest of the improvisation she said nothing but, from her eyes, it was clear she was part of the drama.

The classroom teacher and I talked this over at length. We decided to concentrate upon domestic situations with Sarah in all her classwork. Simultaneously, she began to show a little interest in classroom activities.

The following week when I was working with the class, the social worker called to see us. He had managed to discover some things about Sarah's background. Her mother was a prostitute who brought her clients home. She also largely ignored Sarah whom she called 'a mistake'. Clearly Sarah's first improvisation had been an attempt to resolve a major problem in her home life.

In my first weeks in that school I had learned that dramatherapy can be an effective diagnostic tool — if only I had realised it when Sarah began her drama! — and that, very often, it has a curiously literal character: a concreteness that requires no sophisticated or complex explanation in order to be understood at the basic levels of feeling. In Sarah's case, this kind of diagnosis had been staring me in the face before the social worker brought us the information, but I did not have the background experience to see it. Sarah's drama gave us a brief and realistic glimpse into her interior life. We built on this, the class teacher and I, and she improved steadily. By the second year she was attempting most of the normal classwork and never missed an opportunity to improvise.

Scene two

I also had a single class of highly intelligent eleven-year-old boys and girls, many of whom were also gifted. In fact, the proportion of gifted students in this class was higher than the average in the population and their dramas were often extraordinary.

I had never met a large group of gifted students before so I asked the administration for help. All I received back was a list of IQ scores. It was soon clear that this was of little help. I observed that the differences between the students was quite radical: Tim was a shy, withdrawn boy whose improvisational skills were all verbal; Sandra was a warm-hearted out-going girl who enjoyed the sociality of drama as much as the doing of it; Peter was an odd-beat, less sociable person with a bizarre and absurd sense of humour — and so on.

Any help I was going to receive had to be my own. So I started to write up dramatic profiles for each student with an account of what they did. I continued this for the four years in which I taught them. This document became amplified as I met more gifted students. With its help, I diagnosed that there was a typology of gifted students in drama. This was in an embryonic stage at that time and read as follows:

(1) *Those who want to please me.* They are eager to do anything I want. They do their best improvisations when my instructions are highly directive, their worst when they are unsure of what I want, when my directions are ambiguous. They are extremely industrious, prepare their work very thoroughly (sometimes excessively) and seem unsatisfied if the drama takes an unexpected turn. They are liable to be the most successful in their academic work.

(2) *Those who want to please others.* Equally eager, these students are highly social, popular with their peers, and are often the leaders of improvisational groups. They often lead by a subtle mixture of using the wishes of others and their own skills in decision-making. They are equally at home in conventional and unconventional structures. They are continuously successful in role-taking, however far removed the roles are from their own personalities — often far more so than the other two groups.

(3) *Those who want to please themselves.* It is not that these students are selfish but that their own interior world seems unique to themselves; others do not always understand it, and these

students expect that the others will not understand it. They have an absurd and bizarre sense of humour with wild flashes of association — often too 'wild' for the others to accept. They are full of ideas: often too full, to the detriment of decision-making; sometimes so much so that when others in the group want to make decisions, they can feel rejected.

This typology, however embryonic, was useful with this class and with other gifted classes. It gave me some expectations of gifted students that related to their drama activities. But I soon discovered that this typology was incomplete.

Elsewhere in the school there was another student who was gifted in drama — Timmy. He was totally different from anyone in the first class. His was an entirely different case. Timmy was in a class of less-able students. He had the reputation of being 'a terror' and other teachers told me that, while he was educable, he had no wish to learn and that he made himself a thorough nuisance in their classes.

In drama, however, the situation was quite the reverse. He took to it like a duck to water. Indeed, on the very first day that we improvised, he was amazingly brilliant. Within seconds of the drama beginning, he had dug right down into the personality of an old comic character and had me helpless with laughter. Comedy was his *métier*. As time went on, he got even better. He so affected the rest of the class that, after only a month or so, their spontaneity had grown remarkably.

Later that first term, when I was directing some short plays after school, I cast Timmy in a small part in a farce. The effect on him was electric: it was as if he walked six inches off the ground. It was the first time he had been chosen for anything in his school life. He came early to all rehearsals, even to those of other plays ('to help, if I can') and, far from being a terror, he could not have been more cooperative and willing.

On the night of the first performance, I was standing near him in the wings as he waited for his entry. The audience began to laugh and Timmy's eyes lit up. Offstage, he was already responding to the audience. His role was that of the hotel porter who had to carry people's bags in. He had been extremely funny in rehearsals, but in that first performance, with that light in his eyes, he became hilarious. On his first entry, instead of stumbling in with a pile of heavy bags, he came in horizontally and landed flat on his face! Yet he did not overweight his antics to the detriment of the other actors and the play. As many adults commented to me afterwards, it was like being at the very first performance of a young Chaplin.

The boy was a born performer. Under the right conditions, he had the potential to become a great comic performer in adult life. Yet the rest of his school work, and his attitudes, remained abysmal. Despite this, he was always around the drama room, or he was waiting quietly (almost professionally) during rehearsals of other plays he was not involved in, in case he could help. I did not stop him. He had a wretched home life. He had never known his father. His mother was a prostitute, his elder brother, whom he admired greatly, was in prison having been arrested for theft. Timmy had been his 'look-out' and he was now on probation. If he committed another misdemeanour, he would go to reform school. So I accepted him as my 'gofer': he would 'go for this' and 'go for that' in all rehearsals. Occasionally over the next three years, when there was a farcical part in a play, he would take it and achieve great success.

For those three years, I was rehearsing most evenings and often through weekends and holidays with Timmy at my side. But at the end of that time, I decided to take a holiday with my family. There were no rehearsals in the summer holidays that year. When I returned to the school in September, Timmy was not there. Late in the July, he had been caught stealing and he was now incarcerated in a reform school. I went to visit him the next weekend but he was not pleased to see me. His world had changed and he wanted no part of the one I represented.

Clearly my typology was incomplete. There was a fourth kind of gifted student:

(4) *Those who want to please no one.* Usually boys, these students are gifted in one aspect of their lives: with Timmy it was drama; with others it can be anti-social. Apart from this one aspect, they are often rebellious, surly, unruly.

Many years later, I discovered that this four-fold typology paralleled that put forward for all gifted school students by Elizabeth Drews (1963). I had come to similar conclusions by diagnosing their dramatic behaviour.

One characteristic of drama with gifted adolescent students that I observed during this time has not, however, been commented upon by others (at least, to my knowledge). All such students, whatever their typology, appear to be quite conscious that dramatic action is a meta-drama. That is to say, they are aware that they are performing 'a play within a play'. Where other young adolescents may indicate they have a glimpse of this from time to time, most of the gifted are well aware that an improvisation is a microcosm where life itself is the macrocosm. This is to go beyond abstraction *per se*. Most adolescents explore abstraction through dramatic hypothesis: 'If I hypothesise my role as A then my actions become Y, but if I hypothesise my role as B then my actions become Z.' Unless the student can do this well in dramatic action, he or she cannot hypothesise adequately in mathematics and other forms of learning. But to recognise improvisation as a meta-drama is a leap beyond that. It is very similar in character to what Gregory Bateson (following Alfred Whitehead and Bertrand Russell) called, 'Learning III', a level of human awareness not reached by the majority of people. But it is clearly observable in the spontaneous drama of those adolescents who are highly gifted.

Scene three

Meanwhile I was discovering other things about drama as a 'helping' medium in schools. With some other adolescents, educational drama slipped over into role-play. In the year before they left school, improvisation often centred on jobs, interviews, situations in adult life, and the like.

I came face to face with the 'helping' quality of dramatic action with Fred. A boy of low average ability, he was ingenuous to a fault and his drama showed that he often had little real idea of the practicalities of actual situations. He and another boy had just improvised a scene where they were window cleaners when Fred expressed his desire to take up such a job in real life. The classroom was on the third floor, so I took him to the window and half-hitched him on to the sill (holding him very firmly) so that he could look down for a couple of seconds. I brought him back in and he publicly declared a change of occupation! This led the class, and Fred in particular, to deepen their improvisations — by doing so, the fictional situation became more 'real' to them and they could begin to make valid judgements about their lives.

There was an extreme case of this in a parallel class of pre-leavers. Donnie was of quite low ability and rather simple. One evening, as it was getting dark, he stole a used tyre from the local garage. He was wheeling it round the corner of the garage when he ran it straight into the legs of a policeman. He had not even looked to see if anyone was watching him!

A number of such adolescents do not always realise the obvious practical results of their actions in life. As a result of Donnie's experience, we evolved a drama game (working in pairs) called 'What Do I Do Now?'. At a particular moment in an improvisation I would stop the action and ask each character in turn what their choices were at that specific moment. These games, and others like them, helped these young people to look ahead, to see what might occur from what they did and to take responsibility for their actions.

It is the mentally retarded but educable who need the greatest care in schools. Most students in the Colne Valley High School could generalise from dramatic contexts to life actions. Thus they could work through their improvisations as improvisations. They could live in the dramatic world and, subsequently, their life actions would demonstrably show they had learned from their dramatic experience. But the educable mentally retarded did not demonstrate such learnings. There appeared to be little cause-and-effect relation between dramatic action and life action.

With these students drama as learning and drama as therapy become one. The major goal of a drama programme for them is to lead them to function adequately in life — to do all the simple actions that the rest of us take for granted — to travel on a bus or train, to read road signs, to get to work and hold down a job, to occupy themselves usefully and with satisfaction when not at work, and so on. Essential at such a level of functioning is the ability to see that A leads to B, and that they have a choice of action at any specific moment. They can learn this well in spontaneous drama, but they cannot do so without help. It has to be pointed out to them, again and again, while they are in the action. When that action is fictional rather than actual, they are protected: in drama, they do not have to face the often horrendous results of making mistakes in real life. In such circumstances, learning and therapy are united in dramatic action.

SECOND INTERLUDE

While I was teaching during the week, at weekends I was often an instructor on residential drama courses for youth, mainly from poor areas of Smethwick, Stockport, and similar cities. Sometimes we would run even longer sessions at Easter or in the summer.

From 1956 until I emigrated to Canada in 1967, I spent eleven years working with socially deprived youngsters, aged about 14 to

19, who were in school, at work or out of work. While a proportion of these young people would come because they liked drama, others simply wanted a break from their drab existence but they were soon caught up in the activity.

Drama is particularly suitable for the culturally deprived because it is, as Wagner said, 'essentially a social activity'. An improviser soon discovers he cannot work without others who will work with and for him. Spontaneous drama provides a human bonding that leads to social cohesion and a group spirit of considerable power.

I always tried to base these residential courses on social choice, i.e. where a clinical psychotherapist may emphasise the personal and individual choices a patient must make in his or her life, my emphasis was more upon the choices that affected the immediate group.

For one 10-day residential course, we took some 40 young people by bus from Smethwick to a large building on the hills above Stratford-upon-Avon. After an initial acclimatisation to the living routines, we moved straight into group improvisation for the rest of the day — a necessary basis for subsequent work. After an eventful night (for many it was their first time away from home), we had breakfast and then took them on a guided tour around eight different rooms which contained various materials (photographs and other illustrations, books, objects of all kinds), each arranged to depict a specific theme — Egypt, Australia, Norway, oil, houses, wheat, earthquakes, and the nineteenth-century family. We let them browse in these rooms for an hour and then began improvisation again. Afterwards, they could return to the rooms again and again, looking at illustrations, handling the objects, even trying on costumes and using the paraphernalia. We did not deliberately ask them to use these themes for their spontaneous creations but this did in fact happen naturally, the students making their own choices, both as individuals and in groups. Within any ten-day course, we knew after only a few days whether or not they had social needs to present their dramas. If so, then we invited an audience of their parents and teachers to a hall in Smethwick. If not, then we simply developed improvisation throughout the available time. In all cases, however, one dominant theme emerged that demonstrated their social concerns.

One year the selected theme was Norway. Amongst the books they found the stories of Peer Gynt and these became the focus of their drama work. By working from early morning to late at night, they developed a three-act improvised play with one actor as the young Peer in Act I, another playing the middle-aged role in Act II, and a third as the old Peer Gynt in Act III. They staged the play with their own creations (rudimentary scenery but splendid peasant costumes and recorded music) before a local audience. As they prepared it, they entered deep discussions on the conflict of individualism and social needs that were worthy of Ibsen. And they carried these discussions over into a meeting with the audience after the performance.

ACT THREE

Since 1974 at the Ontario Institute for Studies in Education, I have supervised only postgraduate work in the arts as a whole, including that for drama teachers and therapists.

Recently there has been a massive change in special education. Many of the special schools for those with major dysfunctions have been closed and the children placed in ordinary classrooms. The result has been an increased emphasis upon the needs of special children in ordinary teacher education.

I have found that my first requirement is to teach an experiential class to all entering graduate teachers. Most took their undergraduate degree some time ago, some with experience in educational drama, some with experience in the theatre and some with neither. Most have been teaching drama in classrooms for some years but have had little recent experience in practical drama themselves. They are responsible teachers, with excellent classroom reputations, who are seeking information and theoretical knowledge in order to improve their drama teaching now that children with special problems are joining their classes.

The initial experiential activity is essential to improve their capabilities and in this course we work for 2½-hour periods which are divided into two halves. In each, we do mostly practical work followed by a discussion that always centres on the experiences we have just lived through. The practical sections concentrate upon those elements common to all human dramatic action: perception, awareness and concentration; imaging, imagining and methods of connecting thoughts through empathy, identification, association and the like; the styles of dramatic action — being, sounding, moving; and the basic elements of dramatic form such as contrasts, harmonies, similarities, discords and so on.

It is in the subsequent discussion that individuals can discuss

159

drama teaching and therapy. They can, if they wish, concentrate entirely upon dramatherapy. Sometimes they do, sometimes not. But I firmly believe that it is their choice (and specifically at that time in their lives) that reveals their needs and, therefore, the topics that need to be discussed.

Following this principle, subsequent postgraduate course work is a matter of student choice. There are a range of courses for them to choose from, both at the Ontario Institute and at the University of Toronto. They choose their courses in close consultation with me and I try to recommend those that meet their individual needs. Thus student A may choose to concentrate upon educational and academic drama, student B will emphasise educational drama and curriculum design, while student C may focus on educational drama and special education — it is the latter who becomes the therapeutic expert in educational situations.

I follow the same principle with theses. I try to persuade students to choose their topics early and, as a result, select courses related to their chosen theme. This gives cohesion to their work. As they are preparing their dissertations, I also work with their choices. When they select a course of action, I point out the possible alternatives open to them, together with those alternatives they have closed off. This makes the early stages of preparation very slow but the later stages quick because, by making their own choices, they are producing a work they deeply believe in and to which they are committed.

This method of working is, in my view, essential to all forms of dramatic action in education and therapy. Unless the action is chosen, it is not a dramatic action.

EPILOGUE

The vicar back in 1948 or the Canadian Director of Education in 1986 may not have changed their attitudes much, but their contexts have altered radically. Forty years ago there was only a handful of drama teachers and few of us were engaged in dramatherapy in schools. Today there are hundreds in each province of Canada who are using drama as a 'helping' tool to lead children and students to psychological health. Not enough, it is true. But educational revolutions take a long time.

REFERENCES AND FURTHER READING

Bateson, G. (1973) *Steps to an Ecology of Mind*. Granada, London

Burton, E.J. (1948) *Teaching English Through Self-Expression*. Evans Brothers, London

Cook, H.C. (1917) *The Play Way*. Heinemann, London

Drews, E. (1963) 'The Four Faces of Able Adolescents'. *School Record*, January 19, pp. 68–71

Lee, J. (1915) *Play in Education*. Macmillan, New York

Lowenfeld, M. (1935) *Play in Childhood*. Gollancz, London

McCaslin, N. (1968; 3rd edn. 1984) *Creative Dramatics in the Classroom*. Longman, New York

Moreno, J.L. (1946; 1959) *Psychodrama*. 2 vols, Beacon House, New York

Slade, P. (1954) *Child Drama*. University of London Press, London

Dramatherapy with Disturbed Adolescents

Sue Jennings and Alida Gersie

Adolescence, for all young people is likely to be a difficult period of life. Major biological changes are exacerbated by changes in role, expectation and increases in pressures and responsibility. This time of change, before eventual resolution, is lengthy and has no clear cut-off point. For example, complex legislation makes it possible for various statuses and roles to be expected of young people at differing ages. The age of consent for sexual relations is 16 years, at 17 they can consume alcohol on licensed premises, they can marry without parental consent and have the right to vote at 18, and homosexual relationships are legal at 21. We have no definite age at which we confer adult status on the young person with all the responsibilities and rights that go with it. Students and unemployed are often seen to have an extended adolescence, as if somehow, the world of work and the capacity to be economically independent is a major gauge of adulthood. This work status can occur of course at any age and can be lost too.

Many traditional societies ritualise entry to adulthood through various initiation ceremonies and *rites de passage*. It may even be a transition from child to adult roles without the intervening period of adolescence (Jennings 1986). Rituals conferring adult status on both men and women are very intense periods of learning, often involving physical pain, and in which elders teach and transmit the norms and values of the adult life of the culture in question (see Forge 1970). Any of these rites is related to the 'culture as a whole' and makes use of the symbolism and metaphor inherent within that culture.

Although nominally we refer to 18 as the 'coming of age', in our society it has never been invested with the rituals that other societies value. Many people decide to celebrate both 18th *and* 21st birthdays as a glance in the personal column of a newspaper will illustrate. It is difficult to know just what is being celebrated at the age of 18, apart from marriage and voting eligibility.

Therefore we find it surprising that some adolescents actually survive the journey to adulthood rather than being necessarily dismayed by the amount of severe difficulty that many adolescents and their families have to face. Hughes and Wilson (1986) suggest that probably no client group has the possibility of being affected by such a wide range of legislation as are adolescents in an adolescent unit. In Britain, at any one time, an adolescent may be relating to several major Government departments — the Department of Education and Science, the Home Office, the National Health Service and the Department of Health and Social Security.

The range of methods of treatment vary extensively within different institutions. Variations on behaviour modification, family therapy, individual psychotherapy and groupwork methods are among those currently practised. There are centres that believe in the outdoor model of physical hard work, those that work with peer-group models and yet again those that work with the adolescent within the family construct. Often a treatment approach will be the philosophy of the particular intermediate treatment centre or adolescent unit rather than necessarily catering for the needs of the particular adolescent in crisis.

Again, one of the problems is that often we take no action until there is crisis — either in the family, the adolescent or in society itself. There is little agreement on the type of preventative work that should be going on in schools and youth centres.

It is not the intention of this chapter to discuss all possibilities of adolescent therapeutic intervention. What is under consideration is the potential that dramatherapy has both as an approach to adolescent work in itself and also as a way of working that can be integrated into other ways of working — in particular family therapy and adolescent groupwork. Dramatherapy can also be useful as a medium in life and social-skills training.

As Shuttleworth (1975) has pointed out

Unlike most adult groups, adolescents do not often sit happily for an hour or so and attempt to sort out their problems in a mature and civilised way. More often they will be distracting each other by irrelevant chatter or thumping one another or the therapist.

One of the most daunting prospects for a therapist working with adolescents is the constant movement and restlessness, a frequent incapability to be still for a moment. However, as we point out later in this chapter, restlessness in itself needs to be understood in relation to the stages of particpation that the adolescent may be reaching and needs to be understood *within its context*.

We suggest that the adolescent dramatherapy group needs to have firm boundaries with some realistic flexibility. Time, space and rules of physical hurt are three sound starting points. Within the context of the session, there needs to be some firm 'anchoring', rather like signposts through which the young person can feel grounded. Tasks can include completing certain questionnaires which can clarify themes for the young person. A good example of this is the 'Modified Beck's Dysfunctional Thought Form' (illustrated by McAdam, 1986). Identifying strengths and weaknesses is often a useful precursor to action work. Groups that consist of 'all talking and not enough action' can be experienced by young people as nebulous adult-directed communication. Likewise the reverse can place just the same sort of pressures as he or she is experiencing in the outside world.

It is our contention that young people, within a secure framework, also need quiet, time on their own, and sleep. Often dubbed as lazy or drifters rather than in the midst of demanding changes, young people often have their time filled up for them in very daunting ways. Major transition, such as any adult has experienced, if very tiring and the need for lengthy sleep should not come as a surprise. Since the nub of adolescence is emergent identity, time is needed for these many issues to be considered.

We would also like to emphasise the importance of privacy for young people. Many attempts to 'get through', or to adopt the language of the adolescent are experienced as invasive rather than helpful. Often privacy is confused with secrecy rather than something that is everyone's right, whether child or adult. The importance of adults acting as role models for acceptable behaviour cannot be overemphasised. How we treat adolescents will be interpreted by them as a way of them treating other people. Therefore if we take an authoritarian stance, is it surprising that they find their own way of taking power?

We have suggested that dramatherapy can be used productively to work on body and spatial awareness, role identity in its many contexts and projection of past, present and future lives. Within this framework there is the possibility of the adolescent re-experiencing 'self' in relation to the family, to society and also in an existential way.

The following case histories and working methods and suggestions are drawn from extensive work with adolescents of all ages in
a variety of institutional settings, both residential and in the community.

There are times that I feel totally inadequate, wondering whether
my work is of any use at all. So much has gone wrong for them
for such a long time. All I have is me, my insight and care. Who
knows, it might be that that's good enough. But I do feel helpless
in the face of this misery.

A.G. (18 July 1978)

A diary entry made whilst I was working in a treatment centre for
young drug addicts in New York who were in trouble with the law
— multi-problem children from multi-problem families living in
multi-problem areas. Their only way out had been a route of escape
into the fantasy world of drugs, violence and above all 'magic'
money, used to buy the immediate gratifications they so desparately
needed. Too old — too young. With eyes that had seen more than
their hope could support, and ears that heard words which confirmed
their darkest fears.

My first experience of the Intermediate Treatment Centre was
being hailed from an upstairs window of a Victorian house by a
pale, dark-haired fourteen-year-old; on learning who I was she
screamed, 'F*** off', f*** off — we don't want any bleeding
drama 'ere'. Anxiously I knocked on the front door, the same girl
opened it. She beamed, 'Come in — I'm sure you'll do something
'ere'.

S.J. (London, March 1980)

The centre felt chaotic and I was curious about the fantasies about
my role there. The dramatherapy group was the first time that all the
young people had stayed in the room at the same time. The slightest
threat and they would shoot out of the window or climb up and sit
on top of the bookcase. Drama needed, above all, to contain and,
particularly on this occasion, bring about some order.

There are times in any group when the therapist can feel assailed
by a sudden sense of utter powerlessness. This feeling can be
particularly acute when working with adolescents. It is difficult to
pinpoint where the feeling stems from — often there is not a clear
moment or incident. However, these moments feed our doubts about

165

the efficacy of therapy and can eradicate any earlier feelings of confidence. It can take us over, out of all proportion — the 'roller-coaster effect' — seeming to blot out anything we felt even a short while beforehand. This rollercoaster of feelings can be one of the most demanding characteristics of running a dramatherapy group with adolescents. On reflection it is very characteristic of the adolescents themselves — the turmoil of the so-called in-between years, the see-saw of emotions and loyalties.

We hope in this account of our experiences of working with adolescents that we shall be talking as much for the therapist as for the client, not with any magic solutions, but with an optimism about the ultimate potential for change in human nature.

COMMON DIFFICULTIES

'Don't come near me!'

'Don't touch me. I told you don't touch me!'
He was a skinny, ginger-haired boy. His face flushed with a sudden fury. We met in the corridor of the centre, where he attended a club for kids with trouble at school. I was the centre organiser. The main problem with school was that he refused to go. He had decided, many years ago, that he hated teachers and that they had nothing to offer. His home life had been a mess for as long as he and anyone else could remember. There had been no way out for his mum, or for any of his older brothers and sisters. Hadn't one of them just been taken to hospital to recover from overdosing on glue and other stuff? Why should he care. Why should he be made to try? Nothing would ever make a difference. And even if it did it would hurt too much, far too much.

When he saw me approaching, about to say 'hello', he froze and screamed: 'Don't touch me. I told you, don't touch me.' I put my hands in the pockets of my jeans, and stood as still as he did. We measured one another. He looked like a young frightened animal, poised for fight or flight. Then I said 'I'll try not to. And I'm sorry if I scared you with my hands'. He turned round, and snarled over his shoulder, 'You'd better not. Or I'll get my dad to come and sort you out'. He walked off, looked again, and added 'Nice club this'.

'Don't you touch me, pervert!'

It was a video workshop and a group of mixed adolescents were practising scenes of persuasion in front of the camera. One young girl asked my colleague to play the part of the mother trying to persuade the girl not to stay out late. My colleague went into the role immediately and began by putting a gentle hand on the girl's arm before speaking. It produced a whiplash effect, 'Don't you touch me you pervert' — but the recoil with her body was even stronger than her words as she backed off several feet in one movement and stood like a trapped animal.

Both of the above examples illustrate the threat for the adolescent of crossing body boundaries and of sending out threatening body signals. Our non-verbal 'modelling' is of crucial importance, both to establish an appropriate way of being but also to assist young people to re-learn to differentiate between intrusion and care and between violaton and pleasure. We ourselves need sense training, as well as our clients in order to understand what our bodies are conveying.

We must also consider how easy it is to feel overwhelmed by feelings, particularly sexual feelings, which often go with ignorance and misinformation about sexuality. The following example, as well as the one above, illustrates the confusion and latent fear:

'Don't touch me you poof!'

A large group of boisterous fifth formers attended a workshop on fight techniques. The talk at the beginning illustrated various ways one could have combat — unarmed, knives, broadswords and even the odd chair crashing on to your head, all with total safety. The actor asked for volunteers to join in a workshop demonstration and several lads crowded on to the stage. The actor put his arm on the shoulder of one boy to illustrate a posture: 'Don't touch me, you poof', said the boy jumping back. The actor carried on quite unperturbed and the intrigue of the technique overcame the reluctance to be touched.

Similarly, therapists working with adolescents will often report how they will attempt to shock through sexual allusions or explicit sexual comments. For example, using the drama–mime game of 'change the object', they will often say, 'It's a sanitary pad!' 'It's a tampon!' Perhaps we should remind ourselves that we often express in joke form those issues around which we feel anxiety. Perhaps the primary aim is not to shock the therapist but to signal areas of concern and fear.

'It's so f*** boring'

A while ago, I had a chance encounter with a young man who, several years earlier, had attended a 'special needs' group in a centre where I was the director. He had often stormed into my office, using violent language, to tell me 'how boring' everything we offered was. During one particular period he and several other kids had been so very angry at the range of activities offered, and at the threat which this posed to their determined effort to condemn the world, that, night after night, upon closing time, they would throw a barrage of bricks and other objects at the building, screaming as loudly as they could, 'Go away, go away. It's so f*** boring!' We both smiled, somewhat embarrassed. Each of us remembered the good as well as the bad times.

We talked for a while about his life now — how he had to learn to cope with unemployment, unplanned fatherhood, trying to find ways to keep himself occupied and not to get into trouble 'no more'. Sure, he still went round to the club. I asked 'Is it still boring?' He looked at me intently and said 'You must have known, it never was. It's just that when we're depressed we say it's boring. It's easier that way.' We then decided to go and have a cup of tea in a nearby cafe to talk about his position what it's like to grow up without much real hope that anything will ever get better. He confirmed to me that adolescent boredom is often little else than the presentable face of despair — a way of coping with near over-whelming feelings of powerlessness. For once the child finds the courage not to be bored, then he faces the reality of his emotions — of the relationship with his own life expectations. The pain, the fury and the 'dream of possibility' are likely to be unwelcome guests in a house of fragile, but pre-ordained structure where the permissible rules the possible.

Thus the adolescent often uses boredom as the first and strongest line of defence against change. For as long as the world, people and experiences can be reduced to the unifying 'grey' of powerlessness, then the requirement to act upon the world to be within the world, cannot touch the person who is being weaned from childhood, once again, too soon.

'I don't know what you mean Miss'

Playing the 'idiot game' is a common reaction to people who are already under-achieving and have failed in so many areas of their young lives. Therefore, one could suggest that it had some basis in reality. However, we would suggest that it is also a very successful blocking mechanism in terms of any real progress. To not understand means not to engage, and engagement is probably the most frightening step of all. It is through engagement with another that there is any potential for change. If the 'I don't understand you' is repeated too often it is also a very effective way of sapping the confidence of the therapist, who sits there wondering about effective communication and appropriate language.

The opposite of course, is the very bright person who will grasp the essence of what one is saying and immediately try to take on the leadership, re-interpreting what the therapist has said and directing it in their own way. Very quickly the therapist can feel unseated and confused — pleased perhaps that something is 'happening' in the group (what a change from all the feelings of boredom), but somehow aware that this is not quite what he or she set out to do.

'We've done drama before and it was silly'

This often comes in the 'drama is boring, stupid, a waste of time' set of responses. However, this can also have roots in reality that people have been made to feel silly — it can be that approaches and techniques were quite inappropriate to the age and experience of the group. I say 'approaches', because it can be the way we go about it rather than the technique itself.

> The horror of the first mime group in a remedial class. As I entered the school hall I had a feeling of foreboding. The hall was empty. Where was my class? It began to dawn on me as I noticed some jumper sticking out of the grand piano and one or two curtains begin to move with people's breathing. Rather than get caught up in 'hunt the class', I stood in the middle of the hall and began to do the famous ladder exercise. Slowly, one-by-one, the

class came out of hiding to watch what I was doing. I didn't speak but just carried on the exercise. In the lunch hour, I saw through the window that members of my class were practising the ladder exercise to see if they could 'work it out'. It was a challenge.

However, the 'feeling silly' response can be that people have actually felt very exposed and have felt very silly. Drama is an exposing medium and people become involved too quickly and even more quickly can end up bruised. Maintaining it as 'silly' is a way of distancing feelings and therefore protecting oneself.

Some dos and don'ts regarding group composition

These are recommendations, particularly when setting up groups of very disturbed adolescents.

1. Age range: do not mix pre-adolescent (age range 8–11) and adolescent groups.
2. IQ: try to keep an approximation of I.Q. range*.
3. Health and physique: do not mix ordinary mobile people with those who have major physical disability*.
4. Toughness and shyness: do not mix young people who express themselves as being 'at war with adults' with those who have internalised their conflict.
5. Socio-economic background: try to restrict the group to young people from more-or-less similar socio-economic backgrounds.
6. Sadism and violence: do not admit young people who could dangerously jeopardise the welfare of others to the group.
7. Group sensitivity: check that individuals do not suffer from extremes of, for example, sibling 'paranoia'. Some young people need extensive individual work before coping with a group, however, small.

(see also the diagnostic group).

* It would be quite a different matter, of course, if young people, as part of their rehabilitation, were able to help either with groups of mentally handicapped people or groups with severe physical disability.

NUMBERS

This will vary with the degree of disturbance — numbers up to eight seem to be most workable. However, working in pains or groups of four may be more appropriate with certain groups. Sometimes people find that individual sessions are far too threatening and working in pairs diffuses the threat.

STRUCTURE

The structure of the group needs to be 'firm with room for manoeuvre'. If it is not firm, the group will feel insecure immediately. If it is too rigid, then this will prove daunting — it will just mirror the institution. It must be remembered that many adolescents experience the world as either having no boundaries or as being very rigid. The structure of the group illustrates that there is a middle way. (This theme will be returned to — working from polarity to the middle group).

Therefore a group needs to establish basic ground rules agreed by everyone — for example, being on time and staying in the room; no smoking unless there is a break; commitment to attend each session. These can be discussed and agreed at the first session. It could be the group's first chance of having a say in their own destiny.

If there are ground rules — what about sanctions? For example, if everyone agrees that commitment to every session is important, what happens to frequent absenteeism? This also needs to be discussed. The group need to feel that it is not just the dramatherapy group that is important — they as individuals are important, therefore their presence *matters*.

The group enters the room in a reluctant and angry mood. Their fury is quickly focused on the fact that they have to be in this room with me and they don't want to be here. The session is like a return to the days of school. There is a lot of horseplay and once again the sexual allusions and comments are rife.

I feel tense and insecure when some of the boys start flicking knives, whilst expressing their resentment at having to be involved in this group. I feel decidedly apprehensive. But we struggle on. They remain verbally aggressive, shouting one another down. The knives have been put away, following my request to do so. They go on and on saying how angry they are to be here. Then

171

one of them challenges me and says 'You're a f*** woman. What do you know about our lives? What do you know about poverty, unemployment, fighting parents, misery? What do you know about that?' I say, 'A good deal more than you give me credit for. But right now, I'm here to listen to what's going on for you. I've told my story somewhere else. But make no mistake, I do happen to know.' Something clicked. The mood in the room changed immediately. They draw up their chairs and our work begins.

    A.G. (Notes on a second session of a 'life and social skills programme' for a group of long-term-unemployed boys.)

GUIDELINES FOR A DIAGNOSTIC DRAMATHERAPY PROGRAMME

Usually decisions concerning programmes of treatment are made as a result of psychological testing, interview and case discussion. We are proposing that an action-based group yields certain information and experiences that could otherwise be inaccessible. The following is a framework only and can be adapted to the specific situation.

The sessions can be run once or twice a week, or even once or twice a day. However it is programmed, sufficient time must be allowed for closing the session — both group and individual sessions. For example, in a one-hour session at least 15 minutes is spent closing, and with six or eight sessions, the half-way point should be noted and the last two sessions should focus on the process of closure.

1. The individual in the group: use a game structure — a board game which requires working in pairs making decisions and involving negotiations as well as luck. Or use action games that are co-operative as well as competitive (Jennings, 1985). A board game is useful to focus attention, not to threaten bodies in space. Observe how individuals deal with the structure. Do they have to win? Take charge? Give up?

2. The individual in his/her present life: use visual representations such as life pictures, mapping or spectrograms to represent 'my life now'. Encourage the use of colour and shape. Group members should share the pictures, even having a specific time

(2 or 3 minutes) to talk. A second picture, 'how I'd like my life to look', can be created in the same medium and shared. Differences and similarities are looked at — 'What is the first thing I need to do to bring about a very small part of the second picture?' (Jennings, 1983).

3. **The individual in his/her past life**: use life pictures, sculpting or finger painting. Call the picture 'the path of my life'. Encourage the group to think back as far as they can (a moment or two with eyes closed helps concentration) — get each person to create the path through his/her life in any way using pictures, symbols, words, signposts — include the important things, both good and bad, that have happened.

(Time should be taken to *explain* before everyone starts.)

Get the group to share major events in their lives — the good and the bad. Look for patterns and repetitions. For example, one young person with his arm in plaster drew his picture and then realised that all the important events in his life were to do with physical injury — every one or two years he had broken part of his body.

> After being absorbed in his path, Brian said, 'I was even born with an accident'. Assuming the obvious, I said, 'Do you want to talk about it?' 'When I was born, my foot got caught in me mum's ribs — that's why I was born with a twisted ankle!'
>
> (A lesson in assumptions for me! S.J.)

4. **Body image and spatial awareness**: many young people have no sense of the totality of their own body neither can they experience its reality, (e.g. the anorectic client). Similarly, without developed body image, spatial awareness is minimal. Movement games, movement of different parts of the body, co-ordination exercises, exercises on the floor, movement across the floor and those working against gravity are all useful. Plan the session in a developmental sequence, e.g. lying, sitting, crawling, standing (physical development); or working as individuals, in pairs, threes, or fours, or as an entire group (social development).

173

5. **Role repertoire**: many young people with problems get trapped in 'fixed' roles, e.g. bad, deviant, 'thicky' . . . Simple role-play is useful both to gauge the range of roles and also to explore the test 'hot' issues.

> The group were asked to work in pairs, one was a TV interviewer and the other anyone they wanted to interview. Who they were had to be agreed by the pair. All the pairs were interviewing rapists and sex offenders.
> - S.J. (Session notes from a diagnostic session in a YP prison)

6. **Final sessions**: Use these two sessions to review the preceding five. What do they remember? What did they discover? What was helpful or unhelpful? This can be revealed through discussion and also by answering a simple questionnaire.

The ending of the group must be worked through adequately, and should include some indication of what would be useful in the future.

These diagnostic sessions will help informed decisions to be made but must include the following questions:

(a) Does the person need individual therapy, or therapy in either a small or large group?

(b) Is a life and social-skills programme more appropriate than an exploratory insight programme?

(c) What are the prevailing 'hot themes'? (e.g. sexuality, authority, etc.)

(d) Which roles seem familiar — too familiar for healthy living? (e.g. scapegoat, victim)

(e) Are particular behavioural changes necessary? (e.g. glue sniffing, masochism).

(f) Is a movement-and-space orientation necessary before further development?

A SUMMARY OF USEFUL METHODS OF WORKING

N.B. Remember what was said in the diagnostic sessions about working developmentally. One can also include non-verbal-vocal-verbal development. Therefore don't try *sophisticated* role-play too soon. Simple imitations, caricatures, and 'on the spot' role-plays can be used near the beginning.

1. **Training in sensory awareness**:
   - sight;
   - hearing;
   - smell and taste;
   - touch-sensations, evoked by contact with material objects (and only much later with people).

2. **Body Image/Body in Space**:
   - free rolling, roll-resisting (individually and in pairs);
   - crawling (hands and knees/hands feet);
   - stretching everything and containing everything;
   - staying in 'wrapped' position and roll over;
   - tussling without fighting;
   - pulling and pushing a partner across the room and stopping in an instant.

3. **Feeling or Mood-Expressive Sculpts**:
   - using one's own body
   - using the group;
   - using a polarity diagonal (e.g. drawing an imaginary line between two polarities of feeling, everyone standing where they are feeling now. Trust/mistrust, feeling confident/shy are two examples of such polarities.

175

4. Role-play — useful roles:

(a) preparation exercises — learning to say *no* when people ask you for something/try to persuade you to do something, etc.

— learning to ask for something to encourage other people to respond positively;

— thinking of a certain person and exaggerating everything about them;

— imitating the way someone you know walks, eats, etc.

(b) *Social-skills training* — adopting appropriate body postures;

— adopting appropriate verbal expressions;

— negotiating skills.

5. Exploratory Role-Play:

— the start of a scene and the group improvise the ending;

— end of a scene and group improvise the start;

— a story created around a particular word e.g. a strike, an accident, etc.

6. Projective Scenarios:

— 'spectogram' of 'My Life';

— draw masks of two moods;

— finger paint 'a day in my life';

— life maps;

— life paths and journeys;

— family sculpts (can also be used in role-play)

7. **Developed Character Scenes**:

      — improvisations turned into short plays;

      — use of scripts — plays;

      — use of stories.

Footnotes

(i) Selecting sections 1 and 2 will depend on whether you are working with an appropriate group.

(ii) Usually 5. would come before 4. — however, most adolescent groups need prescribed role-play to make them feel secure before trying improvisation.

ROLE-PLAY EXPLORED IN GREATER DETAIL

Reasons given for participating in role-play:

When structuring opportunities for group-exploration of dramatic content, it is important to bear in mind the reasons why the group members are willing to participate in the creation of an enactment. Below are listed some of the most likely ones:

Reportage

Within the play, the young person can report on the occurence of certain events. These events are likely to be presented in an exaggerated, highly charged way. Nevertheless, they bear witness to real life events — mostly those which happened in the recent past.

Ventilation

Though similar to reportage, ventilation is above all an opportunity to discharge emotional content. Here the feelings are represented. The situation which gives rise to the emotions does not need to bear any resemblance to the original happening. What matters is the authenticity of bottled-up emotions, which are released during the play.

Reparation

The major focus of such plays is the attempt to make amends in fantasy. Amends are rarely directed towards another person, but mostly are geared towards the re-establishment of a positive self-image.

Exploration

An exploration of alternative forms of behaviour, mostly interactive, may be witnessed. The group member is trying to find out whether some other way of responding might have been more satisfactory.

Acceptance

There are many role-plays in which the young person attempts to come to grips with the unavoidable as well as with the acceptable. Oscillating between despondent surrender and gracious compromise, he/she tries to find solutions to conflicts which are not experienced as being crippling or stultifying. These plays are often 'given up on', condemned as boring, only to be returned to before too long.

Choice

This involves the selection of a path to follow — the exercise of will on the basis of a consideration of alternatives. It is hard for an adolescent to maintain a conscious awareness of options, to explore their various advantages and disadvantages, and then to make up his or her mind about the preferred choice. For the problem here is the one of the option not taken — it can be so much more attractive to continue to dwell within the realm of the imagined possible, rather than to face up to the limits and limitations of the *realised actual*. Role-plays around the issue of 'choice' therefore tend to involve characteristics of all the previous stages.

Even though we are reluctant to suggest that these 'reasons for participation' bear an absolute resemblance to the likely sequence of development within a group, our experience has taught us that many groups do in fact travel through an exploration of these various areas in the way we have outlined.

THE NEED FOR EXPLORATORY ROLE-PLAY STRUCTURES

Betty was 14 years old when she started work in the shoe trade. London in the 1930s was not an easy place for a child to be, let alone to start work. There was much to lose: and the gains . . .? She was aged about fifty when her thoughts took her back to those early beginnings of her working life. She said, 'I can hear my mother's voice saying, "Liven yourself up when you get there. Move about quick. Don't get falling asleep or they will soon kick you out. I won't have you coming home here telling me you have got the sack."' Her mother's advice had seen her through, and slowly and gradually she had learned that there were other ways of behaving, different ways of being. But the voice had been there — loud and clear.

Many of the children who enter a therapy group do not have access to a constructive, helpful inner voice which guides them initially through difficult situations. They do not know what to listen for or what to hold on to. They have no choice but to learn to develop 'a voice of their own', the inner voice of constructive parental authority. Then they will need to find a way of creating a dialogue between the internalised destructive parental voice, the created constructive parental one and their own stance. Role-play can help this exploratory process and can then make appropriate changes for the future.

THE GROUP PROCESS

Restlessness is the first indication of the longing for change. It is often accompanied by repeated returning to the embrace of sleep (boredom/absence). However, when accepted as an expression of a serious attempt at making progress, it is gradually and slowly transformed into the early forms of experimentation with structure — structure which can only be sustained for a few minutes at any one time.

Thus we are likely to witness the following process of involvement:

- apparent absenteeism — keeping the eyes closed, adopting sleeping postures;
- expressed absenteeism — 'this is boring'; 'what time is it?'
- a struggle to stay absent — rejection of suggestions — more explicit sleeping postures — the first walk outs;
- chaos — throwing of objects, running round, shouting of four-letter words;
- more apparent absenteeism, alternating with expressed absenteeism;
- a struggle to remain absent, accompanied by struggle to awaken — more throwing of objects, once in a while leading to brief moments of interaction with objects/others;

- an intensification of conflict over absenteeism: first ver-
balisation of what's going on — 'Come on man, want to do
something', versus 'This is f*** boring!'
- more walk-outs, more sleeping postures and some participants who say: 'Okay, what shall we do then?'
- engagement in exploration — often only sustained for a few
minutes — return to an earlier process — return to engagement, etc.
- ultimate disengagement resembling the earlier struggle to
remain absent — frequent verbal disowning of interest in
engagement;
- return to 'apparent absenteeism' enables ending and
departure.

Whenever we are faced with a group or an individual whose
response to a suggestion is one of dismissive rejection, we need to
ask ourselves whether it is possible to respond to more regressed
needs, which are not presented, but which become manifest in the
pattern of rejected suggestions. In the meantime we will need to
maintain our awareness that a deprived person often harbours a
greedy person — one who knows no boundaries — and that we will
have to trust our intuition, knowledge and experience when we are
faced with the dilemma of permitting regressive forms of behaviour
whilst encouraging gradual development. In the course of time we
will learn to trust that following a period of successful nourishment
of early needs, and a sufficiently long period of rest; i.e. a stage
when nothing much seems to happen in relation to individual/group
development. The young person him/herself will indicate his/her
readiness for further exploration.

Without this trust, our response to the regressed needs is likely
to be permeated by the very same fear and apprehension which
contributed to the present difficulties. The young person deserves
our faith and above all, can demand that we shall take responsibility
for the implementation of boundaries which will safeguard the
required therapeutic space.

What happens in the course of time

The process of involvement develops so that the earlier stages take
up less time during a session. The engagement in exploration can be
sustained longer, and the regression to earlier forms of behaviour,

during this phase is less intense and above all less committed. The need to disown the involvement in exploration diminishes gradually and is replaced by a growing awareness that the adolescent is willing to allow something good to be generated from within. The young person can permit him/herself to have a reasonable or good time in the presence of an adult who is facilitating the experience. For even though he/she is often only too willing to say that it has been a 'brilliant' time, that description usually refers to a time when carers have been absent. A young person in trouble tends to identify miserable times with the presence of a so-called 'caring' adult. It is the transformation of this experience through the conscious use of a relationship, which characterises the therapeutic process.

Towards the ending phase, the participants in a therapeutic group are capable of initiating and sustaining their own interest in their work, and have grown to value their own contributions and those of others. In the final stages of the work, we are likely to witness a return to the problems and behaviours of the beginning, and all seems to have been in vain.

The journey towards completion will guide the members through the dangers and pitfalls of this tempting conclusion and the gains of the middle period will ultimately enable the group to reach an end, with a new sense of achievement and an awareness of the process they have been through. The group will have moved through manifest trouble, via boredom, chaos, the use of boredom and chaos in structure, and the free use of the possibilities created by structure, into experimentation and the exercise of choice. The dramatherapeutic journey provides both the structure and process to enable young people to complete at least part of this journey.

The girls had spent two days developing a theme about India — dancing — wearing saris — dramatising a famine riot — Experimenting with new 'outer roles', and risking the expression of inner turmoil. They were hungry in so many ways. It was curious that after the girls had been told they must still go to bed at the usual time — 7.30, 'rules were rules' our visiting staff became very regressed and had a midnight feast of food stolen from the kitchen!

> S.J. (Notes from work in a Young Person's Prison.)

I reminded the kids that I would be leaving in a few weeks time. Deirdre said, 'Take me to England will you. Please, take me back with you.' Frank looked at me and said, 'You traitor.' And the other Frank asked, 'Please take a picture of me. And remember me.' Mark looked up saying, 'Are you really leaving?' When I said that I would — my placement was only for 3 months he rushed out of the room, shouted, 'Damn', and slammed the door. I went after him and said, 'Come back and talk.' He came back, and we all did talk. It was very painful for all of us.

A.G. (Private notes on a short term placement in an adolescent drug-addiction treatment unit.)

REFERENCES

Shuttleworth, R. (1975) 'Psychodrama with Disturbed Adolescents'. In S. Jennings (ed) *Creative Therapy*, Kemble Press, Banbury, Oxfordshire

Forge, A. (1970) 'Learning to See in New Guinea'. In Mayer (ed.) *Socialisation: the Approach from Social Anthropology*, ASA Monograph No. 8, Tavistock, London

McAdam, E.K. (1986) 'Cognitive Behaviour Therapy and its Application with Adolescents', *Journal of Adolescence*, vol 9, no. 1

Jennings. S. (ed.) (1983) *Creative Therapy*, Kemble Press, Banbury, Oxfordshire

———— (1985) 'Diagnostic Drama with Young Offenders'. International Seminar, Athens

———— (1986) 'The Inbetween and the Go-between; the triadic relationship of the adolescent', paper presented at the Anglo-Dutch Conference of A.P.S.A.

Hughes, L. & Wilson, J. (1986) 'Social Work on the Bridge'. In J. Steinberg (ed.) *The Adolescent Unit*, John Wiley, New York and Chichester

9

Dramatherapy with People with a Mental Handicap

Pat Brudenell

We adults destroy most of the intellectual and creative capacity of children by the things we do to them or make them do. We destroy this capacity above all by making them afraid — of not doing what other people want, of not pleasing, of making mistakes, of failing, of being wrong. Thus we make them afraid to gamble, afraid to experiment, afraid to try the difficult and the unknown.

(John Holt, 1968)

The field of mental handicap is a very complex area. Although many changes have taken place in recent years, there is still a tendency for practitioners to favour the more traditional methods of 'treatment' in preference for a more holistic approach to care. This has inevitably created a situation whereby the great majority of mentally handicapped people live in a world full of boundaries, often imposed upon them by the limitations of practitioners who are afraid to experiment and afraid to try the difficult and the unknown.

Whilst we must be realistic in terms of the boundaries and limitations placed upon us by our client groups and the environment in which we work, we must also be aware that our objectivity can work against us. Working with mentally handicapped people often leads practitioners to make assumptions about 'what people can do'. In lots of cases, techniques are kept out of reach, because practitioners are unable to go 'beyond the handicap'. Obviously, it is important to have a diagnosis, and background knowledge of what each 'condition' actually means. However, attaching added and unnecessary labels simply complicates issues further and puts greater distance between people working together. The labels can too easily stand in the way of effective programmes of treatment.

Mentally handicapped people are individual people with individual needs. Irrespective of the degree or type of handicap, their feelings are very real, and are in no way diminished by either their physical or their mental complications. This may sound obvious, but unless we can *believe* that we share common ground, then the role of the therapist will be a redundant one.

To enable a greater awareness of how techniques and processes can be applied most suitably and appropriately, I feel that it is important to arrive at some agreed terms of reference. My classification, however, is more concerned with levels of ability than the categorisation of handicaps. Obviously, there are a great many variables in any grouping, but as a basis I would like to suggest the following:

(1) Handicapped people living independently in the community, who are able to manage their own homes and affairs and to take on responsibilities like other members of the community. There are even greater numbers of handicapped people living in residential settings — no less independent — but hindered by a system which cannot accommodate their needs in an independent way.
(2) There are those who cannot live an independent life, but who nevertheless function well within a sheltered environment. Given the right encouragement and support, they are able to acquire the life and social skills necessary for independent living. But restrictions placed upon them by family, resources and services prevent them from practising and incorporating their new skills in normal day-to-day living.
(3) Profoundly handicapped people, children and adults, who not only have to cope with the severity of mental handicap, but often have to live with the added complications of physical handicaps.

Within all three categories it must be remembered that there are an indeterminate number who also have to live with the extra burden of a mental illness. In the majority of cases, the mental handicap is obvious whereas the mental illness is not (Brudenell, 1986). These then are my terms of reference.

LOOKING AT OURSELVES

Before we can move on to look at some of the methods that can be used, there are other issues that need to be clarified. It is never enough to have a compendium of games and armed with this have some sort of automatic magical solution to all problems. Working with handicapped clients is no more demanding than working with any other client group. Before we can begin, we must look within ourselves. How do we feel about handicap? More importantly, how do we feel about the handicap within ourselves?

There are some very emotive aspects involved which must be recognised and acknowledged before work can begin. I should like to spend some time discussing some of these issues, as I feel it is important for all practitioners working in this field to have an awareness of these processes.

The confrontation of handicap, stirs within us the feelings of our own handicap. The discomfort, the pain, the immobility, the withdrawal of the autistic child, brings us face-to-face with the despair inside ourselves. At times the overwhelming sense of helplessness in that child cries out for us to help them. And what can we do? The restrictions of the handicap are obvious. Movement may hinder what we want to do. Incorrect posture may cause further pain and distress. Anxiety levels from the child may block out vision of what could be done. These feelings are real. There is nothing new or strange about them. The reality of the situation is that the profoundness of the handicap renders the practitioner helpless. This experience is known as *introjection* when we internalise unconsciously aspects of others and experience them as part of ourselves. Similarly we can experience *projection* when we project on to our clients aspects of ourselves that are too painful to acknowledge. For example, we may view a client as aggressive, stubborn or bored, rather than recognise these qualities in ourselves. Also, just as clients will often transfer feelings they have experienced towards significant 'others' in their lives on to us (e.g. rejecting parent), we also may counter-transfer such feelings to our clients.

The intensity of these experiences of introjection, projection, transference and counter-transference can often confuse or overwhelm us, particularly if we do not have experience of psychotherapy. However, we must remember that they are part of a therapeutic relationship and, with regular professional supervision, will be understood and lead to insight in our work.

This situation is compounded further by the limiting expectations of our role. When so little is expected of handicapped people, then little is expected from those who care for them. We too need to be validated in our professional role, just as our clients need constant affirmation.

Other issues that I feel necessary to raise are primarily concerned with the attitudes of the practitioner. So many people assume that handicap is apparent — there is obvious lack of comprehension and deficit of emotional and intellectual functioning. The child or adult who has not yet acquired the skills to convey information, in what we blandly refer to as a 'normal' way, is not entirely to blame for the difficulties they may encounter.

Merely because we are professionals does not give us the right to presume that what we are doing is always right. Any non-responsive behaviour from our groups is not necessarily related to their 'inability' — it might well be related to our own.

We must not pursue our lines of 'treatment' with tunnel vision. The language that we use may be appropriate for other groups, but it may be completely foreign to handicapped groups. As much as we must be clear and concise in the messages we give out, equally, we must also be aware of the messages that are being conveyed to us. However, listening to the messages is one thing — being able to interpret them effectively is quite another, as Freidrich Emerson (1977) says, 'I recreate in a friend my own world — or take to me his new one — and we two look at one mirror from different sides.'

In my experience of working with mentally handicapped people of all ages and levels of ability there is one prevailing theme — that of facilitating the opportunities for broadening horizons and widening experiences. The dramatherapist has a very important role to play in this — but so do all the other disciplines involved. We can easily draw up lists to indicate 'who does what' or 'who *should* do what' — and map out plans of action for each discipline to pursue their respective lines of 'treatment'. But this will not go very far towards providing a holistic approach to care. Practitioners cannot work in isolation and having a multi-disciplinary approach is crucial if the service offered is going to be of any benefit.

Within any setting, and with any group, it is from the relationship which develops between carer and cared-for, that results will be forthcoming. If we can agree that establishing a therapeutic relationship is of primary importance, then we must attach the same importance to the relationships between practitioners. The value of forming a relationship must be a two-way process. If the practitioner cannot place any value on the person in their care or the work or the future, then how on earth will that person ever be able to put any value on those things for him/herself? Similarly, if practitioners are unable to understand and trust each other, then how can they ever work together?

Defining relationship as being a 'nearness', we must try to find ways of bringing about this 'nearness' — both for ourselves and for those in our care. The sharing of problems and difficulties with other workers and the ability to contribute our skills and experience to a multi-disciplinary team will be fruitful for us as well as for our clients. The handicapped person needs to feel and know that the practitioner is someone who can be trusted, who is safe and who provides security. Since this involves several people, we must be careful not to set up situations involving conflict. We must be mindful of the double sets of standards that are frequently set for handicapped people. Whichever work we find ourselves involved in, we must be on the lookout to ensure that we are not adding to the conflict that so many handicapped people suffer.

If we are teaching social skills, are we going to be able to look beyond our own area of work to ensure that our session is not going to be isolated? Are we adding to the confusion? Or are we making sure that what we do is in the context of daily living? Are we able to convey and transfer our skills to other members of the team? Good channels of communication are imperative, as without them our work will be isolated — and when that occurs we simply perpetuate the isolation of those in our care. So before we act, we need to think and reflect extensively.

To summarise, the key areas so far discussed have covered:

(1) limitations and boundaries;
(2) transference, counter-transference, introjection and projection;
(3) attitudes to the work;
(4) equal rights, access and communication;
(5) the multi-disciplinary approach and the importance of working together;
(6) relationships *vis-à-vis* isolation.

WHY DRAMATHERAPY?

Dramatherapy should never be seen as being *the* therapeutic medium for all handicapped groups. 'Give them dramatherapy and all problems will be resolved!' The handicapped person's needs are many and the dramatherapist must be aware of what other disciplines are doing, so that the programme will enhance all the areas in an integrated and cohesive way. Dramatherapy has the flexibility to encompass a vast area of therapeutic methods and can have relevance and application to all groups. Through the creative media, self-expression can be developed. Through training in social skills and life skills, independence and confidence can be achieved. Through role-play, gaming and improvisation, new and old encounters can be experienced and rehearsed, and lessons drawn. When the therapist can bring together the necessary skills to enhance the wellbeing and quality of life of the handicapped person, then the therapist has achieved a great deal. The reality of the situation is that the therapist cannot do all this on his/her own.

I used to think that 'some dramatherapy is better than none at all'. Although by and large I still stand by this, I have learned the hard way that the true value is only realised when it is integrated fully into the daily context of people's lives. Dramatherapy can be used as the vehicle to integrate all the necessary components. But standing on its own, in isolation of all the other parts, it easily becomes a stereotyped 'extra' that few people understand or are motivated to use.

THE GROUP

Open or closed groups

Open or closed? This is something that needs to be thought through very carefully. There are groups who benefit greatly from the security of having the same people to work with each session. Having the flexibility to bring in different people might be equally valuable once a group has reached a certain stage of maturity.

The context in which the session takes place often determines whether the group is open or closed. Fitting dramatherapy sessions into an overall programme may be difficult if other activities clash. The practitioners must decide what is going to be in the best interests of all parties concerned.

A great majority of mentally handicapped children and adults need lots of time to adjust to change of any kind. Keeping the membership of the group consistent will help to alleviate anxieties in the early stages. When the group have established their 'culture', then it will be relatively easy to accommodate new members. However, the boundaries need to be clearly defined so that everyone knows where they stand. The advantage of a 'closed' group is that the practitioner can work more on both developmental processes and group dynamics rather than just a variety of techniques.

How long?

The levels of concentration that can be achieved will determine the answer to this question. I believe that anything from 10 to 45 minutes is long enough, shorter than the sessions for most groups of non-handicapped people. If concentration levels are high, then the time limit could be extended. The time limits must be set to fit in with the needs of the group and not simply to suit the needs of the staff or timetable.

How many?

Eight to ten people is the average number for most groups to ensure effective learning. However, for very handicapped people or those with severe behaviour problems, four, or even two may be more appropriate. Practitioners need to consider the frequent absenteeism that can happen in hospitals and encourage other staff to understand the importance of the continuity of group membership.

Where?

Dramatherapy can take place anywhere! However, the best environment is one that is warm and welcoming, preferably with a wood or cork-tile floor (carpets are a hindrance), a place that affords the necessary privacy and allows for a certain amount of noise.

How often?

Handicapped people usually need more frequent and shorter sessions than non-handicapped people. In an experiment I conducted with a control group, it was interesting to note that remarkable progress was made when the time was increased by an extra session each week. This is not always practical, but given the choice, I would say that a session first thing each morning produces the best results.

The importance of planning

The aims and objectives of any therapeutic session will obviously be

189

centred around the needs of the group. For handicapped groups, there are definite criteria that I feel ought to be established.

(1) Enjoyment and personal growth: sessions need to be enjoyed rather than be viewed as an obligation. Although fun is to be encouraged, handicapped people as well as everyone else have the need to express their sadness and other feelings too.

(2) Time and pace: space for expression will prompt spontaneity and creativity. Rushing things will never allow the time that is needed for any of these things to occur. The practitioner must be aware of pace and timing — pace and timing of the members of the group rather than that of the leaders.

(3) Educational development: the learning process is one that is ongoing and needs to be encouraged throughout the work.

(4) The importance of movement: gaining an awareness of space around the body increases body awareness and self-image.

(5) Contact with others: the defensive mannerisms of many handicapped people tend to come across as being a rejection of others. Eye contact may be difficult and, for some, physical contact is frightening and impossible. The practitioner must have an awareness of this and endeavour to bridge some of the gaps.

A session that can incorporate all of these elements in a safe and trusting way, will provide the base and the boundaries for the handicapped child or adult to 'grow'.

Perhaps more importantly, we need to create the opportunity for handicapped people to have some time just for themselves. This aspect is frequently overlooked — the 'being together' rather than always placing the emphasis on 'being occupied'. Having a plan and a sense of direction is also very important, but this will be of little relevance if it does not take account of the needs of the group. It may be necessary to have a 'trial run', say for four weeks to see if the style of group is appropriate.

The structure of the sessions must provide familiarity and security and this can easily be accommodated in warm-up activities. With repetition, this will enable the ritual of the start to remain consistent and will soon develop into a familiar and safe pattern. 'Where the group is at' must always be taken into account. When the group have warmed up, they can be taken through the 'core' of the session. Cooling down towards the end of the session is as important as warming up, and plenty of time must be made available for this to take place.

There are no hard-and-fast rules as to 'what's best' for any of these sections. However, it is important to bear in mind that because a group is handicapped, then this should not lead us into thinking that many techniques are out of reach. The leader must always be on the lookout for ways of adapting and changing methods and techniques to suit the individual needs at the time. There are several books with a plethora of ideas and methods (see the reference section at the end of this chapter for a selection).

I have selected a few of my favourite tried-and-tested techniques — these are by no means exhaustive, but provide a basis for further 'invention' by both therapists and clients.

Warm-ups

Starting off with very simple 'name games' is an excellent introduction to a session. It facilitates movement, eye contact and use of speech and gives the practitioner time to assess the mood of the group. Many handicapped people do not know the names of their peers, but playing name games creates the opportunity for this to happen. The game can be played as follows. Make a circle, and ask for a volunteer to start the game. This person throws the ball to someone in the group whose name they do not know. The person catching the ball, says their own name out loud, and also in turn throws the ball to someone whose name they do not know. When the members of the group have become familiar with the names, move on to a slight adaptation of the same theme. Keep the circle, and ask a group member to throw a ball to another person in the group, this time saying the name of the person to whom they are throwing the ball. The person receiving the ball then throws it to someone else, again saying that person's name. Once underway, both of these games can lead easily into another game known as the 'handshaking game'. Using the circle, one person walks across saying the name of the person they are approaching. He or she shakes hands with that person and says 'Good Morning'. He or she then takes the place of the person who was approached and the contact then repeats the process by crossing the circle and shaking hands with someone else, and so on.

Depending on the ability levels of the group, the leader can start off another line of handshaking, thereby having two people crossing the circle at the same time. As the energy levels rise, another line, could start up and then another, until the entire group is busy shaking

191

hands and greeting each other. By this time the group will be active and moving, allowing the game to help them to approach others whom they may not have previously felt able to approach. This is ideal for groups that are slow or withdrawn. It is not over-demanding, but can raise energy levels and is relatively anxiety-free.

An alternative game is 'Piggy in the Middle'. With the group sitting on chairs in a circle, one person stands in the middle, and their chair is removed. The leader then calls out the names of two people who are sitting. They then have to swap chairs, 'Piggy in the Middle' trying to get to one of the empty chairs first. The person ending up without a chair is the next 'Piggy in the Middle'. If more than one person has the same name, this adds to the fun. Calling out 'all change', or 'all the girls', or 'all the boys' allows opportunities for instigating a move for everyone. Very often the 'posers' in the group will deliberately not find an empty chair — enjoying the attention of being in the middle. But this is a positive attitude. It may be that this is the only time that this person actually feels that they can hold the front stage, and so it is a way of letting this happen in a very structured way. For the more timid or withdrawn person, this might be a game that causes anxiety and raises stress levels. The practitioner must be aware of these signs and give the necessary encouragement and reassurance when appropriate.

With higher ability groups, it may be that something more active is needed. If energy levels are high at the outset of the session, the practitioner may feel that this energy ought to be channelled along more structured lines. If this is the case, then try 'One Minute' games:

One minute to touch all the walls, floor and ceiling.
One minute to crawl under other people's legs.
One minute to walk very quickly.
One minute to . . .

The excitement levels will be lowered, and the group will be calmer and more prepared for the work that follows.

'Tangles' and 'Rolling' can be great fun. Working in pairs, each couple find another pair. One pair 'tangle' themselves together, and the other pair have to try to pull them apart. Then they change over. With large groups, this can be developed into groups of four and eight. The noise levels *can* be over-powering. For 'Rolling', again in pairs, one person rolls their partner round the room. Coming across other partners, negotiation has to be used as a means of overcoming the obstacle. Some groups move gently out of the way, whilst others are quite aggressive in their manoeuvres!

Some cautionary advice for groupwork

Throughout the warm-ups, the practitioner will develop an awareness of how receptive group members are being to the group process. We must remember that many handicapped people have little experience of groupwork. Very often they have extensive experience of being in the same room as other people, or belonging to a club — but opportunities for self-expression and sharing are limited.

For the handicapped person who has spent a great deal of time working on a one-to-one basis with a therapist, being suddenly confronted with a group — where all members have equal access to the leader, can be a quite daunting, even frightening, experience. So we must be careful when introducing groupwork, that we allow sufficient space for people to adjust gradually.

We may be confronted with episodes of anti-social behaviour, screaming self-mutilating behaviour, aggressive outbursts, or simply a refusal to participate. Before we start jumping to conclusions, we must consider how natural such 'outbursts' are. It is unreasonable of us to expect too much too quickly. When a person has spent most of their life being on their own, co-operating with the occasional jig-saw or table puzzle or choosing to simply sit and stare out of the window, is it very surprising that we get some of the results we do?

When the therapist creates a safe environment, the group will come together. But the cohesion will only occur when the group itself feels ready and cannot be imposed by the therapist. We must never underestimate the importance of providing enough time and space for this to happen. Throughout the early stages of the programme, we must endeavour to plan the core of the session to take account of the varying needs. It will serve no purpose to programme very intimate techniques when individuals are not fully prepared for such close encounters. By all means introduce activities that will foster cohesion — but at the same time build in some activities which alllow for distance too.

The core

The 'Yes/No' game involves the group to work in pairs. Arrange the chairs in two rows so that half the group are in one line facing their partners in the opposite line and sitting together as close as possible, with the knees touching. Ask one line to be 'yes' and the other line to be 'no'. Ask each pair in turn to maintain eye contact, with one another and to have a conversation using the words 'yes' and 'no' only. When each pair have had their turn, repeat the game, swapping sides. Those who are normally very good at making their voices heard are often a little lost for words in this game. Similarly those who are shy and quiet seem to come to life with this activity and raise their voices to levels not previously heard. In effect, the practitioner is saying that it's OK to shout if that's what's felt to be needed. The reactions are always diverse and full of surprises.

A good follow-up to this is the 'numbers game'. Rearrange the chairs in a circle. Without using words, that is, using numbers only, ask each person to take it in turns to say something 'nice' to the person on their left. An example may be 'three hundred and fifty four' — said very quietly and softly. When everyone has received their 'nice' message, then repeat but this time round using 'nasty' messages. An example may be 'six thousand nine hundred and ninety nine' — spoken very harshly. In substituting numbers for words, a barrier is removed so that expression can then be made without causing any offence. This can then lead easily into a game called 'Whisper/Shout'. All the members of the group have to whisper something and then follow it up by shouting something. Again the reactions cannot be pre-judged and there are always surprises. For groups who have great difficulties in relating to their peers, it is necessary to incorporate some work that enables contact to be made but in a non-threatening way. The 'back-to-back' game is ideal. The group is divided into pairs, the members of the pair standing back-to-back without holding hands. Each person must try and say 'hello' to his/her partner, just using his/her back. Encourage the group to be completely non-verbal. If ability levels permit, this can be taken a few stages further:

> 'Pretend that this person has made you angry — and you want to tell them what you think of them — just with your back'.
> 'Pretend that you haven't seen this person for a long time, and they have asked you what you have been doing and you want to tell them — just with your back.'

'Pretend that you are very excited about going to the fair, and tell them about all the different rides — just with your back.'

When all the conversations are over, ask them to turn and face each other and to hold hands, and have eye contact. If the group are able to cope with the closeness and the eye contact, ask them to look at each other in such a way that their partner can see their friendship. Then ask them to try to pretend that they can feel this friendship and warmth coming down their arms and through their fingers into their partners' hands. Remind them to try and 'feel' their partner's friendship and warmth coming into their own hands. Ask them whether they can 'feel' it — everyone always says 'yes'! Finish with a cuddle. This is very easy for those partners who have paired up with a friend, but it is equally important that clients are given an opportunity to be able to work with unfamiliar faces. Careful management can bring this about.

We need to use games that help to increase awareness of self and peers, and 'Object games' are good examples. Arrange the group in a circle and ask for a volunteer. Then ask that person to take something from someone in the group. It could be anything, a tie, a shoe, a watch, a bracelet, a sweater. They then keep this object, return to their place in the circle and sit with the object on display in front of them. The person who has just 'lost' something, then takes something from someone else. This continues until all group members have 'lost' something, but have taken something from someone else. If the circle is kept small, this will reduce the anxiety levels as all group members will be able to see the object that they have lost. If the group is threatened by this type of game, then it will be much safer to play it in a circle sitting on the floor. Once the first part of the game has reached its conclusion, one of two options is open. The first is to start with the person who began the game and ask him or her to return their object to its rightful owner. That person then returns the object that they took, and so on.

The second option is to start with the person who was the last to lose something and ask him or her to return an object held by *someone else* to its rightful owner. The second option is much more difficult and warrants good levels of concentration to carry it out. But in the group situation, what very often happens is that the instruction in a way actually promotes improved levels of concentration. Wanting to 'get it right' is a great stimulator. A variation on this theme is the 'Shoe game'. All the members of the group remove their shoes and put them into a big pile in the middle of the circle.

195

Sitting around the heap of jumbled-up shoes, one person selects a matching pair and returns them to their rightful owner. That person then selects another pair and returns them to their owner, and so on, until all group members have their own shoes back. This game takes time and should not be rushed. With object games, the therapist is bringing into play a great many skills for the group to experiment and explore, including eye contact, hand/eye co-ordination, differentiating and matching like and unlike objects, and gross motor skills, trust, anticipation, 'loss', relief, awareness — the list is endless. The important point to note is that within the simplest of games lie the most complex activities.

Projective work provides tremendous scope for self-expression for mentally handicapped people of all ages. Using paint or clay as a therapeutic medium is not just strictly for the non-handicapped sector. Having used both, it is obvious to me that this is an extremely valuable tool for looking more closely at underlying conflicts and emotions which are often suppressed. When I first introduced this way of working to a small group of independent young adults, the idea was so very new for them that it did take some time for them to grasp the concepts. However, once they began to use the paint and the clay, and were able to relate what they were creating to what was happening in their lives, then their outlook on life began to change. The group very soon realised that what they had in front of them in their pots or their paintings was a very real statement about themselves. I was able to gain insight into areas that were previously well hidden and saw areas of conflict that I was previously unaware of. Having this information armed me with the extra pieces of the jig-saw that were necessary to be able to work more progressively. Having 15 minutes to play with the paint or clay, in a very free and unstructured way, was followed by each group member having the opportunity to comment on what they saw in each other's work. The comments were varied — what to one was a loaf of bread, to another was a submarine!

Group-sculpting and group-painting I introduced at a later stage, when the group were better able to cope with the closeness of their working relationship. This fostered the group process and helped individuals to look more closely at their involvement and interaction with each other.

The first group sculpt was very clustered. Lots of bits of clay were placed very close together, giving an almost claustrophobic look to the finished product. In discussion afterwards, they all claimed that the sculpt was a zoo. When we began to explore some of the reasons as to why this may have been, Lisa said, 'Well being here is like being in a Zoo isn't it?' The very real feelings they had about their environment had been projected into their sculpt.

Within a very short period of time, the group discussions that followed a painting session or a session with clay were being directed by the group members themselves. 'Yes we know it looks like a tree, but what is it saying about you?', they would ask of each other.

Using sounds should be part of every dramatherapist's package. I discuss this in detail in *The Other Side of Profound Handicap* (Brudenell, 1986), but for the purposes of this section, would like to put forward some case studies by way of suggestions for the reader. The following examples are all taken from my work with a special needs group in an adult training centre.

Jackie, aged 23, was unable to identify objects by name and became very confused when asked questions such as, 'Can you show me the table?' or 'Can you pass me the cup?' But when I used a cassette of sounds, she instantly recognised each object and rarely made a mistake.

I played her sounds of animals and she squealed with delight as she identified each one. 'That's a lion', 'that's two horses running', and so on.

For this young lady her stimulus was in *hearing* the objects, not seeing them.

Using sounds of various forms of transport, in conjunction with picture cards, I played the sound of an ocean liner. As the funnel noise echoed round the room, Alan jumped up and shouted, 'That's my dad blowing his nose!'

My careful planning had not given enough thought to the response that the group had made. Alan was right. It really did sound like someone blowing their nose. And what did nose-blowing have to do with pictures of boats? What indeed!

One group were reluctant to do anything together. With my co-therapist we had worked hard to introduce changes very slowly, but the group members much preferred to work on their own. We felt that the time was right to bring in 'a project'. The sounds of the animals had stimulated a lot of interest, so we decided to capitalise on this and take it a stage further. We acquired a wooden board to use as a base and painted it green and brown. With the group, we made a house out of card, and constructed a path with sand and gravel. We used left over bits of raffia to make a hay loft, and painted a small area of the board blue to provide the farm with a pond. What we had was a very empty farm, so we spent a few pounds on farm animals. Allowing time for the group to explore the plastic animals, people, fences, trees, etc. we gathered together the picture cards and played the tapes, creating the background noises of the animals. At first nothing happened. Eventually though, David picked up a horse. He looked to us for assurance that he could place it on the farm, and we nodded with excitement. David squashed the horse through the top window of the farm house, claiming that horses lived in horse houses!

Cows were placed in the pond — they could all swim of course and anyway it was a very hot day! The milkmaid milked sheep and the ducks sat on the roof of the house!

We played with the farm for weeks. And by allowing the group to develop and explore their very own project, I soon began to learn how flexible a farm can be!

My only regrets were that we waited as long as we did to introduce project work to the group. With hindsight, it was very clear that the farm was very instrumental in providing the farmework for the group process. The activities that followed were far more cohesive for all of us.

With higher ability groups, sounds can be used very successfully as a format for improvisation. It is important that we remember how imaginative, creative and inventive mentally handicapped people are. Our responsibilities lie in ensuring that there is space for such expression to emerge. Improvisation can create an escape, as well create space for expression — lying on a beach, playing in a park, creeping through the jungle, going to the moon, travelling on a train, shooting cowboys and Indians, shopping in the market — the list is endless. All these things can be tried without the help of sounds as back-up. But by taking in another medium, practitioners are widening the horizons even further — something we should be doing constantly.

Mirror work gives instant feed back. Working in pairs, one person starts off the movement, and the partner has to copy. This allows exploration of space around the body, and 'control' of another person. When confidence levels are low, body space is limited, but as confidence levels improve, you will discover that partners become very adventurous in how far they feel able to move out of their own body space.

Role-play is often thought to be something out of reach for the handicapped client. The attitudes of some practitioners leads them to actually believe that handicapped people have an inability to rationalise situations well, and an inability to understand the concepts involved, and therefore role-play is something that can only be used with more intellectual groups. Not so! Areas of emotional conflict for mentally handicapped people are the same for us all — and *intellect* is not an issue. Strangely enough, role-play is one of the techniques that I rarely plan to use, but one that I frequently employ. Mostly I use its application to look at problem-areas within relationships. Arguments and upsets that have occurred during the week can be given a clearer airing using role-play techniques. By asking someone to be in someone else's shoes provides the insight needed to be able to see a situation through the eyes of another person.

The difficulty in using role-play with handicapped groups is being able to hold the attention and concentration spans of the audience. It may be all very well for the two or three people involved, but what happens to the rest of the group? What happens to those whose concentration spans are not very wide? I find a useful way of involving everyone is to try to engineer the situation so that the entire group can have some part to play. By changing roles around and asking everyone to participate at some point, creates a much wider view of the situation. For the protagonist of course, the more views heard, seen and experienced, the more information there is to be gathered for discussion and resolution. Role-play must be used with extreme caution. It is a very powerful and emotive method and, if not handled with expertise and sensitivity, can lead to all sorts of problems. Practitioners unfamiliar with this way of working, and without training would do well to leave it alone.

Using 'Trust exercises' is probably one of the most difficult areas for the practitioner. It is one thing to develop trust from a relationship, but quite another to test it out using a trust exercise. I admit to not using these methods with any degree of frequency. This is not because I place little value on them, but more a question of whether they are appropriate to the needs of my particular groups. However, I do feel that they have an important part to play in the right circumstances. One such exercise is a trust circle. Ask group members to stand in a circle with their arms around each other, and ask for a volunteer to stand in the middle. With eyes closed, this person has to 'flop' on to the circle. Keeping their eyes closed, they are then gently moved around the circle, able to fall softly against the group members towards whose direction they are moved. To be able to do this, the group member must be able to trust the group implicitly and for many this is far too threatening. For those in the circle it is also very threatening. 'What will happen if I can't hold this person in the middle?' is a question that is frequently asked. A great deal of common sense and caution is needed on the part of the practitioner. A variation of this exercise is to ask the circle to close ranks tightly, and ask the volunteer to try and break through. This can be done from inside the circle trying to get out, or from outside trying to get in. It is interesting to see those who let them through and those who try their hardest to keep the person out!

'Blind walking' is one trust exercise that I *do* use with frequency. Again though, it must be remembered that it ought only to be used with caution. The group are divided into pairs. One member of the pair is blindfolded and takes the other for a walk around the room carefully guiding them around obstacles and other people, and pointing out objects that they may want to touch — windows, floor, tables, chairs and so on. As with most groups there will be those who will never allow themselves to take the risk of wearing a blindfold. Entrusting themselves into the care of someone else, no matter how well they may know them is far too threatening. Insisting on this being done will be harmful to the therapeutic process. The object of the exercise is to develop trust — not raise anxiety levels to degrees whereby all other work is impossible. If the group have physical difficulties, or if balance is problematic, then this will be one activity that will do more harm than good.

'Three wishes' is self-explanatory. With clients who are infrequently asked what they would like to do it can be invaluable in terms of the practitioner being able to see where group members are going — if in fact they are going anywhere. Some memorable wishes shared with me have been:

I wish I could blow up this building.

I wish I could be on my own.

I wish I didn't have to be watched all the time.

I wish I could see my family at Christmas.

I wish I got more money for my work.

We cannot ask people to do things we are not prepared to do

ourselves. When asking mentally handicapped people to share their wishes with us, we must be prepared to share ours with them. Telling fibs doesn't count — our wishes must be as real and honest as we want theirs to be.

'The Magic Shop' is hard work, but worth the perseverance! This rates very highly on my list of priorities. The greatest difficulty is having to work with subject areas that are not tangible. The idea of having a shop and shopkeeper is easily related to. But the goods on offer is a concept which can create confusion and needs to be handled very carefully. The following example is a lengthy one but illustrates the developmental process of the creativity in this method.

When the group had been together for some months, and relationships were developing along very positive lines, I introduced 'The Magic Box'. I asked two group members to help me carry it in, and placing it carefully in the centre of the group, took out a magic key, and unlocked the magic lid. I explained that the box was empty, but that I thought we might all like to put something into it — to keep for emergencies and times of needs.

We started off by talking about all the things that we have too much of. It took some time, but slowly the group involved themselves in very lively discussion about each other's qualities. John had too much giggling and could well do without that! Sarah had some lovely smiles, with quite a few to spare. Beverley had plenty of hugs and kisses, and Robin had lots of love. Those who felt able to part with something, took these magic objects out of their pockets and put them into the magic box. Before very long, the box was so full of good things, we could hardly close the lid!

We locked it, and carried the box to a safe place. We then discussed possible ways of using it. The group were full of ideas, but had not yet fully understood just *how* they would implement them. The following week, one of the girls was extremely upset because her mother had told her that their dog was so ill, it was going to be put down. Laura was distraught and quite inconsolable. Suddenly Nicky suggested that we get the box out, because there were lots of things inside it that would make Laura feel better. Two of the boys carried the box to the group, took the key from the magic peg, and carefully unlocked it. What followed was very moving and came about without any prompting from me. Various group members started rummaging around in the box looking for certain things. Robin was quite frantic — 'I know its in here somewhere 'cos I put it there myself', he said. Then gathering up handfuls of his 'love' he carefully carried it to Laura and ceremoniously handed it over. Laura accepted this gift, and sat holding it with both hands. She soon had to start looking for spare pockets, and eventually had to get her handbag from her locker, as she quickly ran out of space to put all the presents that the group were giving her — and all appropriate to her needs. Although this had not changed her situation, it certainly made her more able to cope with it.

Some weeks later, one of the group asked me where the magic box had come from, and I told them that I had brought it from the magic shop. This caused some interest and they wanted to know if I could arrange for them to visit the shop. I explained as best I could about the goods on sale; that money was never used — but an exchange system was in operation for all customers. If someone wanted something off the shelf, then they could only have their request if they were willing to give something of theirs away. If they had nothing to spare, then an alternative was to throw something away, (something undesirable) into the magic dustbin. To simplify matters, I was the shopkeeper, and opened the doors for business.

The first customer was David who desperately needed some happiness. He said he could see it on the shelf — but he had nothing worth exchanging — at least nothing that we would want. John shouted out that David was a real misery, so why didn't he throw some of that in the bin. Nobody else would want it! David thought about this then took the lid off the bin, and discarded his miserableness. He then jumped up and down on it and swore and shouted and slammed the lid down quickly, stating very clearly, 'so that it won't come back out and upset anyone else'. I then gave David his happiness, and putting it carefully in his inside jacket pocket, he went back to the group.

The magic shop is not always as successful. Customers want to buy ties, and are prepared to swap sweets, or used tissues. Abstracts are difficult to comprehend and the practitioner must be patient.

TV is a great innovator of activity. By using ideas from programmes such as 'Give Us a Clue', all manner of subject areas can be raised. This type of game is something that I do encourage as it is easily related to. The actions do not always go hand in hand with the clues, but for people who watch a lot of TV it is a pleasurable experience to re-enact something seen on the screen.

Group sculpts can not only provide a clear picture of what is happening in the group, but can also give insight into how individuals see their role in relation to their peer group. Russian Dolls, small figures, soft toys, in fact almost any small objects can be used to illustrate the group. Ask people to arrange the figures in such a way as to show the rest of the group 'who everyone is'. Working in pairs, or individually, ask the group to sculpt their own families, or their club, or their workroom, or their class. Allow plenty of time for discussion and explanations. Find out just who is who and ensure that the person moving the figures around has included themselves in the group. All these variations can lead into the 'Family Photograph'. Ask the group to decide who is going to be who in the family, and to arrange themselves for a family photograph to be taken. Each person has to decide their own role. This can be most enlightening!

If the group have been working together for some time, this can be taken one stage further, leading easily into the 'Hot Seat'. Place a chair in the middle of the room, and ask for a volunteer. This person then sits on the chair with their eyes closed. The rest of the group position themselves physically in relation to how they feel about the person in the 'Hot Seat'. In other words, if they like that person, they will probably stand, or kneel quite close to them. If they dislike that person, then they may decide to stand well away from them, with their back towards them. When all the group have positioned themselves, the person in the 'hot seat' opens their eyes and can see how they are seen by the group. This can be anxiety-provoking and should only be used with groups who have worked together for some time.

In trying to build up a group relationship, one of the ways to enhance this is to build the group literally — physically. By asking one person to start things off, ask them to lie on the floor on their back. The next person then lies down, with their head resting on the volunteers stomach. Gradually introduce all group members, so that each person is linked to another, by heads resting on stomachs. By 'Building a Raft', the group becomes physically connected. The options for taking this on to the next stage will be dependent on the abilities of the group. The group can then try and listen to the noises of the stomachs they are resting on, or the group can be led into an imaginary 'Guided Journey'. Building rafts can be done with very profoundly handicapped groups, providing practitioners are careful about posture and comfort. If lying down is not possible, then try building a train, with each person sitting behind the next. For groups in wheelchairs, this is ideal, as all trains need wheels!

Non-verbal techniques are essential. Mentally handicapped people spend a great deal of their time listening to and hearing staff speak. We must try and build into the session some time for being silent. 'Pass the Parcel' is a particular favourite. Introduce an object such as a bean bag, cushion or soft toy — something not too big and easily held. Give the instruction that if anyone wants to say anything they must be in possession of the 'parcel'. To be in possession of the parcel they have to clap their hands. If the group are sitting in a circle, quite close to each other, knowing that they cannot speak, this will encourage eye contact and expression through body language. As the initial silence takes over, the energy levels will rise and non-verbal communication will follow. There is no prescription for what happens next, as this will very much be determined by the group at the time.

Many of these drama games are used with other client groups. They have additional value for handicapped people in reinforcing developmental learning. They enable the handicapped person to acquire 'the parts towards the whole', i.e. it is usually necessary to focus on one area only.

Cooling down

Sometimes, more time has to be allocated for cooling down, than for the rest of the session put together. When the group departs, there are other things to do, other people to talk to, other places to go. The group must never be left 'in the air' — this will do more harm than good. So while practitioners may feel that all the excitement and the fun and the energy has been valuable and worthwhile — it will not be any of those things if it is suddenly cut short. Consistency and reinforcement need to be constant ongoing themes. Memory recall and concentration spans may be limiting. With this in mind, we must try at the end of every session to recap on the work done, so that individuals have the opportunity of recognising the relevance of the work accomplished and seeing it in the context of daily life.

Without doubt, Relaxation is at the top of the list. Mentally handicapped people can never have too much, especially with very new groups. Relaxation cannot be taught effectively unless people are aware of the importance of breathing, and this might take months. Teaching people to breathe correctly, and to use their lung power is essential. Mentally handicapped people are generally unaware of the fact that their lungs actually go round their backs!

At the beginning make sure that the group does not hyperventilate. Ask them to breathe in deeply, resting their hands on their rib cage at the back. Ask them to talk about what they can feel, and if anything is moving. Working in pairs they can check this out with each other. This will be better illustrated by some simple diagrams. A dummy used to demonstrate artificial respiration will be better still. This way, people will be able to see and hear the lungs filling with air, and watch the diaphragm move on inhalation.

Ask the group to lie on the floor on their backs and to tense and then relax various parts of the body. Be systematic and start at the toes and slowly work up towards the head. Constantly remind people about breathing from their stomachs, and to be aware of how different it feels to be tense and relaxed. When using relaxation in the *core* of a group it can lead into 'Guided Imagination'.

Ask the group to close their eyes and pretend that they are going on a journey. This can be anything the practitioner feels is appropriate — a boat trip, plane trip, cruise, trip to the moon, train ride, bus ride, wagon ride, and so on.
Other suggestions can be:

pretend you are lying on a deserted beach;

pretend you wake up to find that you are in space;

pretend that you have climbed to the top of a big mountain.

People can be taught to use this technique when on their own. Beverly informs me nearly every week of her latest adventures. At the end of stressful days when she goes to bed, she pretends she is back on her boat, or her train, and can for a short time, just get away from it all.

Through group discussion, the journeys will illustrate just where people are. The person who is depressed may travel alone, or choose not to travel at all. When asked what they could see from the window, they may say that it was very dark. When asked if they saw or heard any birds, animals or other people, they may say that there was nothing there. These are all things that we need to know. Mentally handicapped people are experts at telling us that they're OK, when very often the reverse is the case. *N.B.* These imaginative exercises should not develop into semi-hypnotic techniques — make sure everyone has 'returned' from the journey and is well grounded.

DRAMATHERAPY AND PROFOUND HANDICAP

Much of what has been discussed thus far cannot be applied to working with profoundly handicapped people, unless it is adapted. When I first began working with this group I was terrified about being able to find 'something to do'. The group all kept to their side of the contract, in that they were physically *there* — albeit not by choice. So I started by saying that I was going to be there too. This is the base — *time* — the most valuable and precious element of care that can be given — time just to be there.

Profoundly handicapped children and adults need to be able to meet people on their terms. They are not going to be able to form a relationship with someone if that person cannot afford any time to be with them. How can any work ever be done if there is no foundation of a relationship upon which to build? Lying on the floor just being close to someone, letting them explore your face and body — allowing them time to recognise your smile, your smell, your voice are all crucial.

Intellectual impairment may well limit the ability to recognise the practitioner easily and readily. So setting aside five or ten minutes will not be allowing enough time for this recognition phase to occur. The practitioner needs at least 25 minutes — an unhurried and non-stressful 25 minutes. This is the hardest part but the most important.

Think for a moment about what it must be like for a profoundly handicapped person to know that there is someone who can allocate this amount of time — not to see to basic needs — but just to be there. Surely the practitioner must be *doing* something? By being there the practitioner *is* doing something, making the statement 'I want to be here. I want to spend time with you. I enjoy my time with you. This time is valuable'. Once the recognition has been made then the next steps can be taken confidently — holding, rocking, comforting, smiling, whispering, talking, singing. It can be very frustrating to spend lots of time with someone and not get any reaction at all. Reaction is the innovator of what comes next. So without any feedback, the resources of the practitioner can easily become depleted. There is also a desperate tendency on the part of practitioners to be constantly *doing* something. It's a sort of rationale as to their ability to function, that is, if nothing is being done, then the practitioner is not working. But this is just not so and all handicapped people easily pick up these anxious feelings from the practitioner who needs constantly to be doing something. All that this will achieve is to transfer the anxiety, and raise the stress levels to such a degree that nothing will be done. Go with this feeling. Do nothing. Just be there. The sense of togetherness that will eventually emerge from this will automatically develop into something being done — telling stories — real and imaginary, using relaxation techniques using rhyming games to improve vocabulary, using massage — the list is endless. Throughout all this will grow the nearness that is necessary for the therapeutic process to work.

The profoundly handicapped person needs to have an environment that can embrace many things. The time for one-to-one work is as valuable as the time spent with the group. The time to be given for exploration and experiment in ways previously denied is also important as is the time for play and laughter. There needs to be time to introduce newness and risk and time for the unknown. I would never advocate that working with profoundly handicapped people is less adventurous or less demanding than working with any other group. What I would say is that the needs are very different and the complexities often much greater. The practitioner must be able to apply techniques appropriately and with compassionate objectivity. How this is best brought about is as individual as the people themselves.

A FINAL STATEMENT?

Dramatherapy is one of those mediums about which one can never make a final statement — whatever is said about it always provokes more thought and understanding. In this chapter my main focus has been on promoting the greater understanding of practitioners themselves and some attention has been paid to the philosophy behind the work and an understanding of dramatherapeutic processes. I hope to have redressed the balance of some of the approaches that often emphasise lots of activities for people to do. In this balance I want to acknowledge the bridges that can be built and sometimes crossed between therapists and their clients, however handicapped.

Dramatherapy will bring about neatness and tidiness, it will often bring powerful feelings to the surface in clients and workers alike. This is equally true for profoundly handicapped people as for other 'more able' groups. Appropriate training and then supervision is as essential in work with handicapped people as it is for other client groups. Lower ability levels should never dictate lower professional standards. The practitioners need the resources to be able to emphasise these, to share joy and pain — yet at the same time be able to maintain the distance that is necessary to retain an overview of the situation in its entirety and context.

Public and professional opinon is changing in its attitudes towards therapeutic intervention. It is up to us as practitioners that we strive irrespective of discipline towards providing a realistic therapeutic environment that will protect the dignity, self-esteem and value that these special members of our community have as their right. Choosing to work with dramatherapy is one way of ensuring that this right has the chance of becoming a reality.

REFERENCES AND FURTHER READING

Brudenell, P. (1986) The Other Side of Profound Handicap. Macmillan, London

Creber, P. (1972) Lost for Words. Penguin, London

Johnson, Abercrombie (1969) The Anatomy of Judgement. Pelican, London

Postman, N. & Weingartner, C. (1973) Teaching as a Subversive Activity. Penguin, London

Holt, J. (1968) How Children Fail. Pelican, London

——— (1970) How Children Learn. Pelican, London

Jennings, S. (1978) Remedial Drama. A & C Black, London

——— (1983) Creative Therapy. Kemble Press, Banbury, Oxfordshire

Knowles, F., Emerson, F. & Satir, V. American National Red Cross Adapted Aquatics. Doubleday, New York. (This book has a wealth of excellent reference/bibliography material listed)

Levete, G. (1982) No Handicap to Dance, Souvenir Press, London

Shaw, M.E. (1971; 1976) Group Dynamics, McGraw Hill Publishing Inc., New York

Many writers and practitioners have contributed to my thinking and their influence is apparent throughout this chapter.

10

Dramatherapy in a Psychiatric Day Centre

John Whitelock

In this chapter it is my intention to describe my experiences whilst working full-time as a dramatherapist in a day clinic in the National Health Service (NHS) in Britain.

THE SETTING

Conveniently located near the new town centre, the psychiatric clinic had previously been a medical hospital and still had a rather austere institutional aspect. It was a shabby 1930s building in need of repair with a long corridor linking a rather dingy hall, a comfortable if exposed lounge and several small, sparsely furnished rooms.

Its function had been changed ten years ago to serve the psychiatric needs of a catchment area of 250,000 people consisting of residents of a new town in Hampshire and the surrounding villages. Seventy people were registered at the clinic but the actual numbers fluctuated between ten and thirty. The dominant tone established by the nursing staff was both benign and authoritarian, it was regarded as a golden past by some of the more dependent patients. Without a clearly evolved or articulated philosophy, the centre became an intersection for some of the changes affecting the NHS, particularly concerning attitudes to community care. Thus pressure on the acute-admissions ward in the local psychiatric hospital resulted in a sudden influx of rather fragile patients who had barely recovered from severe psychotic breakdowns.

Among the staff there was no clearly defined leadership. The staff included administrators, cleaners, a consultant in charge aided by a registrar, a social worker, a charge nurse, two psychiatric nurses, two nursing assistants, an occupational therapist and a part-time art therapist. Attitudes towards the prevalent groups — recreational and therapeutic — were profoundly ambivalent: a mixture of fear and acknowledged necessity. There was only a limited familiarity with psychodynamic approaches.

The patients were very varied, often victims of 'new-town isolation', unemployment and cultural upheaval and showing signs of depressed anxiety and phobias, or suffering because of loss through bereavement or because of marital crisis. Patients suffering from personality disorders were discouraged from attending but often gained admission because of ambiguity with their diagnosis. A group of elderly people attended partly through the absence of alternative facilities.

I was assuming the role of full-time dramatherapist after a lengthy period in teaching in which I had found educational drama to be a reliable source of excited involvement and highly motivated learning with a wide range of application. This in turn had been inspired by experiences in the sixties witnessing experimental workshops and productions by such people as Peter Brook and Joseph Chaikin and those involved with the Living Theatre. One had a powerful impression of the transformative possibilities of theatre as audiences were galvanised in heightened bodily states and quickened into asking fundamental questions about themselves and society.

My part-time two-year training course had furnished me with a wide range of dramatherapy techniques with an emphasis on gestalt theory. I had also been encouraged to further my knowledge of group dynamics and therapeutic process. In particular three books by Yalom (1975, 1980, 1983) influenced me greatly by increasing my self-confidence and my repertoire of tasks and techniques when leading verbal- and activity-based groups. Finally, though I rarely brought material from work into my own personal therapy, I found it considerably enhanced my understanding of quite complex states of mind and encouraged me to use my own feelings when leading groups as a means of comprehending what was transpiring.

I was appointed by the occupational therapy department with which I retained close links and much support, in spite of its location in the psychiatric hospital a few miles away and I had been briefed to 'get things going where possible'. This in fact was facilitated by the gradual departure of some of the long-serving members of staff and the arrival of new nurses keen to get group experience. The resultant state of flux made it possible for me to establish dramatherapy as a respected and valued treatment modality catering for the needs of a varied and shifting community.

ESTABLISHING ONESELF

I share my office with the resident occupational therapist who is a member of the same department. It is connected to the staff room by a door. Sometimes this is closed when sessions are ponderously constructed, evaluated and noted either by myself or in conjunction with the co-leaders. More often it is open as I join the staff to review the progress of individual clients, anticipate the pattern of the day, chatter and drink coffee. In a glass-fronted cupboard are my tapes, death masks, body oil, finger paints and softwear. This is flanked by a steel filing cabinet containing the medical files. Working as a dramatherapist in a psychiatric day centre involves the elaboration of numerous roles if you assume it implies a full commitment to being a member of the interdisciplinary team. During one day I may be a group leader, teacher, counsellor to staff and clients, assessor of students or clients, key worker or member of a working party on initial assessment procedures of the policy management team, of the community meeting, of the occupational therapy department, of a sensitivity group within the department or of a small study/discussion group shared with a few other therapists.

Elaborating such a framework is the initial task of the dramatherapist in response to the specific and sometimes contradictory demands of the setting. In this respect, the diversity of approaches embraced by dramatherapy can be turned to full advantage by making a flexible response to the demands of a shifting heterogeneous community. This consists of clients of a fragile nature, sometimes elderly, prone to psychotic breakdown and in need of continuing support and also people suffering from neurotic disorders receiving short-term group treatments often for as little as three or four months. Varying amounts of supportive treatment are tempered by an awareness of dependency issues. Different approaches co-exist in an uneasy and even contradictory fashion, i.e. a diluted therapeutic community model encourages participation and self-direction whereas the regular administering of psychotic drugs tends to define the clients as passive recipients of treatment. At any one moment the programme reflects not only the balance within the client group but also the resources and availability of other staff members. As an adjunct of the NHS hospital system, which assigns low priority status to psychodynamic approaches, the centre employs nursing staff who are often diffident and ill-prepared for the leadership of groups. This means that staff training becomes a crucial part of my contribution to the centre.

211

Involvement in the staff team, the sharing of mutual tasks and the resultant blurring of boundaries carries its own risks. I have experienced two dangers. One consists of assuming a merely occupational status in face of demand. 'Could you *do* something with these five patients in the lounge? Everyone else seems to be in groups.' The other necessitates a realistic estimate of the limitations of a broadly-based training when marital therapy, family therapy or psychosexual counselling are required at different times without the provision of appropriately trained staff.

During the first weeks of working within the centre I am trying to understand how it works as a total system, locating the centres of power and decision, creating a kind of internal map. I try to understand the implications of geographical location exemplified in the contrasted urban/rural cultural expectations within the client group, e.g. is Alex's slow hesitant drawl either expressive of the slow pace of his background in a farming village or a symptom of his melancholy resignation because of his physical deformity and sense of isolation. I consider the pressures exerted by other professional groups, institutions and society at large.

I discover potential allies co-leaders and sources of support whilst anticipating potential areas of opposition, distrust or anxiety in the staff team. A registrar from Sri Lanka speaks warmly about healing ceremonies at home where locals treat the mentally disturbed with processions, chants and singing. A nursing assistant reveals an enthusiasm for dramatherapy gained after attending a short psychodrama course. I take into consideration the hierarchical distribution of power within the community and between the staff members, opportunities for democratic decision-making and their possible effects on the assumption of responsibility.

As a potential innovator, I try to follow suggestions made by Georgiades and Phillimore (1975) adopting the word 'client' for *all* those people with whom I have contact. I find that influence and credibility are gained by:

(a) effectiveness in the working role;
(b) avoiding the creation of specialist boundaries often caused by using obscure jargon;
(c) a sympathetic awareness of other professional practices;
(d) working *with* those supportive of change rather than fighting against opposition.

During this preliminary period I am frequently asked to define my practice by puzzled professionals and clients. I find it useful to have a succinct and comprehensive account to establish my professional framework and also my complementary role by reinforcing practices already established and demonstrating my familiarity with the needs of the client group. I produce a handout for that purpose, making a point of describing specific procedures whenever interest is aroused. With clients, I endeavour to relieve anxieties by describing typical sessions stressing both the pleasurable and helpful nature of the activity whilst relating practice to what is already familiar such as games, relaxation, charades etc. Usually many anxieties remain but are most effectively dispelled by word of mouth within the client group by participating members.

CHANGING THROUGH ACTING: THE MEDIUM IS THE MESSAGE

Confronting groups of highly complex individuals daily is a reminder that a part-time training course offers merely an apprenticeship. To operate effectively means combining intuitive flashes of perception, imagination and empathy with a conceptual framework concerning the mind of the individual and the group process. The latter is continually subject to refinement and revision as various models are internalised, offering a flexible basis for interpreting phenomena and making interventions, a continuous interplay between practice and theory. Further reading proves invaluable at times, particularly when facing unfamiliar problems such as cases of incest or anorexia. Membership of a small study group where papers and extracts are perused provides a fruitful basis for argument and discussion. Meeting other dramatherapists often leads to productive exchanges of resources and ideas (see Hobson, 1985). However, an over-dependence on one's theoretical orientation can easily close one off from the unique unprecedented quality of each client confronted. Some of the most explorative sessions seem to be a curious mixture of playfulness and anxiety in facing what is unknown. 'Change is the business of psychotherapy and therapeutic change must express itself in action, not knowing, intending or dreaming' (Yalom, 1980).

During a dramatherapy session, the business of getting people moving in the literal sense of the word is closely allied to the process of getting them to acknowledge that they are responsible for and

213

actively engaged in making their own lives. This most often takes place in the face of assumptions held by clients about being totally at the mercy of controlling such feelings as 'my depression', 'my nerves', or the extortionate demands of others, or family conflicts. The exhortation to act, i.e. do something at the beginning of a session combines the possibility of fulfilling an immediate practical objective such as finding a partner or making a button sculpt with an underlying resonant symbolic meaning. 'Assume responsibility and heal yourself'. This gives a different feel to the sessions. When Michael, with furrowed brow, much pausing and muttering to himself finally tilts and interlocks the backs of two chairs depicting the relationship with a close friend that precipitated his breakdown and overdose (this turned out to be his only attempt at self-disclosure possibly even increasing his sense of vulnerability), one is aware of the high level of arousal and anxiety, an increased sense of commitment in reaching towards a precision of statement.

Potentially there is a time for each client — when the reflective process culminates in decision-making concerning the world out there. By adopting action methods at the beginning of the treatment, the transition from relative passivity to appropriate change may be greatly facilitated. Action then, in the sense of a subjective owning or assumption and responsibility about one's life is expressed within the group in the form of an act, i.e. it is made public by being brought into relation with one or more persons. The presence of others in a cohesive group greatly strengthens the sense of choice, purposiveness and intentionality.

Eileen was an attractive nervous middle-aged woman prone to palpitations, panic attacks and anxiety, particularly at moments of conflict within the group; causing her at times to rush out of the room, to return a few minutes later. During an initial session speaking in a lightly pitched girlish voice, she engaged in a fraught dialogue between two 'part selves' of a top dog/underdog nature, utilising two chairs. A bullying disparaging voice turned out to be that of her husband. As a young girl, Eileen had conceived a child to a casual boy friend and then sought security in a loveless marriage to an older man already beleaguered by a sense of his own inadequacies and a will to dominate. In a subsequent series of role-plays, some female members of the group 'sided' with the subordinate 'helpless' part of Eileen, doubling with her and providing suitably assertive responses. In a lengthy complex process lasting nine months she transferred some earliest experiences of her own persecuting parents on to individuals and at times the whole group frequently relapsed into tense fearful states or wept helplessly. The sympathy and involvement of the group enabled her to bring about proceedings for a divorce whilst simultaneously seeking confirmation and support. The group veered between making constructive suggestions, expressing impatience and critically scrutinising their own marriages. Eileen left the group with only a short period of notice after suddenly finding some form of independence in employment as a sales assistant. She was still not completely freed from her anxiety attacks but much more capable of conceiving her future and that of her daughter with increased confidence and hope. During her period at the clinic, she had participated in the social-skills group including much assertion work, a drama group (where her delicate quality of movement evoked favourable comments), as well as the intensive group. I like to think that all three made some contribution to her relative improvement.

The term 'action' is not merely a convenient generalisation, drawing together a collection of disparate practices but takes on a more specific meaning when executed in a dramatic context. As Arendt (1958) points out, 'Drama is the only art whose sole subject is man in his relationship to others.' Dramatic action is self-revelatory, involving an extension beyond self by contacting and interaction with others. Through mimesis, the imitation of previous actions in the presence of others, we open up the possibility of reflection and making further sense of that experience. For Artaud (quoted by Goodman, 1968) the theatre is 'an action in the sense of a physical cause' comparable with psychoanalysis. 'I propose to bring back into the theatre, the elementary magical idea taken up by psychoanalysis which consists in effecting the patient's cure by making him assume the apparent and exterior attitudes.' Goodman points out 'the interesting moment is when one is *physiologically touched* and one's system is deranged and must reform to cope with the surprise.' It seems that this physiological touching and quickening of the whole sensibility lies at the heart of dramatherapy activity though most frequently occurring below the level of a metaphysical awakening. The potency of bodily feeling is a means of expanding the boundaries of self, from the safe and predictable into the threat and excitement of possibility.

This explorative dimension is illustrated by Simon Callow (1984) when describing the preparation of work as an actor:

In this way you celebrate the flexibility of human character. You demonstrate the almost limitless possibilities of personality freed

215

from circumstances and environment. We are who we are, you say because of upbringing and accident — BUT WE NEED NOT BE . . . Few people who are not performers are allowed or willing to vibrate more than a tiny permitted corner of themselves.

However, the existential possibilities of dramatherapy also imply that it can be a source of danger as well as growth. The idea that we are made up of a community of selves and not a fixed readily defined entity can be both an exhilarating discovery or an awesome burden. This necessitates the provision of safety and containment through ritual, group support and careful modulation of levels according to the specific needs of the client group.

I have to consider constraints in the setting that are going to shape my practice and other areas of compromise. A fairly rapid turnover affecting most of the clients encourages an urgency of approach, restrictions around the possibility of 'working through' problems and fears about impending discharge. Fluctuating levels of attendance mean that group size becomes less important, continuity more difficult to attain. At times one can be treating individuals in a group setting or else exploiting the curative potential of a full size group. At times, single sessions become a more useful operational unit. Group cohesion has to be built afresh each time with limited opportunities to rework them, refer back to previous sessions and build on insights.

WORKING WITH A MEDICAL MODEL

Medicine always creates illness as a social state. The recognised leader transmits to individuals the social possibilities for acting sick. Each culture has its own characteristic perception of disease and this its unique hygienic mask. Disease takes its features from the physician who casts the actors into one of the available roles.

(Illich, 1976)

In the day centre the medical model assumes a dualistic role. There is recognition of 'consumer rights', increased informality and information as to illness and treatment, client consultation over some policy decisions and encouragement of the assumption of responsibility. However there is also the sick role reinforced through medication, ritual and terminology. The medical staff will always be

216

dealing with symptoms when I'm encouraging some clients to convert symptoms into interpersonal problems as the first stage of their treatment. Side effects from medication sometimes result in apathy and failing concentration. Groups express confusion about the conflicting definitions of depression available. An anxious client finally experiences carthasis in a verbal group and is rediagnosed as being endogenously depressed. One months treatment of ECT is prescribed in the case meeting. However, the consultant is very supportive, particularly with regard to groups with a behavioural dimension such as social skills. It is important to be continually aware of their place within the whole clinic community. The group treatments are often interdependent and mutually interactive. There are many opportunities for leakage and displacement. Boundaries between groups are frequently challenged and require definition. For example, Julia weeps in an early-morning social-skills session because of the impending late-morning therapy group in which she anticipates confrontation. The support group is preoccupied with non-member Greta's disclosures about her suicidal impulses over lunch. In this respect, the centre has an inherently dramatic aspect, as an arena for performance and role-playing that vary in degrees of authenticity. Thus clients bring to the community their own internal monodramas in which past selves engage in interminable conflicts. Informal groups during the tea break or lunch can be as charged and revelatory as a closed group. An anguished Tom prepares a 'bloodied' wooden stave with which to confront the chaplain in the community meeting and deal, once and for all with his own internal condemning rector. Performed roles are presented for verification, are confirmed or discontinued. Staff and clients become both actors and audience. Some are irritated whilst others become distraught when Greta, having overdosed herself with Valium, staggers into the community meeting and throws herself across the coffee table. The lounge offers ample opportunity for the display of iconic body signs. Nora chooses a chair directly facing the corridor leading to the staff room in which to fold her body into a fetal position and stick her thumb into her mouth.

The physical surroundings also add to the drama of the centre. Health posters, extolling the virtues of bodily fitness, seem to imply comparable courses in mental hygienics. Cracks in the walls and ceilings tell their own stories about the relative status of those designated as the mentally ill.

217

MAKING A START

Finding appropriate rooms for groups can be a difficult task, taking into consideration the size of rooms related to the potential size of the groups and noting the possiblities for bodywork and expansive movement. Hard cold floors can be made tolerable by rolling out donated carpets, though these offer dangers of tripping and sliding, and large cavernous spaces can be reduced by redefining 'working' spaces with chairs, mats and tables. I consider objects in the room both as potential resonators producing sounds or alternatively, energetic activity as a means of getting warm. I contrive to obtain conditions of maximum privacy, though at times one can seem to be operating under seige conditions as doors, curtains and windows thrust open. I try to avoid intervening noise by locating myself away from corridors, car parks, access points or industrial-therapy units. The obliteration of crucial utterances wrung from subjects in agony of mind by a pounding typewriter or vacuum cleaner can be a devastating experience. Obtaining a suitable room is a form of institutional recognition of the status and nature of one's work. Once achieved, I do my utmost to secure its continuous use. The predictable sameness with all its slowly accumulating associations, helps to promote the capacity for risk-taking and confronting the unpredictable. The associated sense of routine has a potentially holding function crucially important for the more fragile clients just emerging from severe psychiatric cases. The timetable serves a comparable function lending shape and order to individual sessions in their relation to each other and the week as a whole. I list the name of each group, its staff and client members and its time and duration. Negotiating changes can never be a unilateral decision — there are ramifications for the whole treatment policy and all the staff are involved. Special consideration has to be given to the late arrival of a client dependent on transport. Friday's timetable must come to terms with the demands of the weekend for lonely or isolated members. When sessions lasting one hour provide the norm, I can introduce longer intensive groups by working into tea and dinner breaks, though this involves careful consultation and an established level of commitment from the client group, particularly when the afternoon tea break provides a suitable mediation point between the centre and the outside world. Balancing the programme involves not merely an arrangement of treatment but decisions about priorities in the whole treatment policy into which dramatherapy is incorporated.

I try to balance my personal timetable to allow time for all my various duties but also to provide breaks and less-demanding periods. I avoid juxtaposing intensive sessions after experiences of failing concentration and fatigue. The day seems packed, lunchtimes often attenuated to meet the demands of the day. I surprise myself discovering that one quarter of my time is spent on leading groups. The rest of the week is devoted to:

Preparation: writing notes, preparing aids, apparatus, materials, tapes and the room. Briefing, planning and discussion with co-leaders.

Evaluation: of sessions sharing observations and feelings regarding the group and individual performances, criticism and noting of points relevant to planning of further sessions.

Record-keeping: personal records of process. Entries in individual patient's files.

Supervision: issues regarding strategies, possible counter-transference relationships with other staff members.

Attending staff groups: Twice daily. Reports on sessions, sharing individual observations. Discussion regarding policy and planning. Analysis of community meetings including own roles.

Keyworker responsibilities: interviews, liasion work.

Assessment-meeting attendances: Anticipating admission. Case meetings.

Individual counselling: improptu and pre-arranged in terms of a contract.

Attendance of study groups with fellow therapists.

Duties connected with staff and student training.

Leadership of training session for other professionals in the School of Nursing and the main psychiatric hospital.

Negotiating for the leadership of fresh groups in an established setting requires both tact and determination. Suggestions usually consist of putting right possible omissions and deficiencies in the programme arrived at through discussion with the staff alongside fresh innovating approaches. Care is needed to avoid offending members of staff by duplicating or implicitly denigrating treatments already in practice. Too much innovation can seem like a criticism of past methods of treatment, raising anxieties about being super-seded or undermined. In particular, introducing intensive groups which do not operate on an established verbal model is to often engage with powerful defences in the staff team. This can result in statements about therapy 'opening cans of worms', and the elevation of 'practical' here-and-now 'brass tacks' approaches as though working intensively were simply an act of excavation. Some staff members restrict themselves to a special interest in the more fragile members in the fear they might be called upon to participate. Many of the fears can only be fully acknowledged in the confines of the staff group when sufficient trust has been established, preferably in the presence of an external supervisor. In leading intensive groups and daily confronting disturbing issues of death and sexuality, it is tempting to assume the heroic status of someone entering the lion's den. The remedy lies in keeping in touch with fears shared with members of staff concerning the precipitation of breakdown and suicide, loss of control, re-hospitalisation, or fears of reprimand by those in authority.

Having decided which groups are needed I set about creating a referral system by conferring with the entire staff. This proves to be a good test of how effective I have been in communicating the nature of the groups and selecting suitable criteria for group membership. It makes good use of the common pool of knowledge regarding the specific needs and present status of particular clients. Individual clients sometimes refer themselves when acquainted with the scope and objectives of the groups. Inappropriate referrals can be made in the early stages of establishing groups. This is caused by unfamiliarity with the demands of the groups or unavoidable ambiguities in the diagnosis of individual clients. Referrals are made during an initial assessment-meeting prior to admission, after a preliminary observation period lasting two weeks, during ongoing daily assessment or at the weekly case-meetings. Though I might take a special initiative to secure the inclusion of certain individuals, I still seek confirmation from other members of the team to avoid errors of judgement.

I find the distinction between the three models, Creative, Therapeutic and Learning (Jennings, 1983), not only useful as a rough guide when forming groups to meet specific needs, but also as a means of determining which approach to emphasise during individual sessions. All three models might well be in evidence, occurring simultaneously or at different points in time as in a classical psychodrama session where new behaviour is learned and rehearsed after a cathartic outpouring. A voice-work session involving *chaotic* speaking can produce a feeling of elation as well as increased confidence for hitherto diffident individuals. However, whether I choose to highlight the learning involved and provide opportunities to extend it into a life-management dimension will depend on my overriding aim. In this respect, the same technique, i.e. mirroring, assumes a different significance according to the particular objectives of the group, the subjective needs of individual members at that moment and its 'placing' through tone of voice and within the structure of the total plan by the leader.

Therefore it is frequently necessary to re-emphasise the particular boundaries of any one group in terms of what is appropriate. Boundaries can dissolve both productively and harmfully. Difficult moral decisions have to be made, taking into consideration the needs of the whole group and the availability of alternative treatments when faced with disruptive or distressed behaviour. When a grief-stricken young housewife breaks down in the course of a social-skills session, the group may temporarily shift its objectives, become therapeutic and self-disclosing on a deep level. Alternatively she may withdraw to receive individual counselling with a chosen member or be encouraged to find ways of coping so that the group may proceed.

I find it essential to set aside part of the day for preparing sessions in advance and producing a brief outline for instant reference during the session. I consider previous sessions when relevant, and my own objectives for the group, whilst acknowledging the specific needs of individual clients. Themes explored in previous sessions are likely to recur. The ending of the series must be anticipated some weeks prior to its completion. It is likely that my planned structures will be jettisoned with a more experienced therapy group providing its own impromptu points of departure. However, the provision of a firm clear supportive structure with many repetitive elements and a predictable outline characterises sessions involving the more fragile clients.

Paradoxically, the content of these sessions is rich in responsibility issues. If I am co-leading or involving student nurses in the sessions, I try to involve them in the preparatory stage. Leading, planning and evaluating alongside other members of staff proves to be a constant source of mutual learning with the pooling of different perspectives. Within the sessions, supervision and observation can be sustained more closely when sub-grouping. Sharing mutual difficulties heightens trust and levels of support. Shared roles however, necessitate careful planning to avoid confusion and to allow for flexibility. Though I find it easy to share skills, their extended practice by other members of staff sometimes arouses ambivalent feelings in myself. I found myself compensating by placing a greater valuation on those intensive techniques I had decided were best introduced by those with a trained therapeutic background.

Seeking out professional support that is familiar with drama-therapy methodology and simultaneously responsive to cne's own personal need can be very difficult in this kind of setting. It is essential that support in whatever form is not regarded as incidental but firmly built into the timetable particularly when intensive groups are involved. Confronting themes of death and decay, gross forms of sexuality and violence whilst remaining open and responsive can often be a disturbing experience. Counter-transference feelings such as irritation, fantasies of omnipotence and defensive stances need to be comprehended. Relationships and interactions with other staff members often require reflective attention if undesirable feelings are not to be displaced into the sessions. I have found supervision most useful in the presence of a trained therapist familiar with my approaches and not directly in authority over myself. The granting of such periods can seem like an acknowledgement of the importance of one's practice within an institution. In the absence of this, I have received supervisory help from co-leaders offering mutual support, individual members of the team not directly concerned with the group in question, the visiting consultant, the staff team and a closed support group in the occupational-therapy department.

In the need to establish dramatherapy as a treatment modality worthy of consideration alongside more established treatments or even capable of surpassing them in speed and efficacy, practitioners have helped to elaborate a mythology of powerful breakthrough perhaps reinforced by drama's preoccupation with sudden transformations and states of heightened feeling. However working in the same settting over a period of time, one finds periods of intense explorative activity are most often interspersed with periods of sluggish withdrawal, resistance, quiescence and statements of helplessness. The cycle of readmitted clients in the files over two or three years may be regarded both as evidence of the inadequacy of 'brief' treatments and a corroboration of more traditional ideas about the clients' need to rework continually areas of unresolved conflict before making significant improvement. Moreover, some of the positivist attitudes exemplified in the American contributors to encounter theory expounding 'natural' capacities for growth and self-development are not an adequate preparation when facing those clients who are deeply committed to self-destructive life scripts.

LEADING SOCIAL SKILLS GROUPS

The tone of the social-skills sessions has a brisk, businesslike, even challenging quality with opportunities for reasoned analysis, problem solving and purposive exercise emphasising relevance and immediacy. The group is open and continuous. There is a clearly-determined supportive structure whose content places a high premium on responsibility, decision-making and transferral of learning into the community and the lives of the individuals. Referrals are made from those least conflicted about making changes, no longer attached to the idea of symptoms and capable of understanding their interpersonal problems and motivated to practise new forms of behaviour.

The demands of the group necessitate a fairly high level of cohesion, a basis of trust and a readiness to give other members immediate helpful feedback about their behaviour. The ethos is positive and constructive. This culture has to be maintained in the face of new members entering and the departure of those already established in the group. In these groups, analytical thought and pre-planning anticipate action, experimentation and rehearsal in which role-play occupies a central position. In preliminary work, attitudes are emphasised rather than feelings. The clients' erroneous beliefs, values and sets of internalised rules are explored through sculpts, writing and photographs used as projective devices. The healing potential of the group is maximised by highlighting and encouraging remarks and gestures experienced as helpful. At its most effective, the group provides a background of encouragement and support sometimes taking the form of exhortations 'Go on! Tell her Joan! You can do it!' The sometimes daunting action has to be anticipated by a strong emphasis on personal responsibility and commitment to change. Soon after initiation into the group, members take control of the 'diagnosis' and evaluation of their own problem areas, sharing them with the rest of the group. Grids, questionairres, graphical forms of representation, and objective sheets, both long-term and immediate, are employed to this end. At times problems are identified and sorted out by labelling charts, mats or floor spaces as 'positions' from which members speak, explore and establish complementarity. Often it is necessary to minimise opportunities for action to reduce risks of getting in touch with feelings but also to avoid taking up too much time. Selections from this evaluative self-assessment work provide a basis for action and common-group tasks for my own planning. These might include to make friends, to control anger, or to acquire assertion skills. The feeding in of specific skills in the form of shared exercises must be timely and relevant rather than introducing them as components in a tidily sequential programme. Moreover, there is much value in capitalising on problems incidentally exposed in the progress of the session. Thus a client encountering difficulty when recalling his partner's self-disclosures can initiate an examination of the problems of attention and concentration.

However, the cognitive basis of much of this activity frequently engages with levels of feelings as clients confront their wishes, ambivalence, freedom to change and related assumptions about the fixity of self-definitions. Many transactions are replete with risk-taking existing at a considerable remove from any neat behavioural models. In spite of stringent referral procedures, one is frequently faced with non-investment in change, issues of secondary gain and commitment to self-destructive patterns. It is therefore necessary to maximise opportunities for choice and decision-making whilst carefully assessing the degree of threat experienced by individual clients and matching this with support and considered pacing. At times, the inevitability of choice has to be highlighted; the avoidance of decision-making has to be framed as a form of choosing. Whilst respecting the right of individuals to choose their future action, one is obliged to highlight the process of choosing or the flight into choicelessness when they occur against the background of the individual's stated objectives, simultaneously avoiding a judgemental tone. Sudden confrontation techniques can have positive or adverse outcomes depending on the current ego-strength of the client and the dimension of the task. Helping clients in this respect assumes at least a partial degree of insight into their past in which anxieties are identified before performing hitherto avoided behaviours. The emergence of this kind of issue during a social-skills session often necessitates referring the client to her closed therapy group or a temporary shifting of group boundaries.

Stating one's objective before a group, assumes the nature of a pledge, a commitment or a promise witnessed by other members. It can be useful for individuals to be held by promises to carry out *in vivo* homework tasks though it is often equally necessary to ensure a sympathetic counsel is given to difficulties or failures in completing a task whilst still retaining its value as a challenge. Taking a tough line however, by not immediately offering empathy but alternatively reminding clients of their own resources, can be effective at times.

WORKING WITH THE MORE FRAGILE CLIENTS

A slower more gentle pace characterises work in the closed low-level psychotherapy group whose members consist of the more fragile clients, possessing less ego-strength and bearing evidence of psychotic breakdown and long experiences of hospitalisation. For these clients, attendance at the centre guarantees survival in the community with relatively reduced expectations with regard to improvement and progress. Slowness of response, lowered self-esteem, impaired communication skills and passive adaptations are common. Changes made in the sessions tend to be limited in scope and short-lived. Too much or too little stimulation can be equally harmful. Bouts of active involvement may be followed by a spell of retraction and necessary withdrawal. For most of the time, the maintenance of well-being and the avoidance of re-hospitalisation are desirable aims.

In describing his Focus Group, Yalom (1983) emphasises the essentially supportive nature of the activity and suggests a structuring through the use of exercises followed up by opportunities for recalling and evaluating at the end of the session. I combine these suggestions with greater opportunities for being active to provide a constructive group experience. It is above all supportive with a relatively reduced emphasis on responsibility issues. The structure is firmly established, clear and predictable, involving much repetition of the same items from week to week. The leadership style is open and energetic whilst avoiding the dangers of taking responsibility and initiative away from the client group. Opportunities for time out i.e. in solo activity when group pressure is experienced, are built in. Clients are encouraged to have their special needs acknowledged i.e. reduced eye contact. The provision of the experience of success necessitates careful goal-setting and realistic expectations. Time is devoted to the sharing of feelings, though defences must be respected. Each session includes a warm-up establishing the group, structured exercises and an evaluative loop-back where items are recalled, listed and evaluated alongside individual performances. The use of action techniques allows for longer sessions, sometimes up to ninety minutes, without signs of fatigue. Much of the verbal material requires structuring i.e. through written or spoken sentence-completion exercises.

OPERATION AT DEEPER LEVELS

The intensive dramatherapy groups may exist in their own right or act as a supplement to existing verbal supportive groups from which clients, showing signs of blocked feelings or maintaining defences through excessive verbalising, are referred. The groups are closed, of fixed duration, usually consisting of twelve sessions. Sometimes material released in the intensive group may also be worked through in the support group, though this has disadvantages when clients begin to regard one group as primary to the neglect of the others.

These groups integrate action and interpretative modes by encouraging dramatic enactment of intra-psychic conflicts. Working with clients at this level means arousing other powerful feelings of distress and anger. Though there is no evidence that this in itself is therapeutic, the expression of intense feelings hitherto blocked leads to the discovery of wishes and the ability to will change, a crucial preliminary for translating insight into viable behaviour. The cathartic release of emotion may be accompanied by a restructuring of core-constructs and the birth of insight during the session or at any time in the future. The intervention of the therapist can help to further the process of clarification and reflection. For other members of the group, a sense of identification with the expression of painful or joyful feelings, is sufficient to propel them in turn to take comparable action. Sometimes the observer role may be sufficiently powerful in itself.

Some weeks after witnessing a powerful session dealing with a bereavement issue, Joan exhibited a ring which had belonged to a sister who had committed suicide sixteen years ago. She was now able to wear it for the first time after silently sharing another member's grief.

Leading these groups involves the frequent use of ritual opportunities for metaphoric expression enabling the release of unconscious material, a consciousness of levels which are shifted or maintained and a sense of pacing and timing. Ritual, which may be defined as a sequence of behaviours combining symbolic and concrete elements, is incorporated into sessions to perform a variety of functions. It has a binding function when group cohesion has not yet been established to provide a secure basis of shared trust, reducing uncertainty. It provides individual members opportunities for self-inclusion whilst simultaneously heightening awareness of the collective nature of the undertaking. This can be sensed in the choric effect introduced at the start of the session when group members sequentially complete a sentence beginning 'Today, I feel . . .' It can erode conventional boundaries to allow for a more relaxed and direct confrontation. New phases of activity may be introduced and the group moved on as the group circle is divided into pairs who share their perceptions of the preceding activity. Ritual is most effective when crystallising and offering structure for the expression of nascent feelings within the group. In this way a newly formed group begins to experience its curative potential whilst collectively rocking and cradling a distressed member. Finally, ritual helps to initiate the task and identity of the group at the beginning and end of each session, facilitating the delicate transition between its emotive and disquieting events and the practical demands of the world outside where buses must be caught or young children collected from the day-centre crèche. The slow dismantling of a human sculpt as each member is returned to his original place, the loosening of jointly clasped hands as the group steps back to break the circle, the rolling of the carpets in the hall all suggest the completion of one process and the beginning of something new.

In this respect ritual may be regarded as one means among others of encouraging the contribution of the right hemisphere of the brain to the solution of concrete problems and the elaboration of messages about the interface between conscious and unconscious. Dramatherapy exploits the power of concrete imagery utilised by medicine men and psychic healers for thousands of years by adopting holistic thinking and the power of the part not only to represent the whole but to restructure it (Watzlawitz, 1978). During my practice, I employ primary process in different ways:

(1) By the elaboration and extension of representational forms, verbal and non-verbal. This employs some form of metaphor, i.e. a way of thinking about one thing in terms of another, creating a new pattern of meaning by bringing together two hitherto unrelated parts. The emergent patterns may be extended, expanded or amplified giving immediacy and vitality to a self-perception. One client, Timothy, was helped during a session to break through a highly defensive posture by relating to a chair which 'stood for' and then actualised the denied needy part of himself. He was a tetchy and querulous man in his late thirties, proving inaccessible and frequently behaving aggressively and judgementally towards other group members who had made self-disclosures. I had led him into a guided fantasy after a partial relaxation, in which he had been asked to encounter his childhood self in a mirror. Now sitting up,

227

he appeared dazed and bewildered. After some preliminary talk, I encouraged him to address 'the child' represented by an adjacent chair. He stared fixedly at it, in a state of inner turmoil. At first he had nothing to say. The child just wouldn't understand him. He declined to say that to the child. When I tentatively suggested he might try being that child by sitting on the chair, he slowly and cautiously changed his position. At first he attempted to distance himself by retaining his observer role saying 'He is sitting there looking. People are talking about him. I'm just an observer.' Then nervously flexing his fingers and pleading in a high pitched voice 'I'm here — I'm here, speak to me.'

(2) By discourse and communication within a shared metaphoric framework between members of a group, e.g. when group members address each other whilst in the roles of animals.

(3) By lifting the unconscious into full consciousness through translation and interpretation of the expressive behaviour by the client or the therapist.

(4) Sullivan (quoted in Skynner, 1976) expresses the idea of 'selective inattention' whereby the unconscious is regarded more as the sum total of the experience (inner and outer) we habitually avoid perceiving, than as a box in the attic or basement in which secrets are locked away. Focusing on seemingly incidental behaviours, within the group the style and pattern of communication exemplified in barely audible sighs, ambiguous smiles, flexed limbs may prove to be fruitful points of departure.

In creative activity then, the pleasure of originating accompanies the individual's obsessive interest in coming to terms with his experience. Form and pattern bring order to incoherent energies. At times, the resulting product is then made the subject of further exploration, projection and identification, or even left to germinate as a kind of resolution in its own right. Working with the unconscious thought processes may take a variety of forms. Inhibition of secondary process (thoughts or consciousness) allowing for the emergence of hitherto repressed material is achieved by placing prohibition or restriction on verbal utterances when clients are permitted a one-word discourse, gestures and non-verbal means. This is particularly effective when adopting bodywork exercises as groups mingle or partners silently gaze into each other's eyes for a sustained period of time.

The exploration of metaphorical forms of representation involve engagement with whole-world views. These prove to be less controllable by conscious censoring faculties. By enacting or recreating through mixed media, shared symbols such as fruits fishes, or other animals may be related to current experiences of self. Thus a very shy and withdrawn young man was able to describe himself as 'a rotting apple hanging in the garden of Eden ignored by Adam and Eve'. Other metaphors offer life perspectives in the form of journeys, ladders, voyages and walls. Everyday metaphorical forms of expression may be acutalised and made more concrete. The remark made by a depressed young woman 'I've been covering things up' led to an action of 'uncovering' by slowly removing a blanket to reveal the charred corpse of her father who had recently been burned to death in a fire at a home for the elderly. Sculpting representations of the inner world may involve using other members of the group, chairs, toys and dolls, or any valuable objects, offering a beginning to individual and group articulation. Spatial relatonships between objects may stand in for conflicting attitudes and part selves. Robert was able to overcome his fears of disclosing his feelings of despair by leaving his 'hard' chair and weeping freely on a soft one.

Shifting levels when leading these groups demands paying attention to increasing or decreasing empathy involvement and identification or allowing for more distances, removal and reflectiveness. Thus it is possible to increase the potency of a group-painting by asking group members to adopt an appropriate body position close to a part of the painting offering a possible identification and then speak from within that role. Alternatively, a young woman who became increasingly pained and agitated whilst regarding her own sculpt in which members assumed aspects of herself, was able to find a more detached perspective by standing on the other side of the hall. Expressive media, such as painting and writing, seem to permit a greater sense of being in control to the client. Techniques either involving the direct use of the body as in gestalt work or the use of masks more often result in immediate work at a deep level.

CREATIVE DANCE GROUPS

The creative drama session often seems shaped by the demand that it compensates for the pain and stress experienced in the other groups by providing a holiday atmosphere of fun, escapism and release. This is usually articulated by members joining the group. It seems paradoxical then that the 'recreational' activity makes its own substantial contribution to the treatment programme. A hidden social-skills agenda may be discerned in the opportunities to loosen inhibitions in creative bodywork, dancing, exercises developing vocal expression, games demanding spontaneity and imaginative responses. Exploratory work furthers knowledge about the self. Engaging with a dramatic role implies becoming acquainted with one's depths. When reading an extract from John Arden's '*Live Like Pigs*' a contained and inhibited middle-aged woman surprises herself by letting rip in a part demanding coarse abandon and vulgarity. A spare and ambigious early Pinter dialogue inspires lively warring interpretations of its meaning as members reflect on relations between the sexes. Without prompting, the group members begin to question its truth and relevance to their own lives. Hidden resources emerge receiving acknowledgement from the group. A browbeaten housewife elicits admiring comments as she gracefully turns, creating arabesques in the air with a coloured tape. Activating the creative potential of all members of the group is the main aim of the group, making possible the experience of success in a co-operative venture. It is necessary to balance individual needs when leading the group ensuring that fluent and confident members do not become bored, encouraging the elderly, those with physical disabilities, or the shy client bravely attending a first session. I consider issues of timing, where to place the climax of the session, declimaxing after a 'high' moment, allowing for less-demanding activities, moments of repose and stillness, energy levels. My role shifts between intervening and stepping back, energising and letting things alone as I attend to the creative process deciding whether facilitation is necessary during the four phases of preparation, incubation, illumination and evaluation. Though it is highly unlikely that most members will continue dramatic activity after being discharged, the sessions present creativity as a powerful antidote to a sense of meaninglessness. As such, the sessions not only have their own reason for being but exemplify a deeply rewarding way of living not restricted to the artist.

Working in a NHS day centre convinces me that far from being a fringe or occupational activity, dramatherapy can make a crucial contribution to the treatment programme in spite of the compromises involved. Comparing this with more recent experiences in a social services day-centre organised as a therapeutic community with a rather different membership intake, suggests how different practice might have been. Though action techniques are in common usage, we still seem to be at the beginning of a process of integration with more traditional forms of therapy, let alone evolving ways of work-ing alongside the medical model without dreaming of revolutionary overthrow, making handwashing gestures or colluding in myths of peaceful co-existence. Much still remains to be done in evolving more stringent accounts of practice with specific client groups, methods of objective evaluation and furthering the theoretical assumptions underpinning our work.

I don't want to suggest that action methods offer some kind of magic solution. Getting people off their feet and at times helping them to get back there in the teeth of resistance and anxiety can often make for a rough and bumpy ride without necessarily experiencing a good outcome. A steady influx of re-admissions, the severity of some disabilities, the presence of an often inclement and stressful society guarantee a modest level of expectation concerning 'cures'.

As someone who has been at times critical of the plethora of skills and approaches that make up dramatherapy, and then called upon to be Jack of all trades, there are moments when I find its eclecticism a positive virtue. If sometimes my practice seemed to have been shaped by the setting and all its related constraints and demands, dramatherapy sessions were in turn sought out by people in the hope that they might be helped. In time, some of these were enabled to help themselves.

I can never quite get rid of the idea that my profession is kind of anachronism, something peripheral or frivolous. When facing some members of the medical team, I have to remind myself of the crucial role that creativity can play in the healing process in restoring a sense of wholeness.

The error of Freud and most psychologists is making pleasure a negative thing, progress towards a state of rest. This is only one half of pleasure, the least important half. Creative pleasure is like pain, an increase in tension. What does the psychologist make of contemplation and joy?

(W.H. Auden, 1977).

REFERENCES

Arendt, H. (1958) *The Human Condition*. University of Chicago Press
Callow, S. (1984) *On Being an Actor*. Penguin, London
Georgiades, N.J., Phillimore, L. (1975) 'The Myth of the Hero Innovator in Alternative Strategies for Organisational Change'. In Kiernan. C.

and Woodford, S.D. (eds) *Behavior Modification with the Severely Retarded*, Associated Scientific Publications, London

Goodman, P. (1968) 'Obsessed by Theatre'. In E. Bentley (ed.) *The Theory of the Modern Stage*, Pelican, London

Hobson, R.E. (1985) *Forms of Feeling*. Tavistock, London

Illich, I. (1976). (1976) *Limits to Medicine*. Penguin, London

Jennings, S. (1983) 'Models of Practice in Dramatherapy'. *Dramatherapy*, vol. 7, no. 1.

Skynner, R. (1976) *One Flesh: Separate Persons*. Constable, London

Watzlawitz, P. (1978) *The Language of Change*. Basic Books, New York

Yalom, I.D. (1980) *Existential Psychotherapy*. Basic Books, New York

—————— (1983) *Impatient Group Psychotherapy*. Basic Books, New York

—————— (1975) *The Theory and Practice of Group Psychotherapy*. Basic Books, New York

11

Dramatherapy with Elderly People

Dorothy Langley

INTRODUCTION

This chapter focuses on the application of dramatherapy with ageing people. Although the underlying principles are the same for any other dramatherapy group, there are special considerations that need to be given to groups of elderly people. I shall pay particular attention to Reality Orientation and Reminiscence Theatre which, although practised in their own right, are very appropriate, providing a wide repertoire of methods for dramatherapists to develop and make use of.

Creative work with elderly people is still in its infancy. In the past, various groups have included such work in their overall programme (e.g. the Sesame Kats Group and the Remedial Drama Group) and have taken specially designed programmes into old people's homes and large institutions for the chronically mentally ill. More recently, various groups have developed which specialise in the needs of elderly people such as the Devon Community Theatre who developed their own form of Reminiscence Theatre (Langley and Kershaw, 1982) and the more recent Age Exchange, who have developed their own repertoire of material, which is available to other groups. Similar initiatives have been started in the USA, for example, the Playback Theatre of Jonathon Fox. An initiative by Michaels (1981) called Geriadrama has established drama work in nursing homes and recreation centres for senior citizens and includes pantomine, movement, improvisation, games, poetry and music. Perlstein (1981) and Johnson (1985) both describe their approach to drama methodology with elderly populations. Their methods are discussed and their aims and goals described in Landy, (1986, pp. 195–200).

We have now reached a point where it is being increasingly recognised that elderly people do not only need nursing care but also need active processes to maintain bodily and mental faculties, as well as ways to reconcile problems and conflicts during the last stages of their lives (Hanley and Gilhooly, 1986). There is increasing attention being paid to creative arts in the hospice movement (Frampton, 1986) and it is more readily understood that the arts are important to people at all ages and not just in the younger more active stages of their lives.

THE AGEING PROCESS

The age of sixty onwards seems to be the time when people are considered to be elderly and most people retire from active work between the ages of sixty and seventy. However, chronological age does not necessarily have much bearing on the individual's needs and differences. The ageing process varies with individuals and is also influenced by cultural attitudes. Some societies focus their attention on the wisdom of older people and regard mature years as worthy of respect and even worship. Lewis (1976) has pointed out that we are one of the few societies where people may be socially dead before they are physically dead, where many people are not perceived as active contributing members of society. The ageing process can be exacerbated by sudden retirement, unexpected bereavement and a variety of physical and psychological disorders.

Social attitudes towards elderly people will influence the ways in which the staff who care for them expect to work and also the assumptions made about them by their relatives. In many cases, it is a relationship of increasing dependency, perjoratively referred to as the 'second childhood'. However, we need to recognise that this is a societal assumption rather than necessarily being the 'natural process of ageing'. Furthermore, we need to be able to distinguish 'normal' ageing processes from disability due to stress and physical or psychiatric illness.

PSYCHOLOGICAL AND PSYCHIATRIC DISORDERS

The most common psychiatric problems which occur with elderly people are:

(1) Long-term psychotic illness, often with the added complication of long hospitalisation.

(2) Depression of mood, either as an illness or as a response to loss.

(3) Organic brain disorders, the most common being dementias due to either generalised atrophy (Altzheimer's type) or blocked arteries in the brain often associated with strokes. The latter often leave a better-preserved personality but also specific defects in speech and movement. Here, failure of memory and thinking ability may be profound, but is not usually complete.

Brain damage due to infection or head injury, and the occasional pre-senile dementia may affect younger more able-bodied people. Special provision is needed to ensure that they get sufficient motivation for exercise appropriate to their physical condition.

PHYSICAL DISORDERS

The most common physical ailments connected with ageing are:

(1) Strokes.
(2) Arthritis.
(3) Heart/respiratory diseases.
(4) Post-fractured limbs.
(5) Cataracts leading to poor vision.

When physical illness is present, it is important to liaise with other professionals, particularly physiotherapists, as well as doctors, nurses and occupational therapists, so that dramatherapy becomes part of the total treatment in the same way that it is part of the psychiatric team-work.

DRAMATHERAPY AND PSYCHODRAMA

Dramatherapy and psychodrama are both therapeutic methods which incorporate the drama process. As pointed out by Davis (see chapter 5) they complement rather than conflict with each other. A fuller definition of dramatherapy is described in chapter 1, and for the present purpose I shall look at those areas of dramatherapy that are particularly appropriate for the treatment of elderly people.

There are three broad areas in which drama can be a therapeutic process — they are not definitive categories but give a broad area of focus.

(1) Enrichment of life: the intention is to improve the quality of life and engender a sense of play through creativity.
(2) Goal-specific learning: social skills, rehabilitation and assertiveness can all be stimulated through drama.
(3) Psychotherapy: psychodrama, sociodrama and dramatherapy are all ways in which neurotic conflicts may be resolved and resolutions concerning various endings can be achieved.

THE DRAMATHERAPIST

Usually a trained person will be leading dramatherapy groups though they may well encourage others with drama-based skills to assist. The dramatherapist must be sensitive to the overall therapeutic and activities programme for the elderly client group so that different sessions complement each other rather than polarise them.

The dramatherapist needs to be aware of the varying orientations of different professionals working in this field. New ideas can seem very threatening for more traditionally trained staff. He or she can also be a resource for training needs of the staff so that they may feel a part of the dramatherapy process.

However, the dramatherapist must be particularly aware of his or her own particular needs. Inevitably, working with elderly people will arouse feelings about one's own ageing process and the ambivalence with which we all face our approaching endings. Also there may be unresolved difficulties with the therapist's own elderly relatives which can cloud their perception of the dynamics of the group. Careful monitoring of one's own personal feelings and regular supervision will bring about helpful insight rather than 'get in the way' of helpful therapeutic endeavour.

DRAMATHERAPY APPLICATION

In this section I shall elaborate the broad headings outlined above and suggest various methods that are appropriate for different groups. However the practitioner will soon find that he or she will evolve an approach using these ideas as a stimulus. Always remember that elderly people themselves will also initiate creative ideas from their own lengthy experience which will encourage greater autonomy and self-esteem.

Enrichment of life

Although for many elderly people the increased leisure that comes about with retirement can be a time of increased creativity and activity, for others it can be a period of withdrawal and lonely boredom. Self-esteem can diminish and people can experience a distinct sense of uselessness. Creative drama can be a time for increased potential, for widening horizons, and for sustained enjoyment. Through creativity, people may learn to play again — to use their imagination. Care must be taken that people do not feel they are being asked to be childish — their dignity and self-respect must always be kept in mind.

Creative drama is also useful to counteract the unhelpful effects of institutionalisation. Particularly when there are group pressures towards conformity, it is important that the wishes and needs of the individual are always kept in mind.

Goal-specific learning

Many areas of maintaining social skills can be rehearsed effectively through the drama. With diminishing faculties, many elderly people readily slip into unnecessary dependency and social skills need to be reinforced. These may simply be greetings, initiating conversations or handling social situations in shops or restaurants.

Life transitions may also need practice — whether from the institution to the community or from the community to the institution. As Langley (1983) has pointed out, adapting to disability can itself be a means of personal growth. Therefore not only does the person need to work on the transition and change in itself, but also needs to have means of dealing with the accompanying feelings of loss.

Psychotherapy

Many elderly people need to come to terms with unresolved conflicts in their lives, sudden trauma, major changes and reconciliation of various endings. Traditionally it was considered that psychotherapeutic approaches were not appropriate for people past middle age. However, my own recent work in this area and that of others has shown that psychotherapeutic methods can be usefully applied when working with elderly groups. Psychodrama, sociodrama and dramatherapy can all be used judiciously.

Through the dramatic enactment, people may express thoughts and feelings that cannot be expressed in direct verbal ways (Langley & Langley, 1983). Unconscious and repressed material may emerge through the drama and allow for insight and growth. Fears of death and pain are important dimensions of any psychotherapeutic encounter, but are particularly focused in the final stages of people's lives.

Many elderly people also need to resolve issues concerning members of their own families — early death of children, sudden loss of spouses, feelings of being abandoned and the loss of their personal home. These issues are very powerful and the therapy must be developed with care.

Selection of groups

In day centres or wards especially, certain groups may already be in existence and the dramatherapist will be working with an established culture. Other groups may be formed for specific goals and care must be taken in selection, Diagnosis, chronological age and mental and physical disability can be unreliable as criteria for grouping elderly persons.

I find the most useful gauge is in terms of high and low dependency. Many people with low dependency are quite capable of dressing and feeding themselves and many retain their social skills, although certain people in the early stages of dementia will suffer some loss of memory and others may have the residual symptoms of functional psychiatric illness such as depression and schizophrenia. With low-dependency groups, all forms of dramatherapy can be appropriate, especially that facilitated in a rehabilitation programme which will be discussed under a heading of its own.

High-dependency groups make different demands on the therapist. The achievement of goals will not be spectacular and the illness itself may be progressive. Work is needed at a very basic level, concentration periods are short and there are limitations imposed by physical disability. High-dependency groups need to be smaller in number — for example three or four people with a therapist and helper are ideal.

In my early work I took groups of ten or twelve people. By the time I had managed to communicate with the last person, the first ones had fallen asleep! Movement, however, can be more rewarding in a larger group provided there are enough staff.

DRAMATHERAPY METHODS

Movement

It is a constant problem for elderly people to remain agile and get sufficient exercise. Balance is sometimes affected: people tend to become giddy and this, coupled with fear of falling, can result in a reluctance to move at all. Inactivity breeds inactivity and the motivation to move wanes. Movement for the joy of moving is unusual, so frequent stimulation is required. I find ball games are a very good introduction to movement. They can be played sitting in chairs and eventually the ball will be thrown wide, and someone has to get up to retrieve it. Any throw and catch game can result in considerable body movement. By varying the height of the ball the therapist can encourage movement from the waist, arms and shoulders. Care should be taken not to throw too hard (possibly use a foam rubber or woollen ball). Placing the ball on the floor and kicking it around in a circle enables the feet, ankles, legs and thighs to be exercised whilst remaining seated. Movement can also lead into other therapeutic methods. Use the 'name game' so that people have to name the person who is catching the ball. This helps memory training and social recognition.

For more mobile people, hoops can encourage both interaction and movement. Two people can work together with a hoop to find ways of using it, for example, they can step in and out of it, bowl it along the floor, or use it imaginatively as a mirror or a hole in the ground — which then extends into improvisation and role-play. Left to experiment, most people will draw on past experience of child-hood games. This leads to communication and interaction as people share memories.

Music is also useful to encourage movement. Fingers and feet start tapping when people hear music with a definite beat. Even chair-bound people can move the whole body. More active people can stand up and move to the music, for example they can hold hands and stand in a circle to give support and balance. This exercise also encourages eye contact and interaction. The most 'inactive' person can become active with the physical support of the circle. Ankle and calf muscles are exercised by standing and walking on tiptoe. If this leads to hands being above heads it will encourage deep breathing.

Very soon a group can use the patterns of swinging and raising the arms and legs to lead into an improvised dance. These are often more useful than 'set' dances. They can allow for particular disabilities. Streamers or scarves wafted in time to the music expands the movement and increases co-ordination. For less mobile people, place chairs opposite each other, interaction can be encouraged and 'arm dances' invented. Balloons are also great fun, requiring considerable effort to keep them airborne.

Singing is not only enjoyable but encourages deep breathing. However, singing while moving is added strain on the lungs and should be used with care. A good marching tune is irresistible and most useful to help co-ordination when people are learning to walk again after fractures or strokes. A variety of familiar and unfamiliar music can be used to stimulate movement and singing.

Relaxation can also be part of a movement session. Relaxing in a chair is more practical than lying on the floor, and the relaxation can then be carried into the movement. It is important to be aware of individual physical weakness when taking movement groups as it is possible to do harm from ignorance. If in doubt, consult the physiotherapist. However, movement is exceptionally useful for toning up the whole system as well as for encouraging creativity and interaction.

REALITY ORIENTATION

Reality Orientation (RO) was devised in the 1960s to combat the withdrawal, forgetfulness and disorientation associated with psychiatric illness, principally dementia (see Holden and Woods, 1982). It is designed to help people to become more aware of their surroundings and the people with whom they live and at the same time to locate themselves in the present which they so easily forget. There are two ways of using RO — formally and informally.

Formal

The group meets regularly in a formal session. The date, time and various events are noted and discussed, including current events (both local and distant). Notice boards displaying information about the weather, news and current affairs, together with photographs of local and personal interest, are used to encourage participation. One ward I know of displays photographs of staff and patients (e.g. on outings) and also a brief biography of newly arrived staff and patients enabling everyone to be kept up to date with news.

Informal

This involves constantly orientating people in real-life situations throughout the 24 hours. For example, if a patient gets up in the middle of the night he is greeted with, 'Mr Jones, it's not time to get up yet. It's three o'clock in the morning. See, it's still dark. You have five hours before breakfast.' Day time is mapped out by meal times and routine. All members of the staff contribute and it is their enthusiasm and application that brings results. Research has shown that when RO ceases, patients deteriorate to their former state, so it has to be part of the 'prosthetic environment'.

Time and place

With the drama group meeting at a regular time and place, the therapist can announce, 'It's five to ten. The group begins in five minutes in the recreation room. Let's get ready to move now so that we can start at ten o'clock.' (Note the deliberate repetition.) The end of the session can be marked by, 'It's 10.30 now and time to go into the sitting room for coffee. I'll see you all tomorrow at the same time, 10 o'clock, here in the recreation room.'

Sometimes confusion results in clients being unaware that they are in a hospital or home or day centre. Games can therefore help to focus on a place to reinforce its identity, for example:

(1) I spy with my little eye.
(2) How many colours are there in the curtains, decorations or wallpaper?
(3) How many red items can we see?

    (4) What differences are there between the decor in this place and that of the dining room?

    (5) What is the name of the town or village nearby?

Different areas of the room, ward or hospital, or, for low-dependency groups, the village itself, can be used to represent actual places and people can move between them. Also people can give partners directions to get to the dining room/hospital canteen/village post-office. Answers can then be checked against reality and can provide motivation for movement to other places. If the group are unlikely to go outside it is important to remind them that it still exists. Take the group to the window and ask:

    (1) What can the trees tell us about the seasons?

    (2) What is the weather like?

    (3) How many kinds of trees can we see?

    (4) How many people are there, and what are they doing or wearing?

    (5) Are there houses? Are the chimneys smoking?

Spatial awareness

It is important to use the same space regularly so that the clients know where to meet. Once a group is established some variety of space can then be introduced, moving, perhaps to the other end of the room or out of doors, or arranging the chairs differently. Awareness of the body space we require is important to mobility and social integration. Wheelchairs, walking aids, even sticks increase the amount of body space necessary. Games can be devised to increase spatial awareness, such as:

1. Whether a wheelchair can go through a particular space?

2. Making geometrical shapes from cardboard and guessing then checking which shape fits into the other.

3. Determining how much space there is from leg to walking stick or aid then checking it.

Spatial awareness is important to reinforce body image and co-ordination.

The senses

The use of the senses, failing or otherwise, should be encouraged at all times. The drama group provides an excellent focus for this work.

Smell

(1) Bring a box containing a variety of scented objects — fruit, vegetables, perfume, etc.
(2) Try to get people to recall smells from childhood.
(3) Use a box of outdoor scents — flowers, pine needles, wood shavings, fertilisers, etc.
(4) With smells related to cooking — bacon, fresh bread, etc. — aim to co-ordinate with a cooking session so that there is an end product to enjoy.

Sight

(1) Cut out pictures of flowers and arrange them on a background so that the flowers can be removed. The group or the individual can them put them back in the corresponding position.
(2) Show a large detailed picture. Whan can be seen in it?
(3) Draw a large picture in outline. Individuals can then colour different sections.

Sound

(1) List the sounds inside the room and then those outside.
(2) Make a tape recording of a variety of sounds for recognition.
(3) Play a 'sound effects' record for recognition.
(4) Listen to music.

Hearing is probably the most common failing sense. Some will hear more than others and some will be unable to discriminate meaning against a noisy background. Make sure that those with impaired hearing are not left out. Work in a quiet environment and encourage discussion of the disability and ways of compensating for it.

Taste

(1) Discuss taste — the things that are enjoyable to eat and drink, or those that are disliked.
(2) Bring in various items of food and ask people to taste them with their eyes closed. Can they be identified?

   (3) Cut a variety of fruits into pieces. Can those fruits with a stronger taste be identified?

   (4) Try the same with cheese. (Some medicines are incompatible with cheese — ask the ward staff.)

Combined with cooking sessions, the group can taste the mixes before and after baking!

Touch

   (1) Make a collage of materials that have a variety of textures. This could be a group project.

   (2) Bring in large pieces of fabric and create a landscape that can be walked over.

   (3) Use materials such as plasticine, dough, clay, metal and wood and spend time focusing on how they feel in the hand.

   (4) Provide a bag of objects and ask the group to identify them by touch without actually looking at them.

   (5) Wear a variety of colours and textures yourself and encourage contact and comment.

Any group project can emphasise tactile experiences.

Personal identity

Personal identity is very important and differences should be emphasised to promote awareness of individuality. An interest in personal clothing and appearance should always be encouraged. 'Dressing games' can be used, particularly with high dependency groups. Most hospital patients, even if disabled are encouraged to dress themselves. This can be a slow and difficult process, particularly if the patient is confused or has arthritic fingers. Some games to facilitate dressing are:

   (1) A team race to button a cardigan — one button per person.

   (2) Present a variety of underwear or outerwear and ask the group or individual to place it in the correct order as if they were dressing.

   (3) Select a cardigan, hat, coat and scarf. Each team (or individual) has to dress someone correctly.

   (4) 'Pass the hat' involves passing a hat round to music. When the music stops, the person wearing it describes the clothes

that match the hat. If a sun hat is used, summer clothes should be suggested; if a rain hat is used then a raincoat etc. should be suggested.

Always use personal names when addressing clients. Introduce yourself by name and ask for theirs. If a client is unable to tell you his/her name, make sure you find out from staff as soon as possible. The following suggestions are useful:

(1) 'Name games' of all kinds can be played, e.g. throwing a ball, spinning a platter or hoop.
(2) Ask the group what they notice about other members, e.g. May is wearing a new dress, Ivy has been to the hairdresser.
(3) Obtain photographs of people in the group from their home, on ward outings or at parties. Identify individuals or groups.
(4) Repeat with photographs of families and staff.
(5) Bring in pictures of people at work, including jobs held in the past by members of the group.
(6) Mime jobs and activities and ask people to guess them.

It has been noted (Miller, 1977) that results are better where interaction has occurred rather than the passive receipt of information. The more dramatic methods employed; i.e. active, the more likely we are to see motivation, interaction and change.

SOCIAL SKILLS

Living alone, playing a diminishing role, or suffering from physical and/or mental illness, are all conditions that contribute to withdrawal and sometimes unsociable behaviour. People who, perhaps for good reasons have been dependent on others in hospital, need help to reach the level of social adjustment required in a more normal setting or even to improve their quality of life in hospital. Social-skills groups are valuable to young and old alike, but must be conducted at the appropriate level.

Basically, social-skills groups are about communication, conversation, interaction, knowledge of appropriate behaviour and the confidence that is required to make contact with another human being. For many, the skills learned to date are not enough. Some uses of drama in social skills training are:

Eye contact

Throwing and catching a ball is a simple method to encourage this. It causes less anxiety than conscious eye contact. Building on this, one can add name games and identities are acknowledged. Follow this by more deliberate eye contact like changing places with someone or choosing a partner by eye contact alone. Allow time for discussion of how it feels to meet someone's eyes. When others admit to embarrassment, and people find they are not alone with their feelings, trust and group — identity begin to form. (Many of the suggestions under the heading 'movement' also lead to communication.)

Non-verbal communication can be explored through sculpting. Members of the group work in pairs and one of the pair may be used as if they were a piece of clay to depict an emotion. The partner guesses the emotion. Discussion about this exercise leads to talk of body communication.

Self-presentation

Clothing is less important in a social setting than it used to be. Nevertheless, there are rules of safety and acceptability to be encouraged. Going to the shops in carpet slippers can be dangerous as well as creating a bad impression. Visible shirt tails or unbuttoned shirts can be off-putting, so games about clothing can be introduced to help people be aware of their own appearances. Get people to do the following:

(1) Describe their favourite outfits.
(2) Describe outfits that would suit their partners.
(3) Describe an outfit for their partner to wear to a wedding or the seaside or to a ward social, etc.

This can lead the group into a discussion about appropriate clothing and how to wear it. At this stage, a visit to the beauty therapist or hairdresser can encourage further interest in appearance.

Smiling

Give each person a large mirror, and ensure that they have space and privacy. If necessary, have the group sitting in a circle facing out-wards, or in lines back-to-back. Ask them to do the following:

(1) First look at yourself in the mirror. Look at the lines in your face when you turn the corners of your mouth up and down. Does it affect just your mouth? What happens to your eyes?
(2) Try smiling — a little — a bit more — broadly.
(3) Find a smile that feels comfortable for you.
(4) Walk around the room and smile at everyone.

Greeting

Walk around the room and greet everyone in a different manner. Try to vary your words and style of address. Allow plenty of time to discuss how it feels to greet and be greeted with/without a smile. What were the most comfortable greetings in the group?

Opening the door

(1) Describe a door to the group. Then divide the group into pairs with one person behind the door and the other knocking on it. Let the role-play continue, varying the type of door (office, house, etc.) until people feel comfortable with what they are doing.
(2) Find a real door and practice entering and receiving in dif-ferent rooms and situations.
(3) Divide the group into two ranged on either side of the door, so that the role-play is enacted with an audience who can 'feed back'.

These are simple ideas to start training in social skills and can be developed into role-play depicting social situations. Some clients may not be able to progress much beyond these basics, others will use them as a base for more sophisticated work. It is important to work alongside occupational therapists and others who are develop-ing a range of role-behaviour.

REMINISCENCE

Alongside, and overlapping with RO, is the growing use of reminiscence as therapy. Contact through past interests was recognised as long ago as 1953 (Ginzberg). Reminiscence has also been seen as a 'positive coping strategy' (Lewis, 1971). Past memories are used to solve present problems and to adjust the present concept of self and establish social communication. (For more background see Langley G., 1982.)

Any group which remembers a particular event or era which they shared creates a bond. The therapist, who may not share those memories, but has researched the period, will become part of the present bonding and be included as if he or she had personal knowledge of the event. It has been noted (Bergman, 1984) that the bonding between an elderly patient and the therapist gives confidence to explore other situations (c.f. Bowlby's (1971) bonding between mother and infant). Thus the relationship formed during reminiscence groups can be used creatively in other ways.

Elderly people remember the distant past more easily than the immediate past. Their strivings as children and young people, the joys and sorrows of parenting, their part in war service, and the heyday of their development are more accessible to them than the memory of yesterday's visit from a relative. Start with the easily accessible memories that can lead to communication, interaction and sharing. Families often lose patience when events outside their experience are repeatedly related. When clients take part in reminiscence therapy their memories are valued and this raises their self-esteem. It also allows them to look at past events in a secure non-judgemental atmosphere. Some memories can be sad, as is realisation of loss of roles in the present situation. Displays of emotions are not uncommon, and the therapist should not be afraid of evoking such a response, but use the drama situation to deal with unfinished business from the past, or to face the present conflict. People have their own defences, and usually take care to avoid anything too painful to handle.

I remember a session on the First World War. I was surprised to find that the most communicative member of the group was absent. The following week, she called me aside to apologise for her absence. 'I lost my husband and four sons in war, and I could not face that in the group'. The group could be warned in advance of a potentially painful theme.

Like reality orientation, reminiscence can be used both in formal and informal groups. Clients who comment on the therapist's clothes can be encouraged to compare fashions and fabrics with those worn in the past. Shopping prices can be compared, so can the quality and quantity of goods available. Visits to the hospital shop or nearby village can stimulate memories. Dramatherapists have plenty of resources to engage in reminiscence therapy.

Audio-visual aids

Reminiscence therapy was developed in the UK by Kemp and his co-workers in the Architects' Department at the DHSS (Kemp, 1978). Audio-visual material was produced, and is available as a tape/slide presentation from Help the Aged. Using this as a starting point, the therapist can develop it through drama. Creating scrap books and slides of the locality can be an interesting group project, but they have their limitations. We have discovered that slides of old Exeter do not spark much interest from people who lived a few miles away in Tiverton for most of their lives. In the times most remembered by our clients, there was limited transport and people did not visit other villages and cities as easily as we do today. Several small, localised projects are more useful than a large one covering a wide area. Time and energy are required for research, but museums and county archivists are most helpful. It is a good plan to involve relatives to help with research and bring their own family pictures. When the project is completed, it may not be used again immediately, and should then be carefully preserved until the group is ready to take a second look at it. Individual slides and pictures can be used to stimulate role-play and improvisation. Show a slide of an old street or building and ask the group to:

(1) Recount personal memories of it.
(2) Create a story using the slide as a focus for the imagination.
(3) Imagine the people who lived in the street or worked in the building.
(4) Use the slide as a background to improvise a short scene of something that could have happened (or maybe did happen) there.

Music

Music is often associated with the good things in life — visits to the music hall, theatre, dance hall, the comradeship of military service — so that it is reinforced by the memory of actions. Most people enjoy a sing-song, so allow time afterwards for sharing memories. Music can also evoke painful times and buried memories. Be prepared for unexpected reactions.

In one movement session a lady demonstrated the charleston, and later led the group in the valeta. She had been a dancing instructress and was still fairly nimble. The movement session became a reminiscence one, and within it she was able to bring a past role into the present, actually creating a new one as she became temporary group-leader. Physically active clients may be able to dance, and an old time dance session can be arranged. I find that men can become very courteous in dance sessions — the old-time grace and good manners. As well as being a source of enjoyment, music is also another subject for discussion.

Costume and props

Things that can be handled, demonstrated or worn can add another dimension, for example:

(1) Bring in articles from a bygone era so that they can be passed around, demonstrated and discussed, e.g. a mangle.
(2) Bring in costume hats for people to try on. Be sure to have large mirrors available.
(3) Ask each member of the group to bring an object which holds memories for them that they can recount to the rest of the group.
(4) Invite the local theatre company to have a fashion parade of period costumes.

Hats are most useful because they are easy to put on. Too much clothing is too tedious and time-consuming for dressing-up. The group tends to lose interest if the pace is too slow. It is better to use a few experienced models than give complicated clothing to everyone. Importantly, it is not only women who find fashion interesting. One man told me his wife had worn a hat, similar to that of the model, when they were courting!

Radio and recording

(1) Tape stories round a theme to play to another group.
(2) Tape stories for the hospital radio.
(3) Approach the local radio for a reminiscence programme.
(4) Record the local primary school children singing hymns and singing songs that are part of certain games.

Community

Involve the local community whenever possible.

(1) Invite amateur dramatic groups to give a recital performance of a suitable play.
(2) If more appropriate, take the group to the theatre.
(3) Involve relations, local WI, Church groups etc. to help with research and supply pictures and objects.
(4) There is a natural affinity between the old and the young. Invite the local schools in to sing, play and perform.
(5) Involve the school or, if possible, a whole community like a village in a day of reminiscence. Everyone can contribute a picture, an object, song or poem, anything that is precious to them. The day could initiate lasting relationships with the community and help break down barriers between its different sections.

Reminiscence Theatre

We were fortunate in Devon to have a community theatre group who were interested in working with the elderly. They developed their own form of Reminiscence Theatre (Langley and Kershaw, 1982). They used techniques based on music-hall skills and worked in two ways:

(1) Selecting events or songs from a certain era and presenting them as an informal show, encouraging audience participation and subsequent discussion.
(2) Visiting a hospital ward or residential home, listening to stories and noting them. The company would then improvise scenes around suitable stories, returning to the group with a performance compiled from its own memories.

251

This would be followed by a further meeting a few days later to rein-force the points made in performance. The company developed con-siderable skill in 'freeze-framing' the action in order to step out of role and talk with the audience, returning to their roles to complete the rehearsed performance. Although the company disbanded through lack of funds, there is some record of their work (Langley and Corder, 1978). The actors need to be skilled in coping with interruptions and able to judge when a spontaneous comment from the audience can be built into the overall performance.

I would like to see spontaneous theatre (such as that used by the Playback Theatre in the USA) developed as another form of Reminiscence Theory with elderly people. The actors arrive prepared with basic props and costumes. They invite members of the audience to tell personal stories, which the company then improvise. In this way, members of the audience see their stories come instantly to life. It would require people with theatre skills who are prepared to risk instant improvisation. It has taken the interest of some actors in Devon, and I hope we will soon be in a position to give it a trial. It would be suitable for people living in the community such as senior citizens' clubs, as a means of stimulating interaction, as well as being of value in therapy.

Group Reminiscence Theatre

No theatre group was available when I first thought of the develop-ment of 'Playback Theatre' in reminiscence therapy, so I decided to try out a group performance myself, using my local senior citizens' club who agreed to be 'guinea pigs'. My intention was to produce rehearsed improvisations from their real life experiences. I intro-duced the concept of reminiscence to them first, and we demon-strated games we played as children. Later we told stories of events in our lives, but the group were reluctant to improvise them for per-formance. So we produced a topical improvised sketch, with songs, readings and simple dances drawn from our past experiences, if not directly reminiscence. In retrospect, I realise that the group did not believe that their memories were interesting enough to be enjoyed by others. The group have continued both to share memories and to produce another entertainment, and I hope one day to return to work on a reminiscence performance.

I have discussed reminiscence in a form mostly applicable to low-dependency groups. However, many of these ideas can be modified to suit high-dependency groups.

ROLE-PLAY

Old age is a time of changing roles. Work and family roles diminish. Some are replaced by new roles as people take up hobbies, become grandparents and great grandparents, but illness and disabilities tend to restrict roles rather than extend them. Responsibilities decrease with loss of role and can leave a feeling of impoverished life. People who live in institutions can succumb to the 'blanket' role of being a patient, relinquishing all independent decision-making and activity to the passivity of institutionalisation. Staff today are more aware of these dangers and take steps to encourage independence in as many forms as possible. As part of a team, the dramatherapist should encourage role-development, as well as keeping the memory of past roles alive. Role-play is a term frequently used in therapy as relating only to behaviour. In theatre, the concept of a role is to do with attitudes and feelings, and the behaviour springs from them. The background of theatre and drama is unique to dramatherapy, so it is important for the dramatherapist to make full use of these skills. These are our special contribution and other therapists are unlikely to use them to any marked extent.

(1) Role-play, as a means of preserving remembered roles, can be part of a reminiscence programme. Using audio-visual aids as a background, group members can play themselves in a familiar situation.

(2) It is useful to use fantasy role-play as a projective technique (Langley and Langley, 1983). Enactment of myths is a way of reaching archetypes and looking at ourselves 'once removed'. Sometimes the therapist can leave the client to make his or her own discoveries. At other times, some discussion and personalisation is appropriate. It would appear that some clients do not wish to work at a 'reality' level, but resolve the problem through the imagined role.

(3) Clients who face new roles may feel ill-equipped for them. Returning home after bereavement, moving to a residential home, living with relatives after years of independence, are some of the new roles we see frequently. Talking about the future may help, but it does not have the same impact as 'living' the future in the imagination. In a group setting, the experience can be reinforced by others who can share their experience, perhaps of coping with a similar situation. The same scene can be rehearsed several times, trying out different ways of managing it, so the

client has a choice. The role-play can be followed by trial visits to the new situation — perhaps an afternoon or weekend at home — then back to work in the drama group based on knowledge of the new situation. This builds up both familiarity and trust in the new role, which is halfway to achieving success.

(4) Role-play can be used in all forms of rehabilitation. Care must be taken to ensure that the rehabilitation goals are realistic.

PSYCHODRAMA

Bereavement frequently leaves unfinished business with the deceased. People who become depressed after the usual period of grieving may find psychodrama helpful. I have not held a group specifically for elderly people, but have had elderly members in a mixed group. Blatner (1973) describes 'act hunger', a situation where the protagonist has a need to relive a situation, handling it differently. I suggest there is also 'role hunger' when people realise there are roles they will never have in reality — rebellious teenager, spouse, parent and so on. Psychodrama gives an opportunity to encounter these roles in fantasy and come to terms with their unavailability.

I can also see the possibility of using psychodrama with groups of relatives. The feelings aroused by caring for an elderly mentally ill relation can be very intense. The difficulties in communication, and the reversal of roles as the child becomes the carer, can give rise to feelings of guilt, anger and remorse which are often repressed. Support-groups for relatives are becoming common and could include psychodrama to work on problems and feelings.

THEATRE

Taking part in a theatre production can be an intense experience of group cohesion and activity. There is so much value in the interaction and compromise of group creativity in itself (Langley, D.M., 1982). The main problem in productions with elderly people is remembering lines. I recommend either rehearsed improvisation or rehearsed play-reading. This releases people from a major anxiety so they can give full attention to the communication, both verbal and non-verbal.

It helps to play to an invited audience who are interested in being part of the experience than staying at a distance. Theatre should be approached with a positive representation of what we *can* do, and not be an apology for age or disability. Attention must be paid to details of production. Each section — acting, scene, props, etc. can become a project in itself, involving more people than those on stage. Some sections requiring special skills such as make-up and costume can involve people outside the group or even the institution. In one group, a lady of nearly 70 went on stage for the first time in her life. Another made props for the first time. Both were equally successful, gaining considerable pleasure and confidence from the experience. In the same production, an 80-year-old man, with experience of amateur theatre in the past, was delighted to find he could still hold the attention of an audience — something he thought his failing memory would never allow again.

When using scripts be realistic in your goals. Start with one-act plays or selected scenes from longer ones. If scripted performance is not appropriate, try a rehearsed improvisation.

Inevitably, a feeling of 'let down' follows a performance. It is important that the therapist recognises this, acknowledges it with the group, and helps them through the difficult period, otherwise the feeling may be projected into other situations, thus devaluing the therapeutic experience.

CONCLUSION

In this chapter, I have endeavoured to present an idea of the breadth as well as the depth of potential work with ageing populations. I have suggested some broad headings for dramatherapeutic work including movement, reality orientation, social skills, reminscence, role-play, psychodrama, and theatre. These ideas are in no way exhaustive. Thurman and Piggins (1982) give a plentiful account of methods with older adults, and many books on drama contain ideas that can be suitably adapted, such as Barker (1977), Levete (1982), and O'Neill (1982), to suggest but a few.

Dramatherapists must be aware of their own attitudes and feelings towards growing old as well as assumptions and sometimes pre-judices determined by society. Additionally, they must be conversant with the various physical and psychological disorders that affect elderly people in particular. Their work will be enhanced by being part of a multi-professional team and perhaps using their own skills as a resource for staff-training groups.

Dramatherapy cannot reverse the ageing process but can help us discover an enhanced vitality and creativity and can help maintain our imagination and mental faculties as well as assist us to face our ending with dignity and a sense of reconciliation.

REFERENCES

Barker, C. (1977) *Theatre Games*. Eyre Methuen, London

Bergman, C. (1984) Personal communication.

Blatner, H.A. (1973) *Acting In*. Springfield, New York

Bowlby, J. (1971) *Attachment*. Pelican, London

Frampton, J. (1986) *British Medical Journal*, forthcoming.

Ginzberg, R. (1953) 'Geriatric ward psychiatry; techniques in the psychological management of elderly psychotics. *American Journal of Psychiatry*, vol. 110, pp. 296–300

——— (1954) 'Attitude therapy on psychogeriatrics'. Conference Report, *Old Age in the Modern World*, pp. 457–63. E. & S. Livingstone, Edinburgh

Hanley, I. & Gilhooly, M. (1986) *Psychological Therapies for the Elderly*. Croom Helm, London

Holden, U.P. & Woods, R.T. (1982) *Reality Orientation*. Churchill Livingstone, Edinburgh and New York

Johnson, D. (1985) 'Expressive Group Psychotherapy with the Elderly: a Drama Therapy Approach'. *International Journal of Group Psychotherapy*, no. 35

Kemp, M. (1978) *Audiovisual Reminiscence Aids for Elderly People Including the Mentally Frail*. DHSS, London

Landy, R. (1986) *Drama Therapy Concepts and Practice*. Charles C. Thomas, Springfield, Illinois

Langley, D.M. (1982) 'Theatre in Therapy'. Conference paper, *Art and Dramatherapy*, College of Art and Design, St Albans

——— & Langley, G.E. (1983) *Dramatherapy and Psychiatry*. Croom Helm, London

Langley, G.E. (1982) *Quality of Life in Extended Care*. Royal College of Psychiatrists, London

——— (1978) 'Workshop on the Contribution of Reminiscence Therapy with the Elderly'. *Seminar Report*, Exe Vale Hospital, Exeter, Devon

——— & Kershaw, B. (1982) 'Reminiscence Theatre'. *Theatre Paper No. 6*, Dartington College, Devon

Levete, G. (1982) *No Handicap to Dance*. Souvenir Press, London

Lewis, C.N. (1971) 'Reminiscing and Self Concept in Old Age'. *Geront.*, vol. 262, pp. 240–3

Lewis, I. (1976) *Social Anthropology In Perspective*. Penguin, London

Michaels, E. (1981) 'Geriadrama', in Courtney and Schattner (eds), *Drama in Therapy*, vol 2, Drama Books, New York

Miller, E. (1977) 'The Management of Dementia: A Review of Some Possibilities'. *British Journal of Social Psychology*, vol. 16, pp. 77–83

O'Neill, C. & Lambert, A. (1982) *Drama Structures*. Hutchinson, London

Perlstein, S. (1981) *A Stage for Memory — Life History Plays by Older Adults* Teachers and Writers, New York

Thurman, A.H. & Piggins, C.A. (1982) *Drama Activities With Older Adults*. Haworth Press, New York

12

Dramatherapy in In-patient Psychiatric Settings

Ross Mitchell

> So I wish you first a
> Sense of theatre; only
> Those who love illusions
> And know it, will go far.
> W.H. Auden: *Many Happy Returns*

> But men must know that in this theatre of man's life,
> it is reserved only for God and Angels to be lookers on.
> Francis Bacon: *Advancement of Learning*

This final chapter examines the role and functions of the drama-therapist working in clinical psychiatric settings. Currently in Britain, there are few full-time dramatherapists working in the NHS, with some rather more part-time therapists. Other freelance therapists seek work wherever they can get it on a sessional basis, while other professionals — occupational therapists, psychologists, psychotherapists — who have undertaken training through the 2-year post-graduate dramatherapy courses, may use dramatherapy techniques and processes, but in the context of their own professional work.

In practical terms therefore, for most dramatherapists hoping to work in psychiatry, it will mean seeking employment in the larger psychiatric institutions (the remaining mental hospitals) rather than in psychiatric units of district general hospitals, or in psychiatric day-centres, because it is only these large institutions that may feel that they have enough work to justify paying the salary of an attached dramatherapist. However, having established a base in the mental hospital the dramatherapist can then, if he or she wishes, extend the work outwards into smaller more specialised units, if time and energy allow.

The task of this chapter then is to examine how such dramatherapists can exercise their skills and expertise within these psychiatric hospitals, and how they relate to other staff and to the daily life of the institution as a whole.

HISTORIC DEVELOPMENTS IN PSYCHIATRY

The word 'psychiatry' is derived from two Greek elements: *psukhe* and *iatreia*. Psukhe (Psyche) was the goddess of the soul or spirit, beloved by Eros, the god of love, and came to personify the breath of life. Thus the immaterial psyche (mind) becomes the complementary component of soma, the material body (Larousse, 1964; 1981). *Iatreia* is the art of healing, and thus *iatros*, the healer or physician (Partridge, 1979). This leads to two interesting and differing interpretations of what psychiatry is about — either it is the art of healing those disorders which express themselves through the mind, or, as was originally intended by Johann Christian Reil when he coined the term in 1800, a method of medical treatment in which the physician uses his own mind (psyche) as the primary therapeutic agent (Walmsley, 1984). The first interpretation has won the day, and psychiatry is understood by most to be that branch of medicine which deals with the mental consequences of disease of the brain, and of the body as a whole. As a result, there is an unresolved tension between the use of physical objective techniques to diagnose and treat the pathology thought to lie inside an individual, and the use of psychological and emotional methods to help to heal the fragmented internal worlds of troubled people, and to build bridges between them and those with whom they live. In practical terms, this tension can be seen in hospitals involving decisions to spend more money on drugs, or on more doctors and nurses, rather than on the salary for a dramatherapist. Doctors and nurses deal with practical and 'scientific' matters; dramatherapists work in a shadowy world of as yet unproven benefit to acutely or chronically disordered psychiatric patients.

In order to understand how dramatherapists come to be working in psychiatric settings at all, it is important to see how the practice of psychiatry has developed through three significant phases. In the beginning, the asylum phase grew naturally out of the medieval understanding of what constituted mental disorder, when the main purpose of psychiatric care was to protect and generally look after the mentally disordered and destitute. Originally, the motivation was clearly a truly religious concern and a humanitarian desire to care for the needs of the very vulnerable and severely disadvantaged members of society. However, with time, this phase became less humanitarian and more authoritative, leading in the eighteenth century, to the second or custodial phase. Then, the main purpose was frankly to lock away the mentally disturbed for the protection of others, and to safeguard the susceptibilities of the general public. By now, mental disorder was equated with dangerous madness. There was, however, in the mid-nineteenth century a return to an age of enlightenment when the moral treatment movement spread across Europe, and the egalitarian ideals of the French Revolution led to 'striking the chains off the lunatics' (Masters, 1977). Finally, with the onset of the scientific diagnostic and treatment philosophy of medicine as a whole in the early twentieth century, the third or remedial phase emerged in which the principal concerns have been the identification of the widely different patterns of mental disorder, and the development of effective means of treating, or at least managing, the underlying causal illnesses.

We are currently working through this remedial phase, within which there have been in turn three very significant evolutions, or revolutions of thought. The first was the medical revolution brought about by the scientifically-based understanding of the relationship of mental disturbance to disease of the body, and particularly to disease of the central nervous system. General paresis of the insane was proven to be due to the spirochaete of syphilis, and not to excessive self-abuse through masturbation. Antibiotics could bring about miraculous cures of infections, and the barbituate drugs provided an apparently safe and effective means of calming distraught patients, as well as being powerful anaesthetics, and anti-convulsant in action. After the Second World War there was an explosion of effective medical treatments for mental disorder — newer sedatives, hypnotics and tranquillisers; electroconvulsive therapy (ECT); psychosurgery (leucotomy) and insulin-coma therapy. It was also possible to treat other non-psychiatric illnesses which, if left uncontrolled, could lead on to mental disorders, for example, venereal disease, metabolic illnesses, hormone disorders and various neurological conditions such as brain tumours or epilepsy. Latterly, the introduction of the antidepressant drugs, together with lithium for the treatment of the extremes of emotion, has made possible the effective medical treatment of a very large number of psychiatric disorders, especially those presenting for the first time in general practice.

At the turn of the century, and parallel with the slowly emerging medical advances, came the psychological revolution, based on the work of Pierre Janet in France and of Sigmund Freud in Vienna.

Mental disorders could now be seen as not always arising out of bodily illness, but out of internal derangements of the inner psychological world of the patient. The psyche was now being recognised by the medical profession as being as important as the soma. The internal world of imagination, fantasy and symbolic representations was now available to the psychiatrist as a right and proper arena for investigation and treatment. Psychoanalysis was about to give birth to a vast array of progeny — transactional analysis, behaviour therapy, gestalt therapy, rational emotive therapy, Rogerian therapy, confrontational therapy, family therapy and so on.

The conditions prevailing in the Second World War focused attention on the behaviour of people in groups, and this helped to usher in the social revolution which declared that individuals and their behaviour cannot be taken out of the social context in which they live, but can only be fully understood and helped within that context. The family, societal pressures, cultural determinants, all shape and influence the internal psychological world and the body systems of the presenting or nominated patient — he or she who is said to be acting in a mad way. Each individual person is susceptible to a whole host of interpersonal influences which are as powerful in the genesis of mental disorder as physical illness in the body, or psychological conflict in the mind.

Modern psychiatry has the task of bringing together and trying to synthesise the insights into the nature of man and madness which these three revolutions force upon us. No one revolutionary insight is enough: the problem is to weigh up the relative contributions of each, and how each shapes and modifies the effects of the other two. People inhabit society and live by their wits, and thus body and mind together reflect the stresses and strains to which such a tight-rope existence daily exposes them. The dramatherapist is concerned with theatre which is society in microcosm, with the emotional and psychological responses of the actors and of the audience and with bodies which can be so eloquent in telling us who we are, and how we relate both to those who struggle on the stage with us, and to those who sit silently, watching in the audience.

RECENT TRENDS IN PSYCHIATRY

There has been considerable political pressure of late to move the venue of psychiatric practice away from large institutions because of the fear of institutionalisation (Goffman, 1961) and of regarding psychiatric care as oppression (The Radical Therapist Collective, 1974). The setting up of smaller psychiatric units in district general hospitals was the first response, but following on from important publications in Britain such as 'Better Services for the Mentally Ill' (DHSS, 1975), and 'Changing Patterns in Mental Health Care' (WHO, Regional Office for Europe, Copenhagen 1980), the pressure is on for more and more psychiatric care to be provided in the community where people live, by setting up a network of contact and care points — in general practice, by community psychiatric nurses, in psychiatric day-hospitals, and day-centres shared with social services departments, after-care hostels, group homes and community mental-health centres. This will mean a fragmentation of the present psychiatric service, with more of the psychiatric staff leaving their hospital base to work elsewhere alongside other professionals and voluntary agencies. Large numbers of psychiatrically disturbed people will be dispersed across the care networks, and as far as the dramatherapist is concerned, one of the few surviving advantages of the 'old fashioned mental hospitals' — large numbers of potential clients brought together conveniently in one place and under one roof — will be lost. Nevertheless, a 'mass exodus' into the community has not yet taken place because it has been discovered that to set up a properly funded and properly staffed community-care programme is as expensive as institutionally based care. Such a move would also require much more education of the public, politicians, administrators, patients and relatives, and not least the psychiatric hospital staff, that has been carried out so far. Large psychiatric institutions are thus likely to remain for the time being, despite forecasts of their impending closure (Tooth and Brooke, 1961). Dramatherapists may have to be prepared in the future to move out of their hospital base into various community projects, just as patients and other staff will if this community orientation continues, and if the necessary funding is ever provided.

As well as this shift in location, there has been a shift of emphasis away from mental illness or disorder towards mental health. This is not just playing with words, but represents a true change in philosophic direction. Mental disorder, and particularly mental illness, implies that the medical, pyschological or even the social model of understanding is saying that the person is deviant in some respect, and that therefore some 'sickness' is present which will require the intervention of some external curative agency if the person is to be 'better' or 'well' again. Although the patient will

261

have an important part to play in getting better, the diagnosis of the 'sickness' and its 'cure' will lie in the hands of others. This eventually tends to foster a regressive dependency of the patient on those others. Mental health on the other hand, although it eludes firm definition, is something in which everyone is involved, and something for which everyone has a responsibility. It allows for gradations of 'healthiness' and does not require the patient to cross over that invisible line which sets him or her apart from others in a dependent sick-role. No matter how deficient in 'mental health', the patient can always be challenged to seek out that which is lacking, and be encouraged to find out where it might be obtained. Mental health approaches emphasise self-knowledge and self-help on the inner journey of self-exploration. There is the belief that there is a healing potential in everyone, no matter how disordered, but it has to be located, activated and then channelled into effective expression. Dramatherapists can function in a mental-illness framework, helping in the assessment or diagnostic process, and in the treatment of the patient. Their own tradition, however, fits them better to work in a mental-health framework, where client and therapist, actor and audience, are interchangeable roles as each pursues the same pathways to self-fulfilment. Each can help the other in a manner that the traditional 'illness/treatment' model does not allow. Here, doctor and patient, fit person and sick person are roles which are defined and static through one therapeutic transaction.

The emphasis on mental health brings out other factors, recognised but only given lip-service in the 'illness/treatment' model, but which are central to the work of the dramatherapist — self-discovery, self-exploration, self-determination, self-help and the release of innate creativity and flight away from constrictive and restrictive labelling and categorising processes. Creativity, or the possibility of creativity, is essential to this view of what psychiatry is about. The 'illness/treatment' model has by its nature to emphasise disability and disorder of function; to emphasise what is wrong rather than what might be potentially right; to emphasise what the patient cannot do rather than what he might be able to do; to emphasise that what requires to be done is carried out by others rather than what the patient might do for him/herself.

Dramatherapists, and others working in this mental-health perspective, must believe that no matter how apparently deranged and defective someone may be, the urge to be creative, and to be healed in the process of creating, is present in all of us. This urge to create, even if in the beginning it brings forth more chaos than cosmos, is there deep down. It may have to be drilled for with many a dry tap, but eventually the well spring will gush forth, whether the person is locked in an acute psychotic illness, lost in a deeply felt neurotic conflict, or grasped in the deadening effect of chronic, long lasting mental impairment.

Currently in psychiatric practice, particularly under the influence of the psychological and social revolutions, there has grown up a premium on what are loosely called the 'talking treatments', whether this is sitting down with an individual to talk through a variety of personal problems, or a large group-community or ward-meeting at which events on the ward are submitted to a social analysis, or fully established psychodynamic or psychoanalytic psychotherapy. The power of the word is held to be paramount. The emotional substrate of the word is recognised to be as important as its semantic content, but this trend results in people sitting down and spending long hours speaking, talking, listening, interpreting, with an aversion to what is called 'acting out'. This is held to be an escape into action as a defence against what is being talked about, and at times it may well be so. But the premium on talking, and 'being' through talking, creates a resistance to 'being through doing', or 'being through being' in other parts of the ward programme. Initially, occupational therapy was thought of as a means of combatting destructive boredom by offering diversionary activity in between the more important daily episodes such as 'talking to the doctor' or 'going to the ward meeting'. The dramatherapist will have to struggle against this trend, and show that mime or sculpting are other equally valid ways to self-discovery and self-awareness, which do not set themselves against 'serious sitting down and talking through problems', but offer a complementary way by which troubled, and often singularly inarticulate people can be helped to confront aspects of themselves, and the daily dramas of life they are caught up in.

It has been necessary to go through this detailed and historical review of the developments of psychiatric care and present trends, because no one can come into current psychiatric practice and hope to work efficiently with patients or with other staff, without some awareness of where psychiatry has come from, and where it seems to be heading. These revolutions of philosophy, models of care and current trends are not just academic issues, but are present everyday in the ward, in the unit, in the hospital and at management meetings. They underlie so much otherwise-inexplicable conflict and tension which rise to the surface every so often, and lead to confrontations and struggles between patients and staff, between one professional group and another, between administrators and clinicians, and even within the large professional groups themselves. They have to be understood if they are to be recognised, and if, despite the real differences that yet remain to be resolved, the work of the unit or hospital is to carry on.

THE DRAMATHERAPIST AS MEMBER OF THE CLINICAL TEAM

The dramatherapist is the latest recruit to the family of non-medical team members known collectively as the creative therapists. This is not to imply that other therapists not of this group are uncreative, but that this particular team of therapists consciously work to 'a theory of creativity' in relationship to mental disorder. The dramatherapist is thus expected to work in ways similar to, and to have the same kind of goals with patients as the art therapist, the music therapist, the dance therapist, the recreational therapist, the creative-writing therapist and so on. As these other therapists use materials to help in the creative work, so the dramatherapist uses the material of theatre — a stage, props, costume, make-up, lighting, musical effects, a script and so on. Sometimes the drama is complicated and sophisticated; sometimes it has its greatest effect through its simplicity. But there is one fundamental difference — the dramatherapist uses the body and experience of the patient directly in the action in a way that the other therapists do not, except perhaps for the dance therapist (dance after all is drama expressed through movement and music). Only if the drama is video-taped and played back, can the participants see themselves in the creative act. They can only relate to a semblance of what was created. This is similar to music therapy — a tape or video-recording is not the music; only a vivid shadow of the musical event now past. There is the picture painted, the figure sculpted, the music composed, the poem written; each has an objective reality separate from the creator, and can be experienced in its own right separate from the creator. The drama and the dance in this respect are different; the actor and the dancer can never really step out of the drama without changing it irrevocably. The drama can only be experienced by being in it and sharing in its creation; the dance only by being danced. In this respect there cannot ever really be an audience as in commercial terms. Only God and the Angels have that right! The therapy lies in the experience of doing and being, and in sharing that experience with others who are doing and being at the same time.

Other members of the clinical team may get confused over socio-drama, psychodrama and dramatherapy, imagining them to be the same. The dramatherapist will have to make the difference clear. Sociodrama operates in, and makes full use of the social-system setting, helping the client to learn how to function in a group of others in a shared social task. This might be learning how to run a party, or how to conduct a ward discussion-group. Psychodrama is a highly specialised technique developed by Moreno for explicit goals achieved by explicit means, as described by Martin Davies in Chapter 5. Dramatherapy is different from the other two systems, and uses its own techniques for its own aims. It makes use of drama-derived ideas and methods, directed primarily towards helping clients to get in touch with moods and feelings. It uses verbal and non-verbal symbolic expressions. It teaches the client to use the whole of him or herself and experience, as the vehicle of com-municating with others.

In theoretical terms, the dramatherapist has to show the other members of the clinical team what his or her work is based upon. There is the creative model, through which it is possible to discover that it is fun and enjoyable, despite reservations to the contrary, to explore oneself and others. There is the learning model, which is task-orientated, and directed towards the acquisition of social skills. And there is the therapeutic model in which there is a deliberate and structured exploration of the psychodynamic connections between the inner and outer worlds of the clients. Using these three models, the dramatherapist can make a number of contributions to patient care:

(1) Working directly with patients, using his or her particular skills and experiences to reach an intensity of contact.
(2) Supporting, teaching and supervising others who may wish to use their own skills and professional perspectives in a new way with patients.
(3) Participating in the assessment of selected patients, as a means of establishing the diagnosis.
(4) Participating in the subsequent management and therapeutic programme derived from that diagnosis.
(5) On occasions, working with the clinical team itself where dramatherapy skills can be used in the analysis and 'dia-gnosis' of a malaise, which may be reducing the effec-tiveness of the clinical team through hidden conflicts or

blocked 'performance'. The dramatherapist will only be able, and be asked, to work in this way when he or she has successfully built up a sense of mutual trust and respect.

As with anyone who is going to work closely with others in a multi-professional team, the dramatherapist will have to struggle quite hard initially to earn the right to be listened to, and be consulted. He or she will have to be able to declare clearly and unambiguously, what he has to offer, and that his or her contribution is not 'just a nice frill', an expensive luxury compared to such effective treatments as drugs and ECT. The dramatherapist has also to persuade others that what he or she is offering is not another or a more sophisticated way of 'keeping patients occupied'. The occupational therapist has had to struggle hard to escape from the 'basket-making and weaving' image, and the dramatherapist will have a similar struggle, especially in hospitals where there has not been a dramatherapist before, or any other creative therapists. This is not easy to do, and it takes time to overcome what is often not frank and informed hostility, but largely ignorance and lack of understanding.

WORK WITH PARTICULAR PATIENT GROUPS

Patients in acute-admissions wards

These are psychiatric patients who have either been admitted for the first time, or with recurring but time-limited episodes. Some are psychotic, suffering from acute schizophrenic illnesses, or from manic-depressive psychosis, in either the elated or hypomanic phase, or the acutely withdrawn depressive phase. Others may have confusional states of uncertain origin, or may be showing acute behavioural disturbances which render them a danger to themselves or to others. Some may have neurotic disorders — acute anxiety attacks with panic states or phobias, or short-term depressive reactions sparked off by bereavements or losses. Some may have more or less continuing disorders of their personalities.

In such a setting, the dramatherapist will find it convenient to do groupwork, each session lasting about 1½ hours. The session will often begin with warming-up exercises, but then go on to pick up a theme and develop it through the rest of the session. Such themes are taken from the life of the ward and reflect daily issues such as 'the staff are not caring for us any more' or 'why can't we all go home?'. Role-play can be used to look at what it is like to be a patient who is literally pushed around by everyone else, or what is it like to be a staff member who is always expected to have the answers. It can involve the exploration of conflictual messages — 'Do grow up and make some decisions for yourself, but you must keep to the ward rules.' 'We expect you to be responsible for your own life, but we can't allow you to go home next weekend.'

In the acute-admissions wards, the patient population is constantly changing, with new people coming in, and previous patients going home or on leave. Each session therefore has to be self-contained because there is little chance of getting anything like the same people together for on-going work the following week. It is essential then for the dramatherapist to have other ward staff help in these sessions, not only to provide some semblance of continuity, but also to take back to the other team members the themes which have been worked through. Despite the shifting patient population, with time, a series of themes emerge again and again — the nature of mental upset and what causes it, just what is normality and who is to say who is normal and who is not, how to cope with going back home and facing the 'outside' world again, how to live with loneliness or the indifference of others. Work with acutely disturbed patients is mostly concerned with finding ways of self-expression: finding ways of sharing feelings and circumstances which of their nature are confused and very difficult to convey to others, even if the words were to hand which usually they are not.

On the acute wards, there is ample scope for the dramatherapist to supervise other team members, and it is difficult to strike the right balance between working with patients and working with other staff. On such wards, the supervisory work consists of:

(1) reviewing and teaching appropriate drama skills which the staff can use themselves with patients.
(2) setting limits appropriate to the needs of the patients, and to the skills and experience of the staff.
(3) encouraging a self-critical, self-observing attitude in the staff so that they learn to monitor themselves as they go along in the work of drama with patients.

Also on these wards, the question of making the best possible use of the limited time the dramatherapist has available is crucial, and raises issues as to whether his or her time is best spent either sitting in on the consultant's ward round to aid in assessment and diagnosis, or working directly with patients in another place. There may not be time to do both all the time, so which is to be chosen, and when?

PATIENTS IN LONG-STAY (REHABILITATION) WARDS

These are patients who have come into the hospital through the acute admissions wards but after a number of admissions there, have now been transferred to the long-stay wards for a variety of reasons such as being unable to survive outside, there being nowhere willing to have them, or because they are going through a time-extended rehabilitation programme to try to offset the disabling effects of chronic mental disorder. In such settings, the dramatherapist is working with a more consistent, but more damaged group of patients where assessment and diagnosis are of less importance than getting the patients in touch with the creative part of themselves, which may have lain dormant and atrophied through misuse for many years. This work requires a lighter touch, but applied over a longer and more consistent period of time, compared to the acute-admissions wards. The dramatherapist has the challenge of using all kinds of engaging activities — masks, puppet work, group play-writing and group theatre, film-making, video and so on. Creative fantasies require to be evoked to fill the emptiness of chronic disablement. Such work needs privacy as well as many technological aids, and whereas work on the acute wards can be done wherever there is a bit of space, work with the long-stay patients is best done away from the wards where they spend so much time each day, and done in an 'activities area' specially created and set aside for this purpose. The very act of getting up to go to the activities centre is the beginning of motivation. Music in this context can be used to induce relaxation and self-confidence; techniques of body massage and sculpting help alienated people to get in touch with themselves as a prelude to getting in touch with other people. Dramatherapy here can comfortably overlap with art therapy, music therapy and dance therapy. The borderlines become blurred, and each approach complements the others.

Psychogeriatric patients

This is the rather unflattering term used to describe the old folk said to be elderly mentally infirm (EMI). Many sadly are demented and locked away in a world of their own, or locked into a past which no longer exists. Some may be depressed and anxious, and may recover sufficiently to go home, but for others, these wards are their home and they will spend the rest of their days here. The dramatherapy work here is an extension of that done on the long-stay wards, but recognising the importance of memory and the tendency to return to the past that was. Reminiscence therapy is concerned with acting out stories from the past, myth-making and story-telling. Work of this type complements reality–orientation techniques designed to draw out the elderly confused patient from a now mythic past into contact with the real people of the present. Allowance has to be made for frail old bodies, the restrictions of arthritis, the awkward gait and the loss of balance. There may be a fight to regain control over bladder and bowels, but what continues to cause surprise is how often inaccessible, frail elderly people can be helped for a time at least to come awake and come alive by these measures, and what seemed an empty shell, now becomes an actual person with a story to tell.

Patients in the special units

In many psychiatric services there are units catering for special client groups — those with alcohol-related disorders, those with drug misuse and dependency problems, those who are disturbed adolescents or children. There are also the family units, mother-and-baby units, as well as the day hospitals and day centres. Each of those units could employ a dramatherapist if there were enough to go round. Each unit has its own special needs defined by age, or by the dynamics of the disorder. Dramatherapists would obviously mould their methods to these special needs, but would find commonly occurring themes of dependency versus independence, creativeness versus destructiveness, self-confidence versus reliance on others, maturity versus being a child.

In a sense, there is no limit either to where the dramatherapist might work, or with whom dramatherapy methods would be useful. The only limitation is the small number of dramatherapists fully trained, and available to the NHS. Sadly, the limitations on time and energy of the existing dramatherapists can detract from research in the psychiatric field, and also the discovery of new and exciting ways of work with new client groups, whether they be in hospitals or in community settings.

269

AN ACTIVITY CENTRE

In a large psychiatric hospital, where there may be a group of creative therapists on the staff, including the dramatherapist, it helps to be able to set aside an area away from the wards which is reserved for creative activities. This gives a focus for these activities, and provides privacy and confidentiality away from the everyday life of the hospital, both for patients and for staff. It can house special resources which are better centralised rather than spread about the hospital, or carried from ward to ward.

The motivating effect of getting to the centre has already been discussed, and the existence of the centre gives the activities undertaken there a special status, which they often lack if squeezed into a corner on the wards. The creative therapists also feel more secure with a definite location of their own, where they can have an office in which to keep records, and in which to hold confidential staff-meetings. A single dramatherapist working in a large hospital needs a peer reference group both for personal support, and as an anchorage for some of his or her sessions. The centre can also be used as a venue for staff training, and as a place in which to build up demonstration material or collect data for research.

Such a centre need not be elaborate, but does require a number of rooms — one big room for larger groupwork, and two or three smaller rooms for more personal activities. There should be a lockable office, storage space, basic audio-visual equipment (TV, music centre, audio-tape player, slide-projector, overhead projector, video camera and recorder with TV monitor) and sufficient toilet facilities on site or very close by. It also helps to have minimal facilities for making tea or coffee, and for the occasional more ambitious catering project.

The large room can be fitted out as a drama studio properly lit with a stage area and comfortable seats or preferably cushions for the 'participating audience'. Most modern video equipment operates perfectly well with ambient light, but with more sophisticated lighting better results can be obtained. If the activities centre is shared with the art and music therapists, there is obviously scope for combined activity such as a theatre production with its own music and its own visual effects, make-up and publicity departments.

Often, such centres grow out of the enthusiasm of one person or of one department, and provided there is a flexible approach towards the use of the centre, avoiding territorial disputes, the actual costs of running the centre can be kept to a workable minimum, and the budget gathered expeditiously and discreetly from existing departmental budgets by agreement. A small expenditure results in considerable gain both for the staff who work there, other staff who are trained and supervised there, and above all, for the patients who are encouraged to use the centre.

Having a place of one's own, is vital for a sense of personal identity, as well as for codifying the work that one is doing. In this, the dramatherapist is no different from everyone else.

Difficulties and obstacles

Anyone who wishes to work as a dramatherapist in a psychiatric unit will be faced with a number of difficulties and obstacles. Some will be philosophic in origin, some will be administrative, and some will be mainly practical.

The philosophic difficulties are to do with finding a secure identity within the multi-professional team. There is the problem of personal identity for dramatherapists: do they have a clear concept of what skills they are offering, and the therapeutic goals towards which they will be working? Are they clear on where their responsibilities and skills lie, and where they share and overlap with others in the team? There is the problem of credibility: can they persuade others that what they have to offer is worthwhile, and worthy of consideration among all the other therapies that are being made available to patients? Dramatherapists must search for a definite and established theoretical base from which to argue their position cogently with the others. Possible theoretical bases for the dramatherapist are described earlier in this book — systems theory, psychodrama, creativity theory, but there are also gestalt psychology, and a psychodynamic view both of family development and of the genesis of mental disorder and disablement.

The administrative difficulties relate both to the training programmes in dramatherapy and to the subsequent career structure for trained dramatherapists. There are needs of recognition and validation for both. In times of financial restraint, dramatherapists in Britain who wish to work either in the National Health Service or in social services departments will have to continue to fight for recognition of their speciality in competition with other vocal claims for pieces of the shrinking cake. They will have to fight for recognition at the level of the clinical team, and persuade administrators that their services are not just a luxury item, but essential to any

271

psychiatric service which wishes to claim it is comprehensive. Work in the private sector is always a possibility, but here too there are struggles for the available budget, and payment is more often dependent on visible results. Once accepted into a psychiatric hospital or unit, the dramatherapist is well advised to learn how to use the political and administrative structures of the organisation for his or her own benefit. It may be tedious and time-consuming to write annual reports, especially if there is the not unwarranted suspicion that few will read it. However, presenting this report to the unit management group or to the executive of the division of psychiatry, will at least remind others that there is a dramatherapist, and will hopefully educate them to a degree about what the dramatherapist is trying to do. He or she will also have to learn how to make political alliances with other professional groups on the staff in order to pursue common aims, such as the establishment of an activities centre, or an increase in the number of creative therapists.

The practical difficulties mainly arise from the limitations of one person trying to do effective work against the pressures of time and of conflicting demands. How should the time available best be spent? How should dramatherapists divide time between working directly with clients, and teaching, supporting and supervising other staff? Should they spend time in the activities centre where they will have all their equipment to hand, or should they take themselves, bag and baggage onto the wards and struggle for time and space with patients? There is the difficult question of autonomy and accountability. In legal terms, the consultant physician or psychiatrist is the responsible medical officer, and has the ultimate responsibility for saying which type of care each patient shall receive. Should dramatherapists bow to the doctor's decisions, or should they try to influence the doctor, and if so, how are they to go about it? How are dramtherapists to respond to the inter-professional rivalries which rise to the surface every now and again? How are patients to be referred to dramatherapists, or will the dramatherapists have to take whoever comes along? How should they apportion time between the various patient groups described? None of these difficulties is easy to resolve, and priorities may have to be determined as there will inevitably not be enough time or energy to do everything. What these priorities should be, and how they should be arrived at, is a primary task for the dramatherapist in conjunction with others in the clinical team, and ideally, with patients as well.

THE ROOTS OF DRAMA IN PSYCHIATRIC SETTINGS

Psychiatric institutions have always been, and remain, very dramatic places. In the dark archetypal days, they were places where dangerous madness was confronted and confined. In more recent times, they have become in the public mind both places of miracles and places of scandal. Here the depressed should discover joy, the lonely should find companionship, the anxious and panic-stricken find an inner peace. The confused and disordered should grasp towards a semblance of sense, and the staff should care for those whom others cannot love. If reality does not accord with fantasy, then there is an outcry, and someone has to be found to be the scapegoat.

The staff too, have their expectations. They feel that they should be able to improve, if not cure, the disorder, and generally ameliorate the lot of those they are asked to treat: the acutely ill should get better and go home again to make room for the next new patient; the long-term disabled should respond to the rehabilitation programme, and if the lame are not expected to pick up their beds and walk, they are expected to make their beds at least, and come to terms with what is called 'the realities of the outside world'. To remain locked into the inside world of fantasies, is to be truly institutionalised.

In the everyday world of psychiatric practice there are roles and scripts. The name badges worn, the notices on doors, staff designations within the unit, and especially the status of patients, all declare clear-cut 'roles' which evoke certain expectations in the minds of others. One's role says who one is in the organisation and what one can be expected to do; it sets out the limits of one's choices and declares what one can and what one cannot do. Roles define existence, and may either enable or frustrate the ambitions we have for ourselves and others. Some roles facilitate, other roles de-skill. 'Scripts' are the instructions for daily interaction and daily living. Sometimes they are written down by others, and are to be followed explicitly — the standing orders of the unit. Sometimes we write them for ourselves — job descriptions, option appraisals or plans for action. Sometimes scripts are created spontaneously as we go along — in a therapy session, at a staff-sensitivity meeting. This can be exciting, but there have to be controls, and the scripts seen to operate within certain restraints.

Within psychiatry there are 'hierarchies of roles' — the Gods and mortals. These hierarchies can be acknowledged or denied, but they

273

are always there, in the line management-structures — the heads of departments, the unit management group, in the ward round, and in the multi-professional team at clinical level. In a therapeutic democracy we may all claim to be equal, but some are still more equal than others. We are equal in that we have common aims and objectives, and are working for the benefit of patients and their relatives. We are equal in that we try to co-operate with each other, and respect what each other stands for. We are equal, but at the same time, there are external constraints — the legal responsibility and accountability of the consultant, the authority of the management group, the dictates of the regional plan. Although everyone should be given an equal chance to have their say, decisions cannot be made by 'clinical committees'. The consensus view on occasions may have to be over-ridden, and someone must be charged with making that decision on behalf of all, and recognised by the others as having that responsibility. Who that person should be varies with circumstances and with times; the sign of a true democracy is that this need is accepted and recognised.

There are established sanctions for rule-breaking. The roles define us, the scripts set down our scope for action, the hierarchy tells where we stand in relation to others. If anyone steps over an invisible line — a line drawn in the water — then there are sanctions. There are the official sanctions taken when professional codes of conduct are flouted. There are the informal sanctions when 'upset' is caused by stepping out of role, or altering the script without agreement. Conflict and confrontation are at least positive and can be reacted against, but to be ignored as if invisible, is the most hurtful sanction of all.

Finally, in the practice of psychiatry, there are 'mysteries and miracles'. Things are done in a way that produces results, but no one may really know why if they are being honest. Mysteries are to do with the way things are done, because to do them any other way could be disastrous. Newcomers have to be inducted into the ways of these mysteries. Miracles are to do with certain practices which seem to proceed from charismatic as much as scientific bases. Good examples are the now-abandoned insulin — coma techniques, the still-used abreactive methods, and above all, the current use of electroconvulsive therapy (ECT). Under this heading, some would want to include the more sensational of the psychotherapies, and the cults that spring up from time to time.

This is the world of drama that dramatherapists enter in psychiatric settings. It is here that they will be expected to exercise special skills. They will have the unique opportunity of revealing this drama, whether it be within the staff organisation or within a patient, or within a family. The drama is there, but the others may not be fully aware of it.

RETROSPECT

To return to the beginning, and to the two quotations which head this chapter. Auden, thinking of a birthday gift for mankind, wishes us a sense of theatre first of all, because he claims that only if people have a sense of the drama of life and the illusions involved in the evolution of that drama, will they be able to survive the rigours of this life, and even prosper into the bargain. Mental illness is one of the most dramatic happenings that anyone of us may have to face in the unfolding of our personal drama. In it, we are confronted with powerful primitive forces, latent in all but usually kept well under control so that they do not seem even to exist. Now they burst on to the stage of our minds, accompanied by the weird sisters of hallucination and delusion and alienation. Bacon, in his turn, reminds us that we cannot stand idly by as mere spectators of these events, but that inevitably we are drawn into the drama whether we like it or not. This is the stuff of drama, and right in the centre, the dramatherapist has the chance to weave his or her magic, partly as director and producer, partly as scriptwriter and script editor, and partly as erstwhile actor bringing us gently on to the stage, and giving us courage to speak the lines that nature, kindly or otherwise, has prepared for us. It is natural and proper that dramatherapists should find themselves in this psychiatric world, and through finding themselves, help others to find that which they may have lost along the way.

REFERENCES

Department of Health and Social Security (1975). *Better Services for the Mentally Ill.* Cmnd 6233, HMSO, London
Goffman, E. (1961) *Asylums.* Penguin, London
Graves, R. (1981) *Greek Myths.* Cassell, London
Larousse (1964) *Encyclopaedia of Mythology.* Larousse, London
Masters, A. (1977) *Bedlam.* Michael Joseph, London
Partridge, E. (1979) *Origins.* Routledge and Kegan Paul, London
Radical Therapist Collective (1974) *The Radical Therapist.* Penguin, London

Tooth, G. and Brooke, E.M. (1961) 'Mental Hospital Populations and Their Effect on Future Planning'. *Lancet*, vol. 1, pp. 710–13

Walmsley, T. (1984). 'Teaching Psychiatry: Scientific Myth'. *Bulletin of the Royal College of Psychiatrists*, vol. 8, no. 6, pp. 109–10

World Health Organization (1980) *Changing Patterns in Mental Health Care*. Regional Office for Europe, Copenhagen

Appendix

Training Courses, Associations and Journals

GREAT BRITAIN

Hertfordshire College of Art and Design, 7 Hatfield Road, St. Albans, Herts.
post graduate diploma in dramatherapy: 1 year full-time, 2 year part-time; summer school and short courses.

College of Ripon and York St. John, Lord Mayors Walk, York.
post-graduate diploma in dramatherapy: 2 year part-time.
dramatherapy supervisors training course; summer school, short courses.

South Devon Technical College, Torquay, Devon.
post-professional diploma in dramatherapy: 2 year part-time.

Dramatherapy Consultants, 6 Nelsons Avenue, St. Albans, Herts AL1 5RY.
advanced dramatherapy training; short courses; Easter school; supervision; clinical referral for individuals and groups; applied research including infertility and child abuse.
publications: Dramatherapy Bulletin.

British Association for Dramatherapists, P.O. Box 98 Kirbymoorside, Yorks YO6 6EX.
Professional Association for dramatherapists with registered, full, and associate and student membership; conferences and seminars.
publications: Journal of Dramatherapy; Dramatherapy Bulletin.

GREECE

The Arts and Therapy Centre, Haidariou 4, Etolias, Athens.
4 year dramatherapy training course; International seminar programme; short courses; client referral.

USA

University of Antioch, Pine Street, San Francisco.
Masters course in dramatherapy.

University of New York, New York, New York.
Masters course in dramatherapy.

National Association of Drama Therapy, 19 Edwards Street, New Haven, Connecticutt 06511.
professional association for drama therapy with registered, full, associate and student membership.
publications: Dramascope.

Index